STAR WARS®
❦ L E G A C Y ❦

LEGACY

(Forty years after the Battle of Yavin and beyond)

As this era began, Luke Skywalker had unified the Jedi Order into a cohesive group of powerful Jedi Knights. It was a time of relative peace, yet darkness approached on the horizon. Now, Skywalker's descendants face new and resurgent threats to the galaxy, and to the balance of the Force.

The events in this story begin approximately 137 years after the Battle of Yavin.

STAR WARS®
LEGACY

VOLUME THREE
❖ CLAWS OF THE DRAGON ❖

STORY
John Ostrander and Jan Duursema

SCRIPT
John Ostrander

PENCILS
Jan Duursema

INKS
Dan Parsons

COLORS
Brad Anderson

LETTERS
Michael Heisler

COVER ART
Travis Charest

DARK HORSE BOOKS®

PUBLISHER
Mike Richardson

COLLECTION DESIGNER
Scott Cook

ART DIRECTOR
Lia Ribacchi

ASSISTANT EDITORS
Freddye Lins and Dave Marshall

EDITOR
Randy Stradley

Special thanks to Elaine Mederer, Jann Moorhead, David Anderman, Leland Chee,
Sue Rostoni, and Carol Roeder at Lucas Licensing.

STAR WARS: LEGACY VOLUME THREE—CLAWS OF THE DRAGON

Star Wars © 2008 Lucasfilm Ltd. & ™. All rights reserved. Used under authorization. Text and
illustrations for Star Wars are © 2007, 2008 Lucasfilm Ltd. Dark Horse Books® and the Dark
Horse logo are registered trademarks of Dark Horse Comics, Inc. All rights reserved. No portion
of this publication may be reproduced or transmitted, in any form or by any means, without the
express written permission of Dark Horse Comics, Inc. Names, characters, places, and incidents
featured in this publication either are the product of the author's imagination or are used ficti-
tiously. Any resemblance to actual persons (living or dead), events, institutions, or locales, without
satiric intent, is coincidental.

This volume collects issues fourteen through nineteen of the
Dark Horse comic book series *Star Wars: Legacy*.

Published by
Dark Horse Books
A division of Dark Horse Comics, Inc.
10956 SE Main Street
Milwaukie, OR 97222

darkhorse.com
starwars.com

To find a comics shop in your area, call the Comic Shop Locator Service toll-free at 1-888-266-4226

563   First printing: June 2008
ISBN: 978-1-59307-946-8

1 3 5 7 9 10 8 6 4 2
Printed in China

Seven years ago, Darth Krayt sent his legion of Sith followers to destroy the Jedi Academy on Ossus. In the battle that followed, Jedi Kol Skywalker sacrificed himself to ensure the escape of his son, Padawan Cade Skywalker.

Overcome with anger, fear, and regret, Cade turned away from his training, joining the Pirate Rav before becoming a bounty hunter. As captain of the *Mynock*, Cade, along with crewmates Jariah Syn and Deliah Blue, turned in anyone for a reward, even the Jedi Hosk Trey'lis.

That was, until a confrontation with the Sith who killed his father convinced Cade to face his legacy. No longer running from the past, Cade has undertaken a solo mission to Coruscant, capital of the Galactic Empire, where he intends to rescue Hosk from the depths of the Sith Temple . . .

STAR WARS

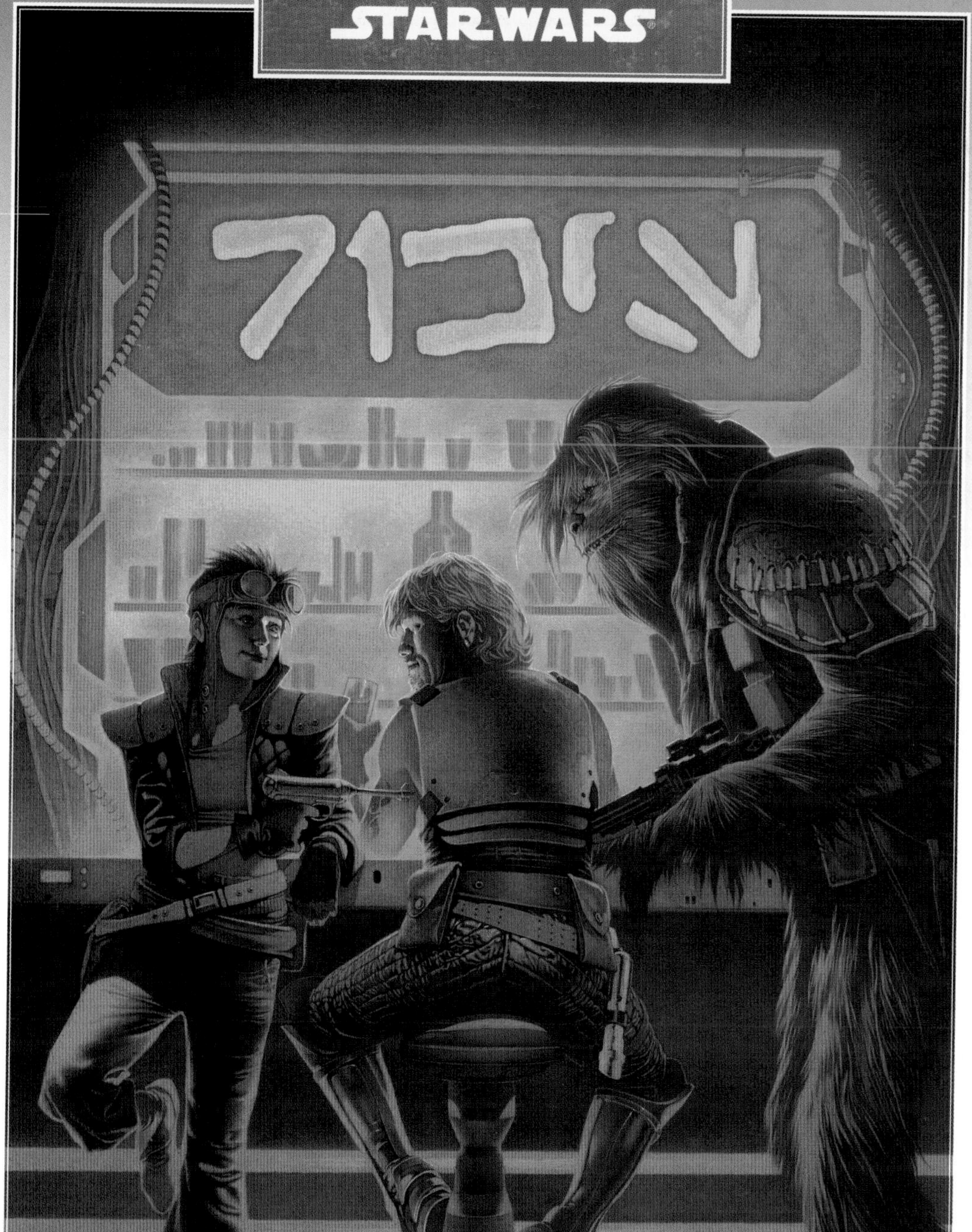

TRAVIS CHAREST

CLAWS OF THE DRAGON

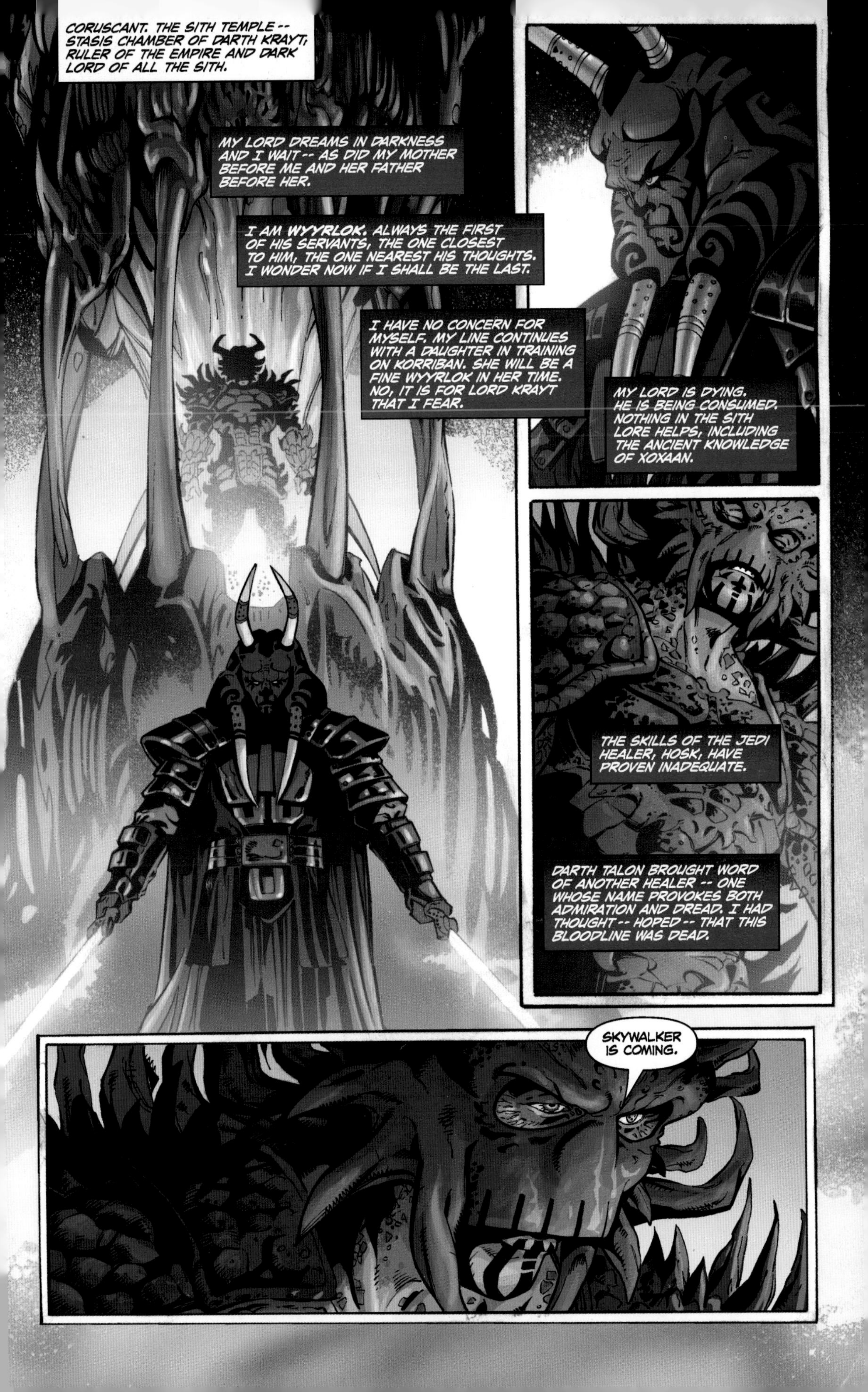
CORUSCANT. THE SITH TEMPLE -- STASIS CHAMBER OF DARTH KRAYT, RULER OF THE EMPIRE AND DARK LORD OF ALL THE SITH.
MY LORD DREAMS IN DARKNESS AND I WAIT -- AS DID MY MOTHER BEFORE ME AND HER FATHER BEFORE HER.
I AM WYYRLOK. ALWAYS THE FIRST OF HIS SERVANTS, THE ONE CLOSEST TO HIM, THE ONE NEAREST HIS THOUGHTS. I WONDER NOW IF I SHALL BE THE LAST.
I HAVE NO CONCERN FOR MYSELF. MY LINE CONTINUES WITH A DAUGHTER IN TRAINING ON KORRIBAN. SHE WILL BE A FINE WYYRLOK IN HER TIME. NO, IT IS FOR LORD KRAYT THAT I FEAR.
MY LORD IS DYING. HE IS BEING CONSUMED. NOTHING IN THE SITH LORE HELPS, INCLUDING THE ANCIENT KNOWLEDGE OF XOXAAN.
THE SKILLS OF THE JEDI HEALER, HOSK, HAVE PROVEN INADEQUATE.
DARTH TALON BROUGHT WORD OF ANOTHER HEALER -- ONE WHOSE NAME PROVOKES BOTH ADMIRATION AND DREAD. I HAD THOUGHT -- HOPED -- THAT THIS BLOODLINE WAS DEAD.
SKYWALKER IS COMING.

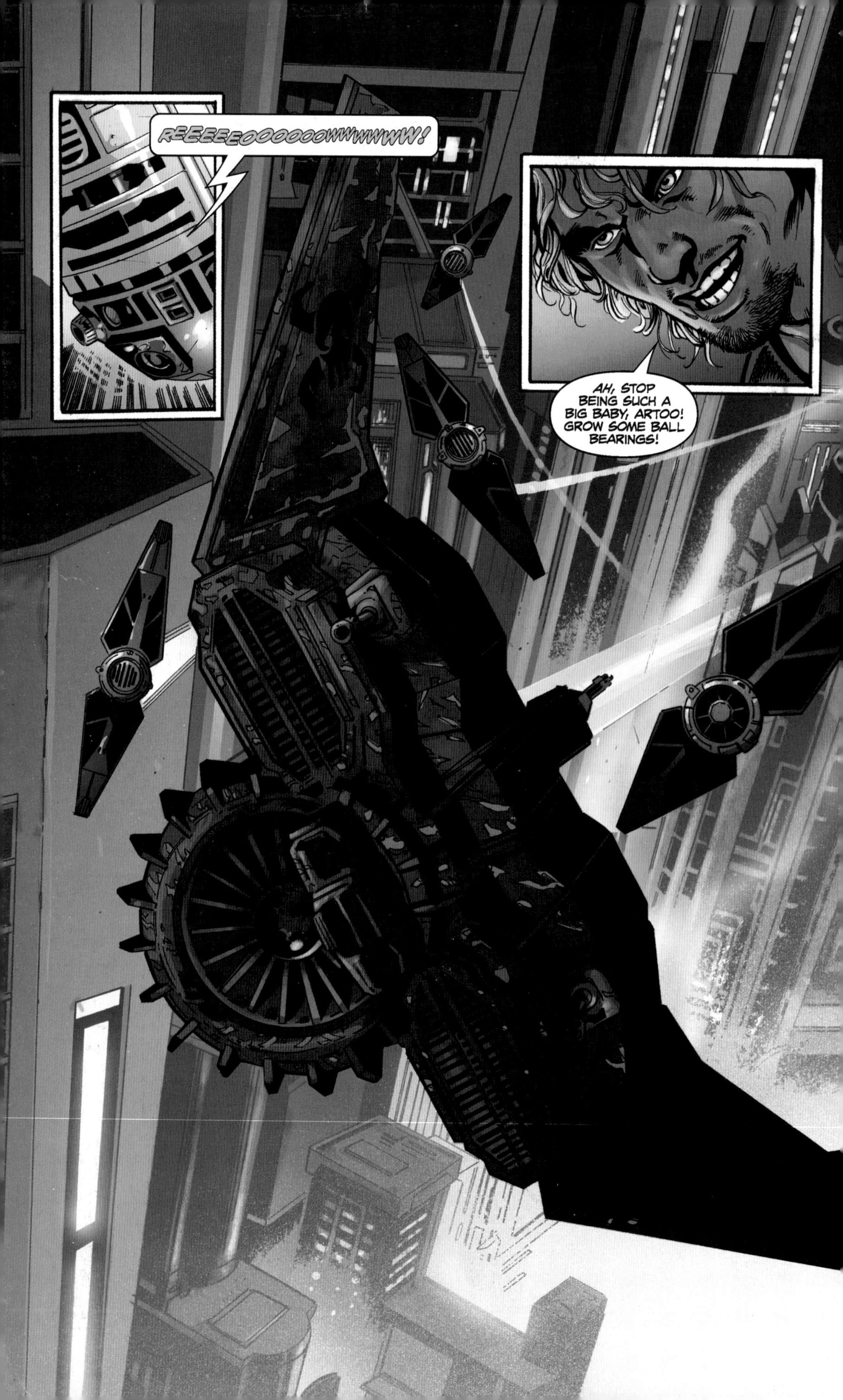
REEEEEEOOOOOOOWWWWWW!
AH, STOP BEING SUCH A BIG BABY, ARTOO! GROW SOME BALL BEARINGS!

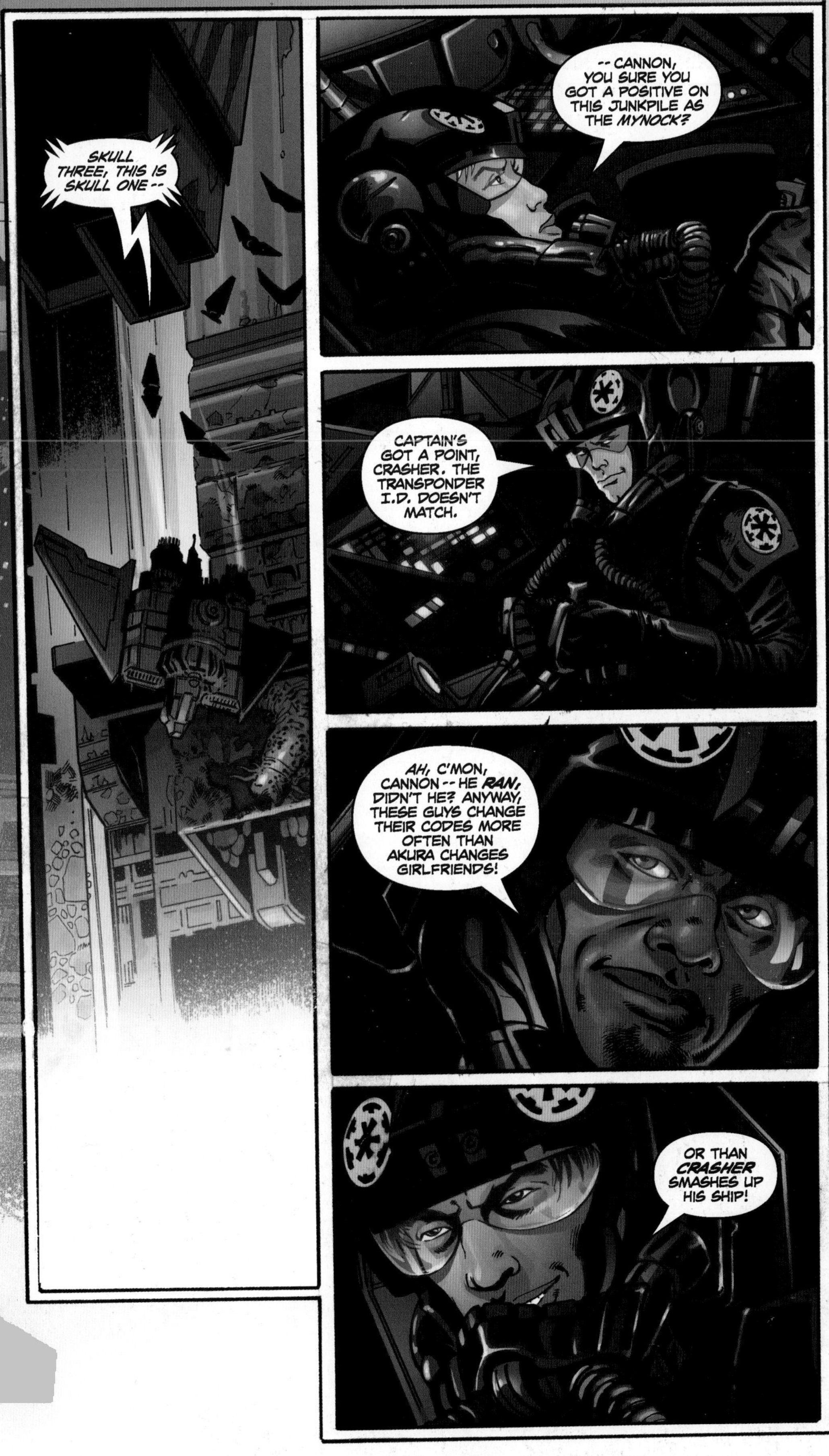
SKULL THREE, THIS IS SKULL ONE --
-- CANNON, YOU SURE YOU GOT A POSITIVE ON THIS JUNKPILE AS THE *MYNOCK?*
CAPTAIN'S GOT A POINT, CRASHER. THE TRANSPONDER I.D. DOESN'T MATCH.
AH, C'MON, CANNON -- HE ***RAN,*** DIDN'T HE? ANYWAY, THESE GUYS CHANGE THEIR CODES MORE OFTEN THAN AKURA CHANGES GIRLFRIENDS!
OR THAN ***CRASHER*** SMASHES UP HIS SHIP!

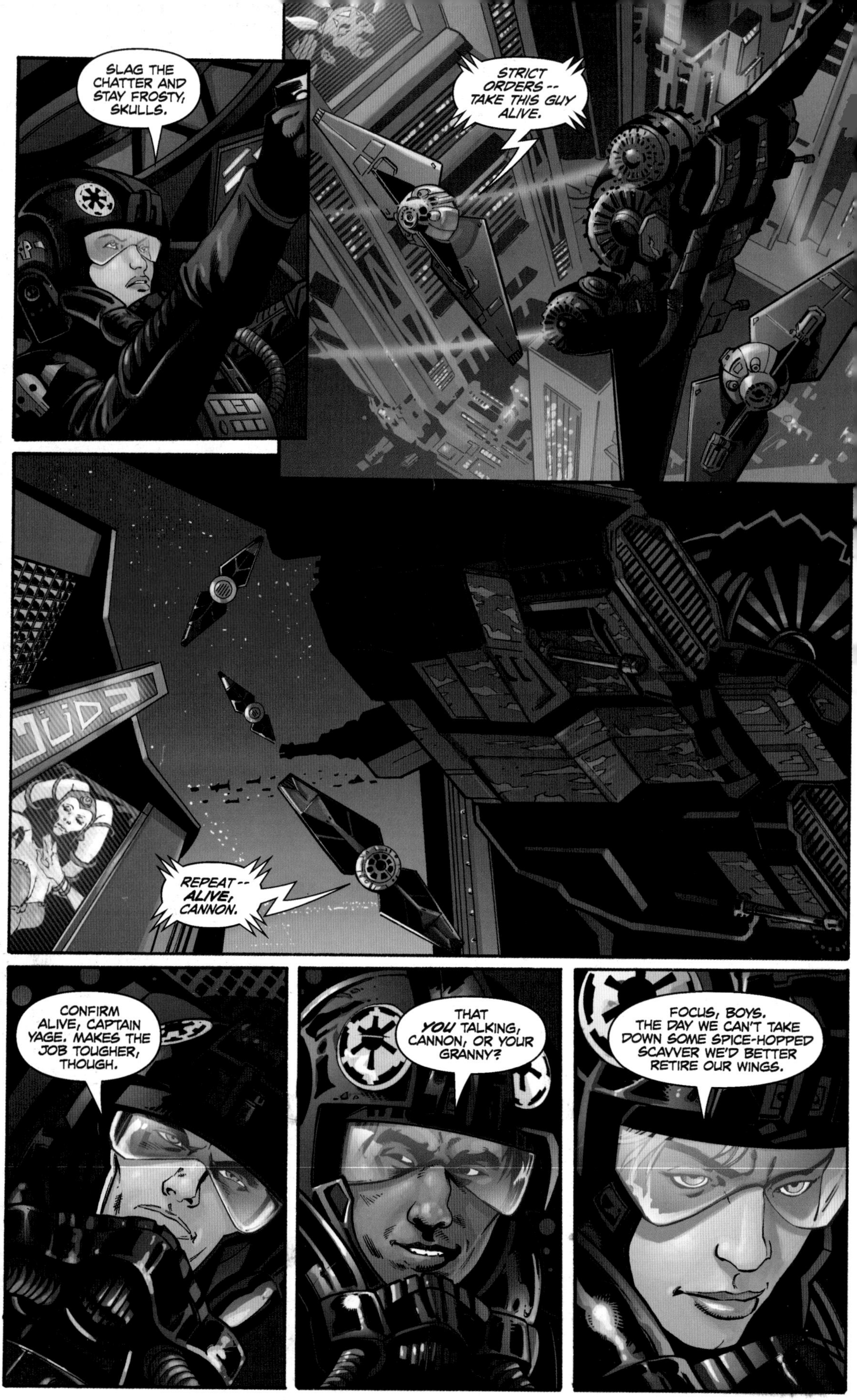
SLAG THE CHATTER AND STAY FROSTY, SKULLS.
STRICT ORDERS -- TAKE THIS GUY ALIVE.
REPEAT -- ALIVE, CANNON.
CONFIRM ALIVE, CAPTAIN YAGE. MAKES THE JOB TOUGHER, THOUGH.
THAT YOU TALKING, CANNON, OR YOUR GRANNY?
FOCUS, BOYS. THE DAY WE CAN'T TAKE DOWN SOME SPICE-HOPPED SCAVVER WE'D BETTER RETIRE OUR WINGS.

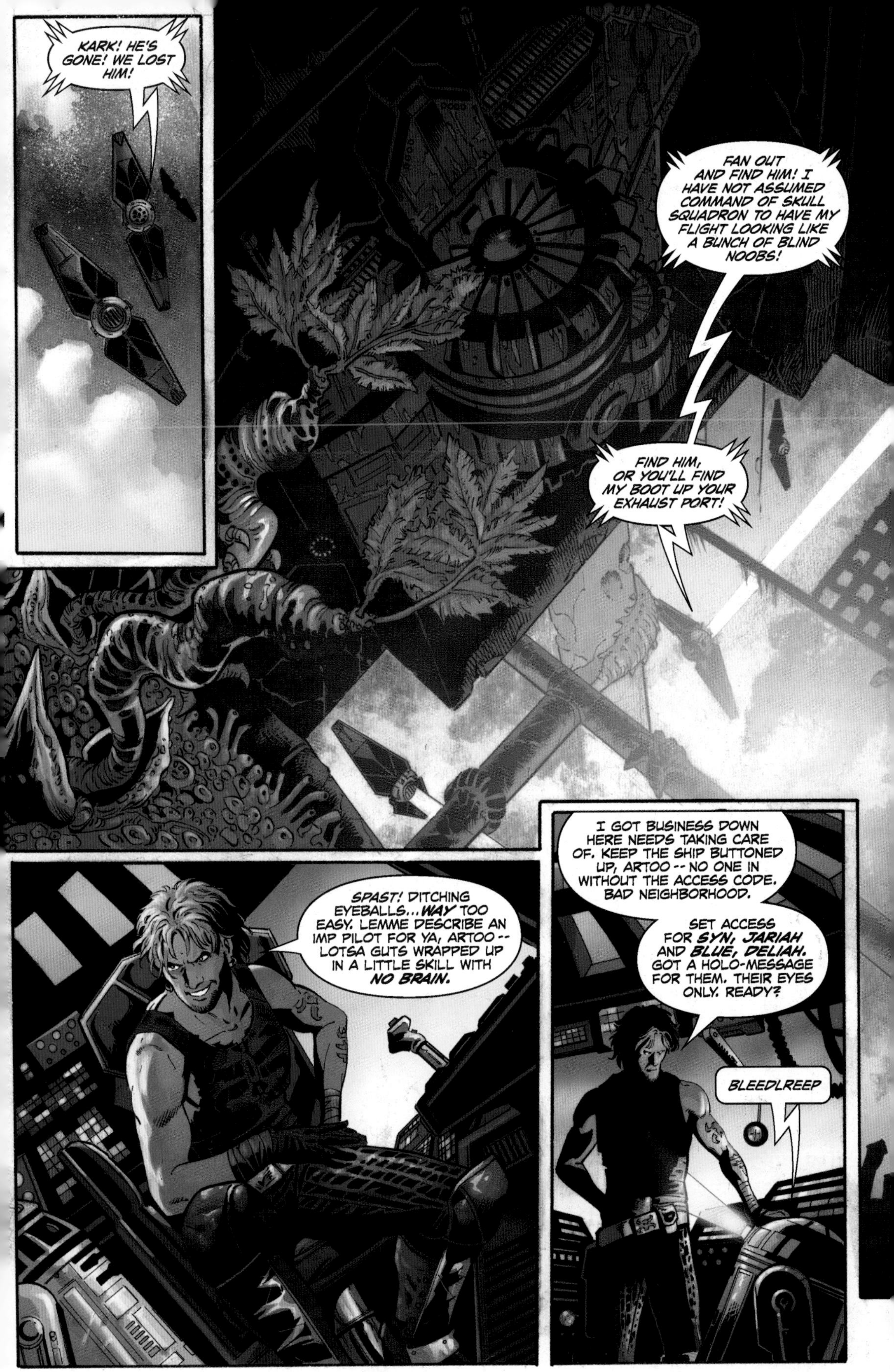
KARK! HE'S GONE! WE LOST HIM!
FAN OUT AND FIND HIM! I HAVE NOT ASSUMED COMMAND OF SKULL SQUADRON TO HAVE MY FLIGHT LOOKING LIKE A BUNCH OF BLIND NOOBS!
FIND HIM, OR YOU'LL FIND MY BOOT UP YOUR EXHAUST PORT!
SPAST! DITCHING EYEBALLS... WAY TOO EASY. LEMME DESCRIBE AN IMP PILOT FOR YA, ARTOO -- LOTSA GUTS WRAPPED UP IN A LITTLE SKILL WITH NO BRAIN.
I GOT BUSINESS DOWN HERE NEEDS TAKING CARE OF. KEEP THE SHIP BUTTONED UP, ARTOO -- NO ONE IN WITHOUT THE ACCESS CODE. BAD NEIGHBORHOOD.
SET ACCESS FOR SYN, JARIAH AND BLUE, DELIAH. GOT A HOLO-MESSAGE FOR THEM. THEIR EYES ONLY. READY?
BLEEDLREEP

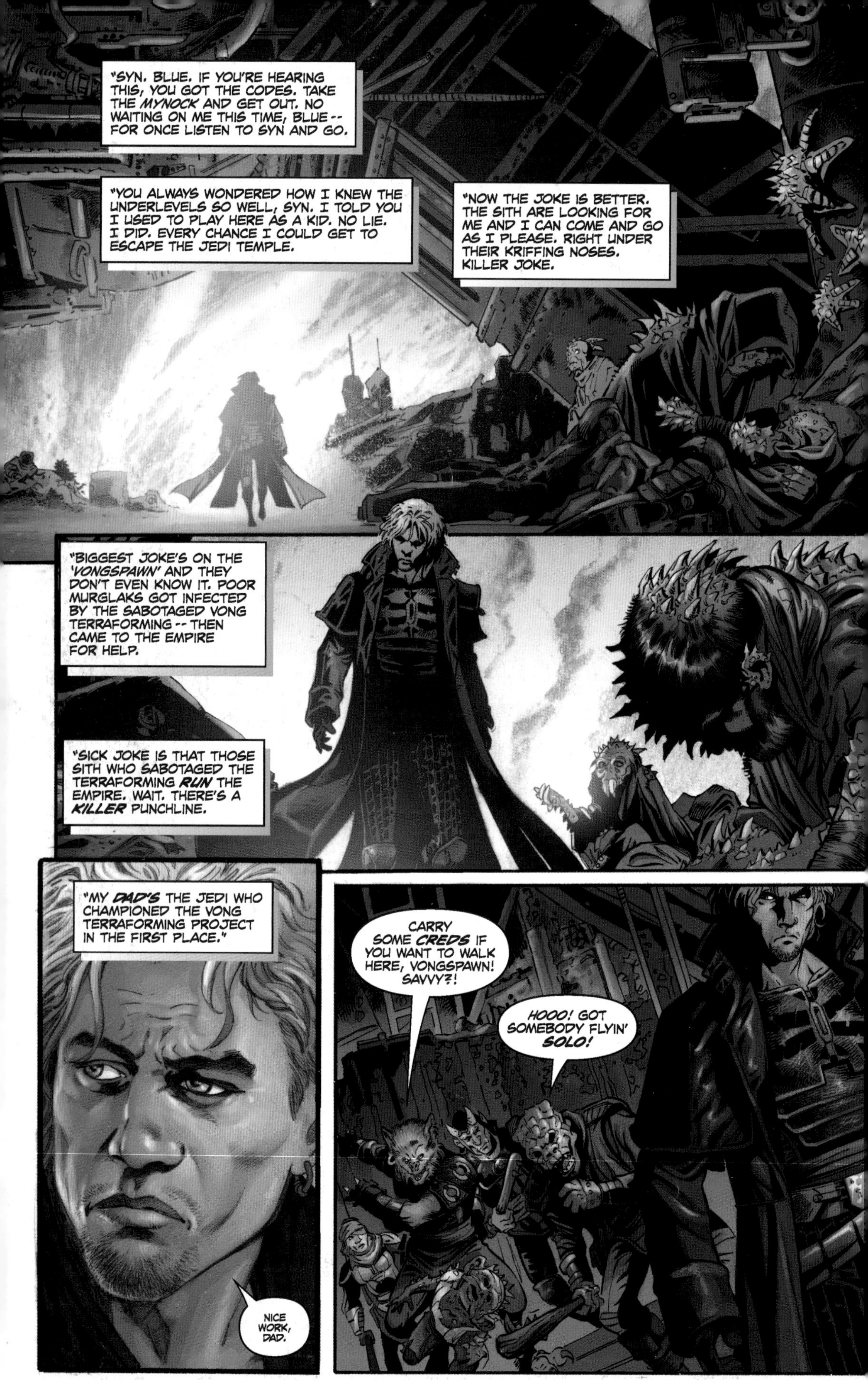
"SYN. BLUE. IF YOU'RE HEARING THIS, YOU GOT THE CODES. TAKE THE MYNOCK AND GET OUT. NO WAITING ON ME THIS TIME, BLUE -- FOR ONCE LISTEN TO SYN AND GO.
"YOU ALWAYS WONDERED HOW I KNEW THE UNDERLEVELS SO WELL, SYN. I TOLD YOU I USED TO PLAY HERE AS A KID. NO LIE. I DID. EVERY CHANCE I COULD GET TO ESCAPE THE JEDI TEMPLE.
"NOW THE JOKE IS BETTER. THE SITH ARE LOOKING FOR ME AND I CAN COME AND GO AS I PLEASE. RIGHT UNDER THEIR KRIFFING NOSES. KILLER JOKE.
"BIGGEST JOKE'S ON THE 'VONGSPAWN' AND THEY DON'T EVEN KNOW IT. POOR MURGLAKS GOT INFECTED BY THE SABOTAGED VONG TERRAFORMING -- THEN CAME TO THE EMPIRE FOR HELP.
"SICK JOKE IS THAT THOSE SITH WHO SABOTAGED THE TERRAFORMING RUN THE EMPIRE. WAIT. THERE'S A KILLER PUNCHLINE.
"MY DAD'S THE JEDI WHO CHAMPIONED THE VONG TERRAFORMING PROJECT IN THE FIRST PLACE."
NICE WORK, DAD.
CARRY SOME CREDS IF YOU WANT TO WALK HERE, VONGSPAWN! SAVVY?!
HOOO! GOT SOMEBODY FLYIN' SOLO!

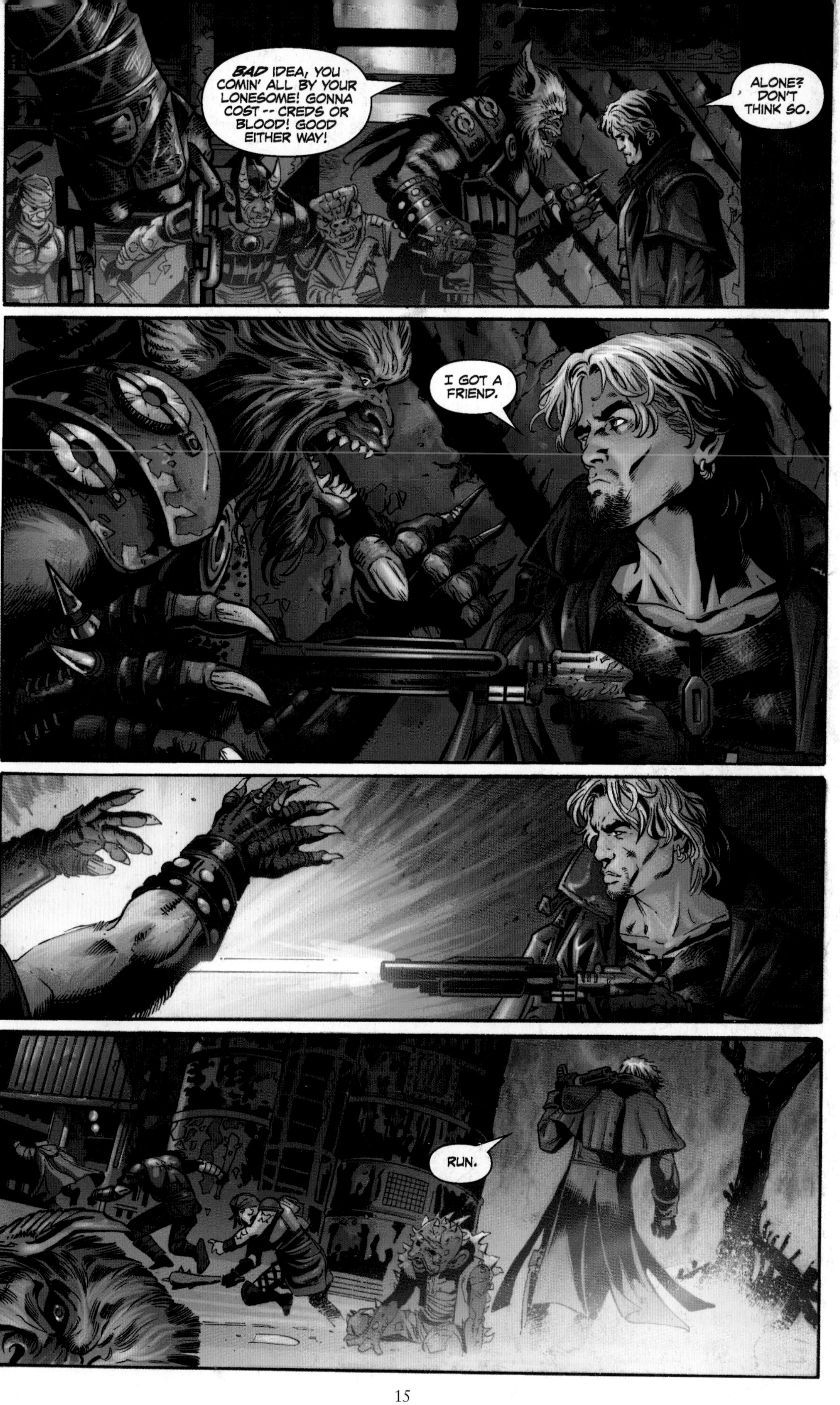
BAD IDEA, YOU COMIN' ALL BY YOUR LONESOME! GONNA COST -- CREDS OR BLOOD! GOOD EITHER WAY!
ALONE? DON'T THINK SO.
I GOT A FRIEND.
RUN.

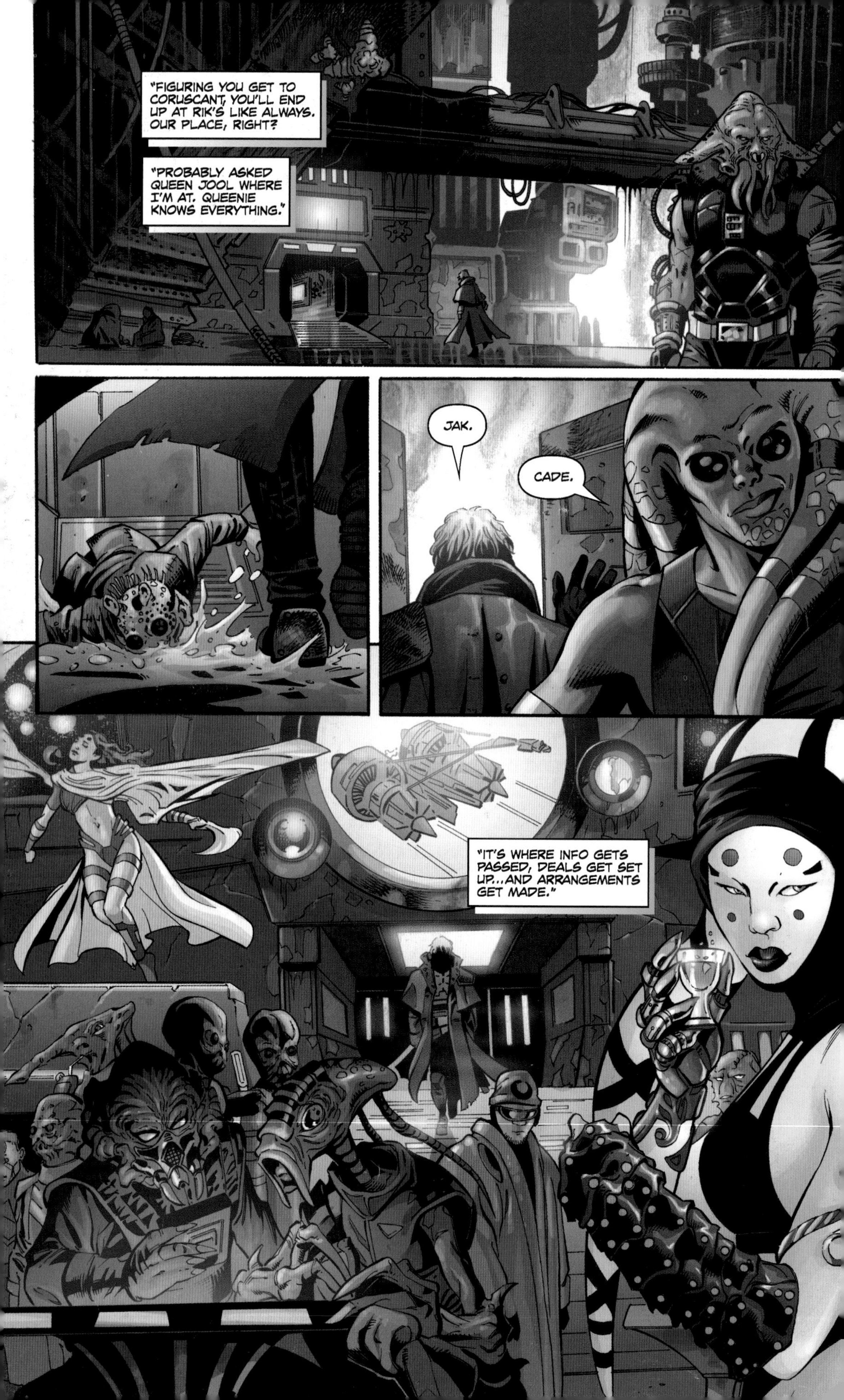
"FIGURING YOU GET TO CORUSCANT, YOU'LL END UP AT RIK'S LIKE ALWAYS. OUR PLACE, RIGHT?
"PROBABLY ASKED QUEEN JOOL WHERE I'M AT. QUEENIE KNOWS EVERYTHING."
JAK.
CADE.
"IT'S WHERE INFO GETS PASSED, DEALS GET SET UP...AND ARRANGEMENTS GET MADE."

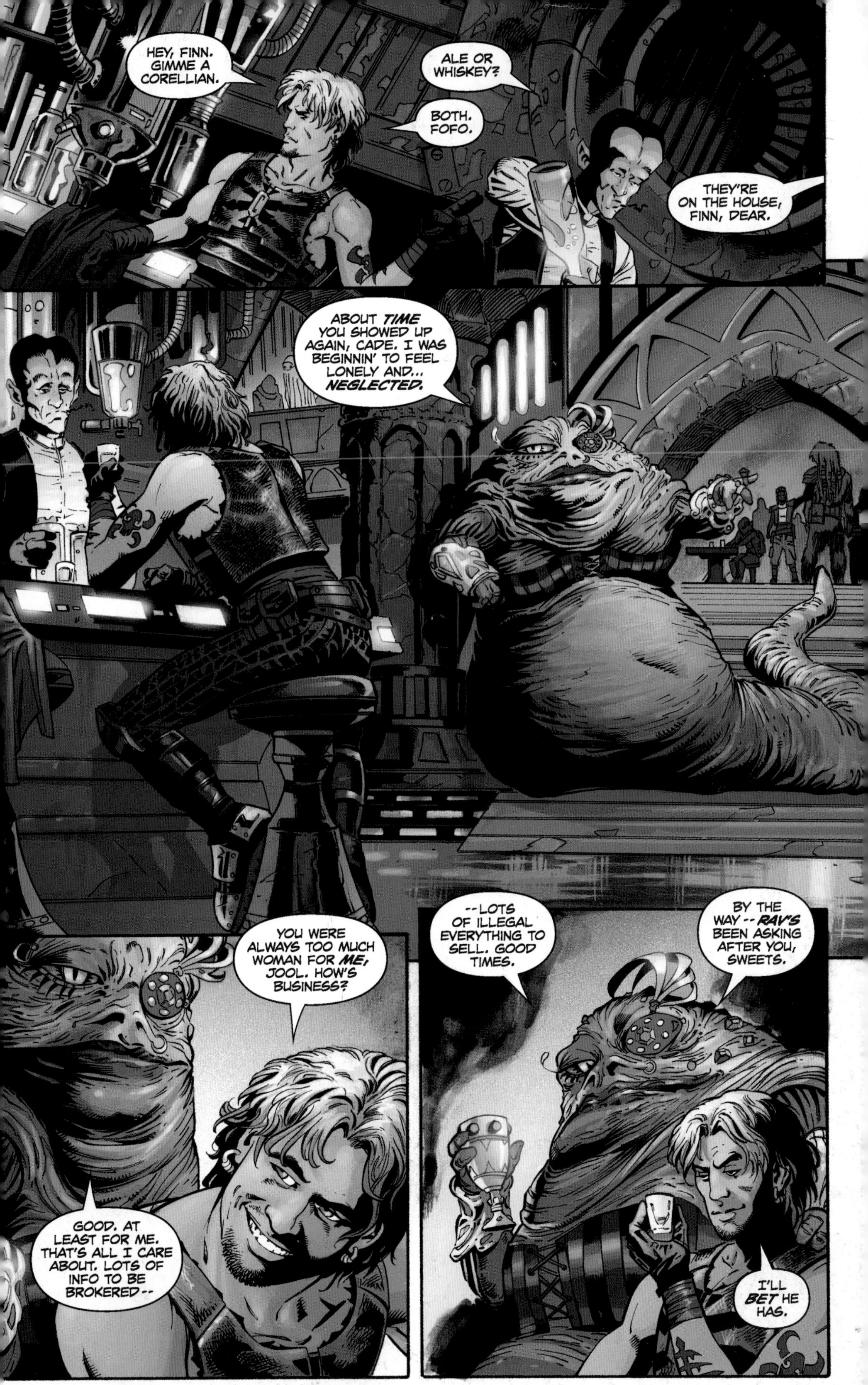

HEY, FINN. GIMME A CORELLIAN.
ALE OR WHISKEY?
BOTH. FOFO.
THEY'RE ON THE HOUSE, FINN, DEAR.
ABOUT TIME YOU SHOWED UP AGAIN, CADE. I WAS BEGINNIN' TO FEEL LONELY AND... NEGLECTED.
YOU WERE ALWAYS TOO MUCH WOMAN FOR ME, JOOL. HOW'S BUSINESS?
GOOD. AT LEAST FOR ME. THAT'S ALL I CARE ABOUT. LOTS OF INFO TO BE BROKERED--
--LOTS OF ILLEGAL EVERYTHING TO SELL. GOOD TIMES.
BY THE WAY--RAV'S BEEN ASKING AFTER YOU, SWEETS.
I'LL BET HE HAS.

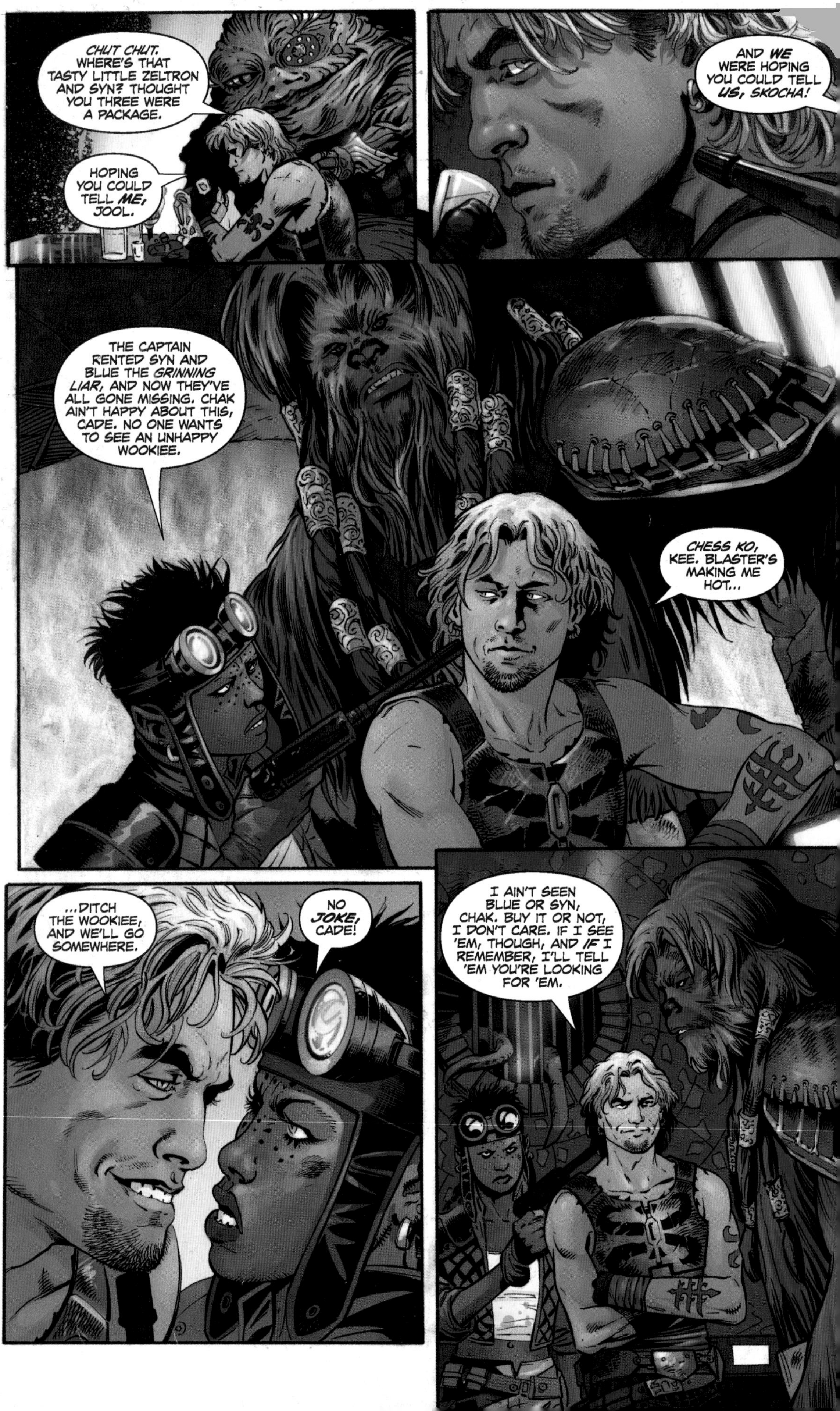
CHUT CHUT. WHERE'S THAT TASTY LITTLE ZELTRON AND SYN? THOUGHT YOU THREE WERE A PACKAGE.
HOPING YOU COULD TELL ME, JOOL.
AND WE WERE HOPING YOU COULD TELL US, SKOCHA!
THE CAPTAIN RENTED SYN AND BLUE THE GRINNING LIAR, AND NOW THEY'VE ALL GONE MISSING. CHAK AIN'T HAPPY ABOUT THIS, CADE. NO ONE WANTS TO SEE AN UNHAPPY WOOKIEE.
CHESS KO, KEE. BLASTER'S MAKING ME HOT...
...DITCH THE WOOKIEE, AND WE'LL GO SOMEWHERE.
NO JOKE, CADE!
I AIN'T SEEN BLUE OR SYN, CHAK. BUY IT OR NOT, I DON'T CARE. IF I SEE 'EM, THOUGH, AND IF I REMEMBER, I'LL TELL 'EM YOU'RE LOOKING FOR 'EM.

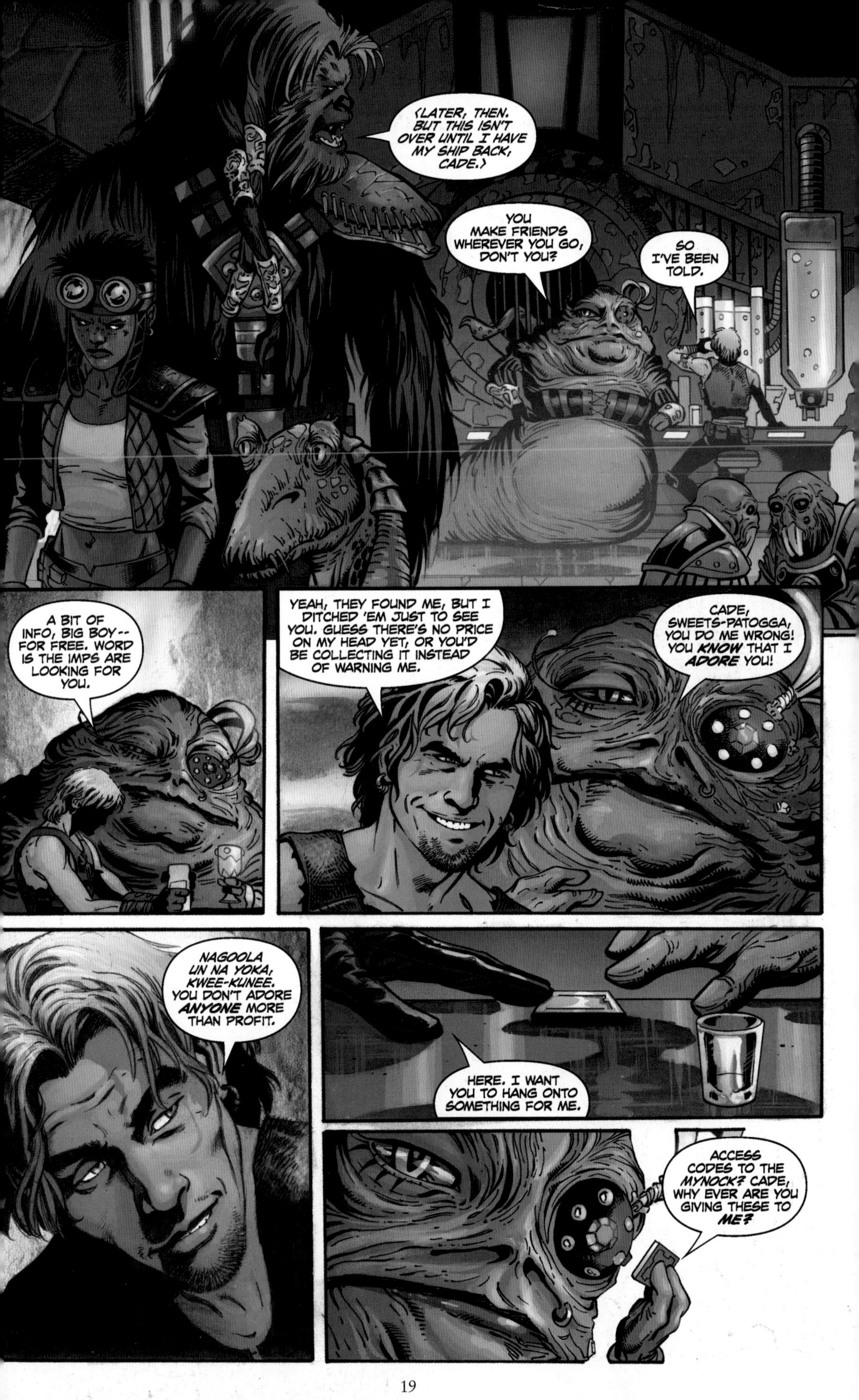
<LATER, THEN. BUT THIS ISN'T OVER UNTIL I HAVE MY SHIP BACK, CADE.>
YOU MAKE FRIENDS WHEREVER YOU GO, DON'T YOU?
SO I'VE BEEN TOLD.
A BIT OF INFO, BIG BOY-- FOR FREE. WORD IS THE IMPS ARE LOOKING FOR YOU.
YEAH, THEY FOUND ME, BUT I DITCHED 'EM JUST TO SEE YOU. GUESS THERE'S NO PRICE ON MY HEAD YET, OR YOU'D BE COLLECTING IT INSTEAD OF WARNING ME.
CADE, SWEETS-PATOGGA, YOU DO ME WRONG! YOU KNOW THAT I ADORE YOU!
NAGOOLA UN NA YOKA, KWEE-KUNEE. YOU DON'T ADORE ANYONE MORE THAN PROFIT.
HERE. I WANT YOU TO HANG ONTO SOMETHING FOR ME.
ACCESS CODES TO THE MYNOCK? CADE, WHY EVER ARE YOU GIVING THESE TO ME?

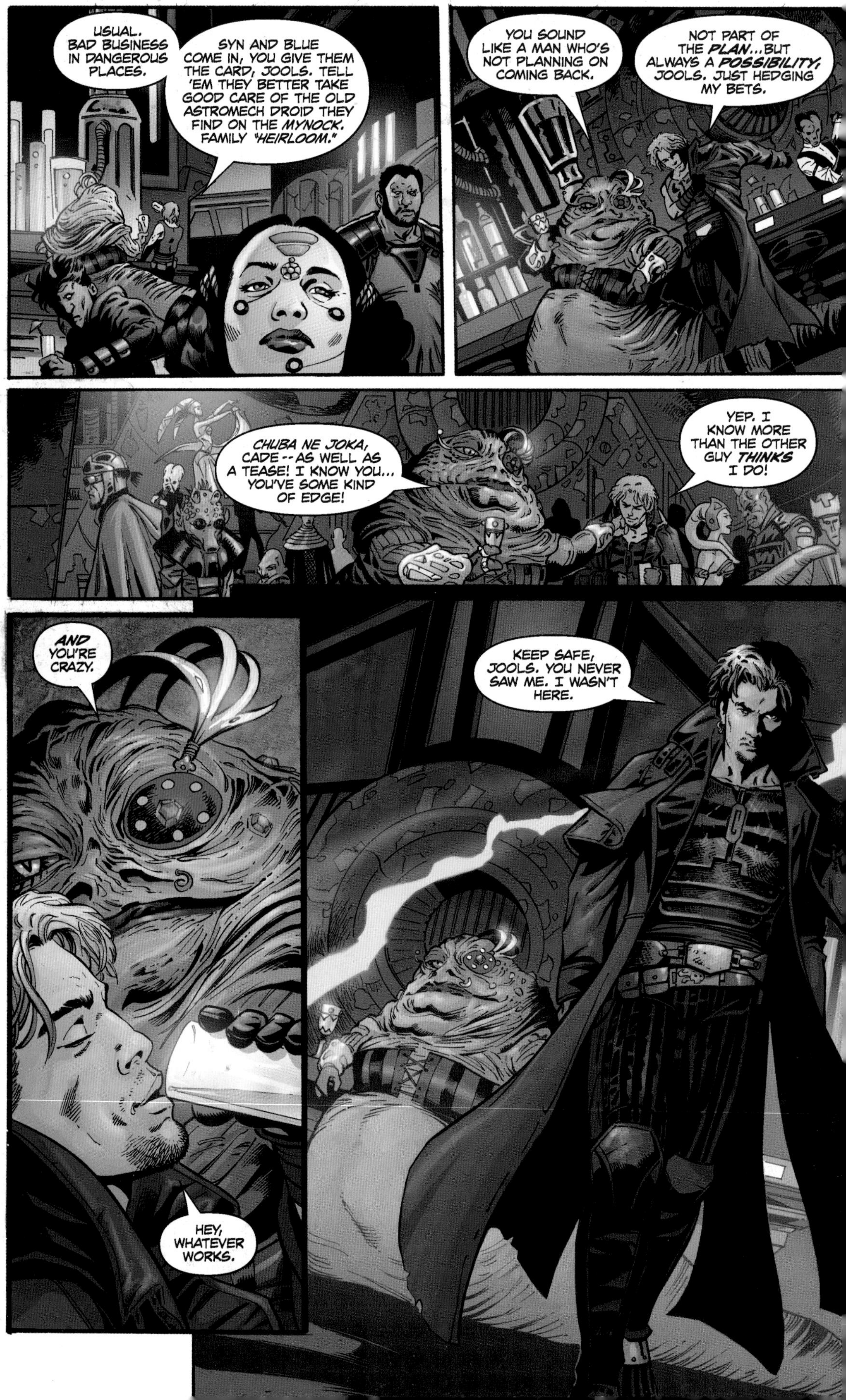
USUAL. BAD BUSINESS IN DANGEROUS PLACES.
SYN AND BLUE COME IN, YOU GIVE THEM THE CARD, JOOLS. TELL 'EM THEY BETTER TAKE GOOD CARE OF THE OLD ASTROMECH DROID THEY FIND ON THE *MYNOCK*. FAMILY *"HEIRLOOM."*
YOU SOUND LIKE A MAN WHO'S NOT PLANNING ON COMING BACK.
NOT PART OF THE ***PLAN***...BUT ALWAYS A ***POSSIBILITY,*** JOOLS. JUST HEDGING MY BETS.
CHUBA NE JOKA, CADE--AS WELL AS A TEASE! I KNOW YOU... YOU'VE SOME KIND OF EDGE!
YEP. I KNOW MORE THAN THE OTHER GUY ***THINKS*** I DO!
AND YOU'RE CRAZY.
HEY, WHATEVER WORKS.
KEEP SAFE, JOOLS. YOU NEVER SAW ME. I WASN'T HERE.

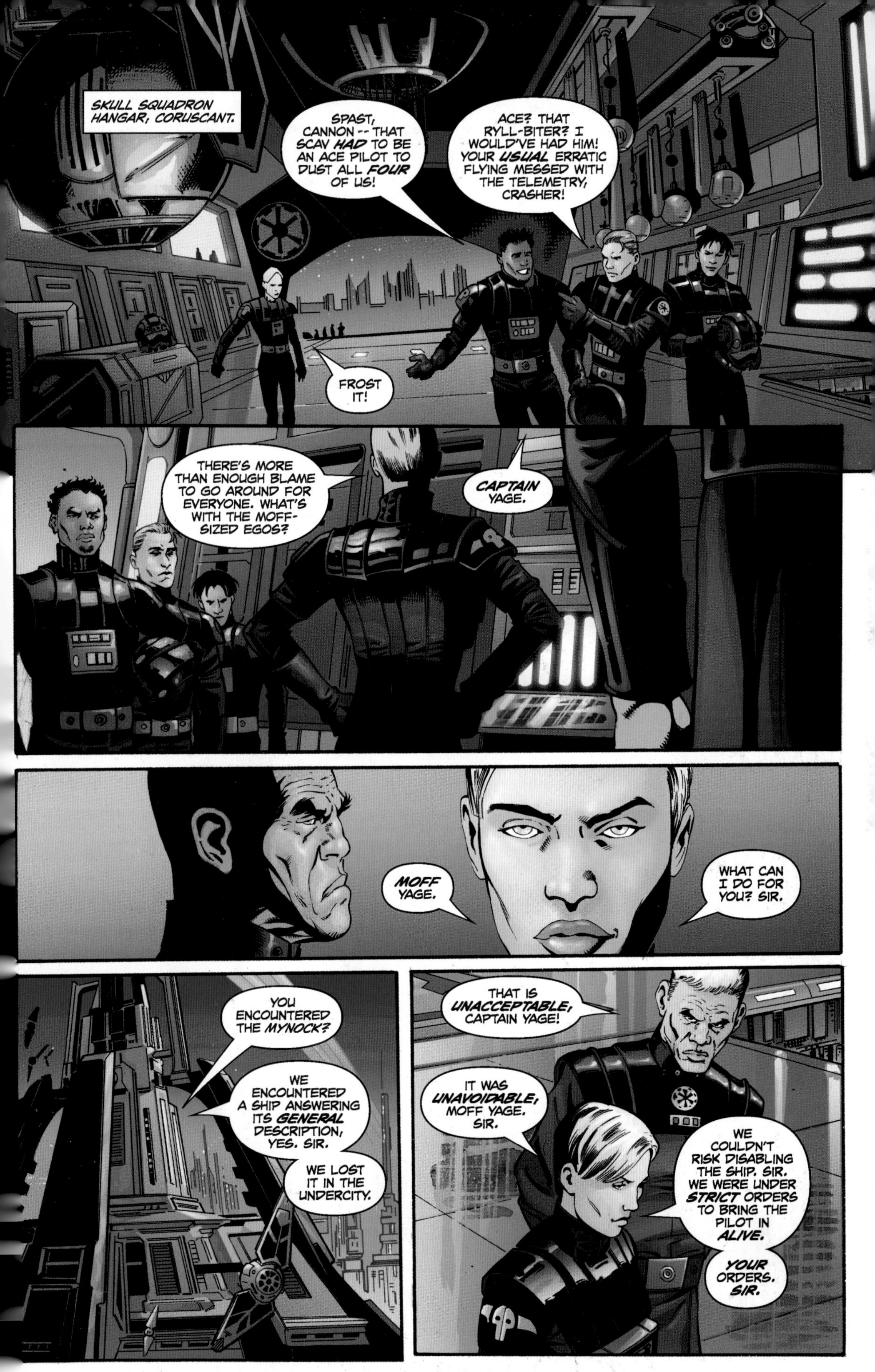
SKULL SQUADRON HANGAR, CORUSCANT.
SPAST, CANNON -- THAT SCAV *HAD* TO BE AN ACE PILOT TO DUST ALL *FOUR* OF US!
ACE? THAT RYLL-BITER? I WOULD'VE HAD HIM! YOUR *USUAL* ERRATIC FLYING MESSED WITH THE TELEMETRY, CRASHER!
FROST IT!
THERE'S MORE THAN ENOUGH BLAME TO GO AROUND FOR EVERYONE. WHAT'S WITH THE MOFF-SIZED EGOS?
CAPTAIN YAGE.
MOFF YAGE.
WHAT CAN I DO FOR YOU? SIR.
YOU ENCOUNTERED THE *MYNOCK*?
WE ENCOUNTERED A SHIP ANSWERING ITS *GENERAL* DESCRIPTION, YES. SIR.
WE LOST IT IN THE UNDERCITY.
THAT IS *UNACCEPTABLE,* CAPTAIN YAGE!
IT WAS *UNAVOIDABLE,* MOFF YAGE. SIR.
WE COULDN'T RISK DISABLING THE SHIP. SIR. WE WERE UNDER *STRICT* ORDERS TO BRING THE PILOT IN *ALIVE.*
YOUR ORDERS. *SIR.*

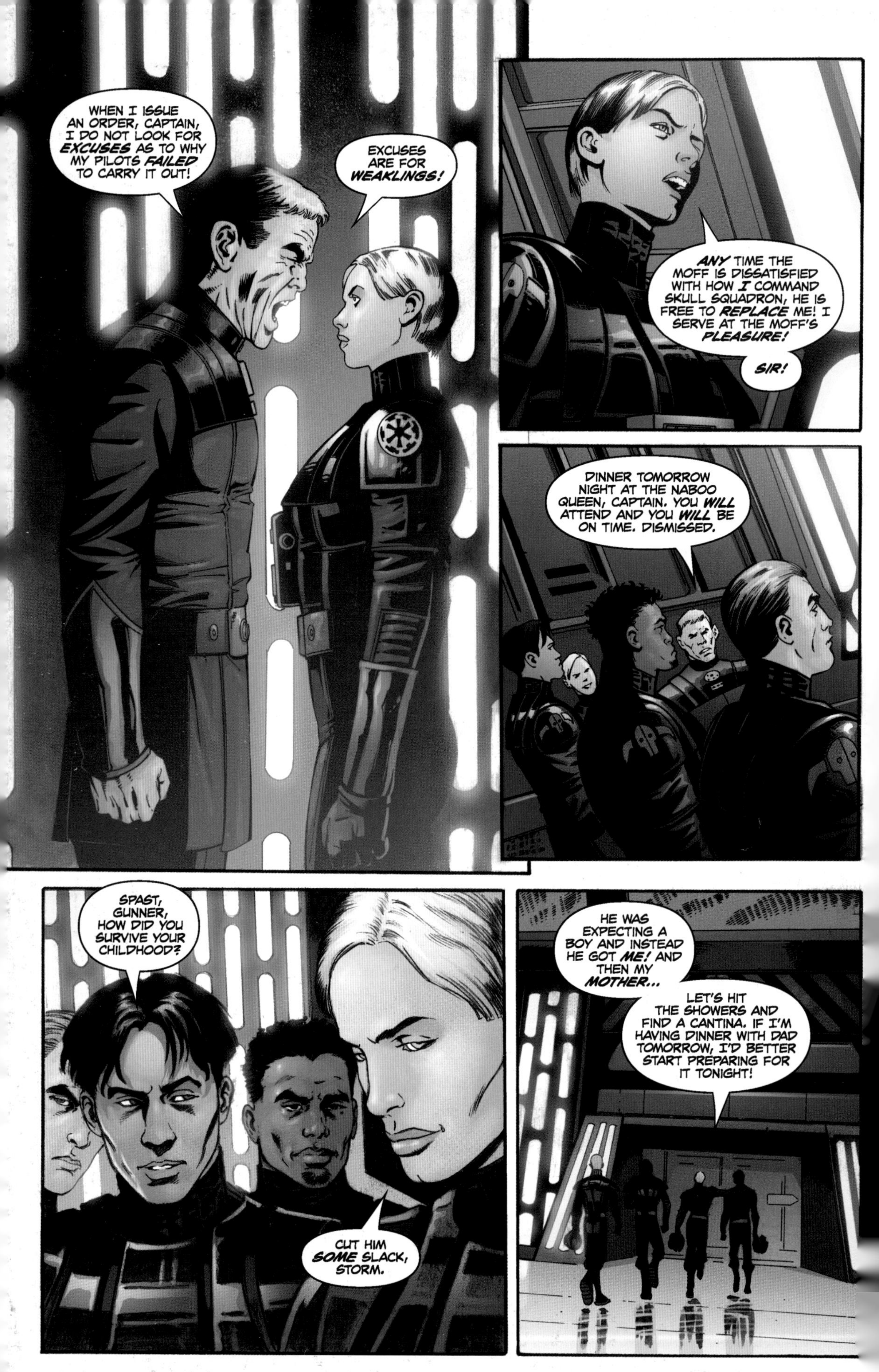
WHEN I ISSUE AN ORDER, CAPTAIN, I DO NOT LOOK FOR EXCUSES AS TO WHY MY PILOTS FAILED TO CARRY IT OUT!
EXCUSES ARE FOR WEAKLINGS!
ANY TIME THE MOFF IS DISSATISFIED WITH HOW I COMMAND SKULL SQUADRON, HE IS FREE TO REPLACE ME! I SERVE AT THE MOFF'S PLEASURE!
SIR!
DINNER TOMORROW NIGHT AT THE NABOO QUEEN, CAPTAIN. YOU WILL ATTEND AND YOU WILL BE ON TIME. DISMISSED.
SPAST, GUNNER, HOW DID YOU SURVIVE YOUR CHILDHOOD?
CUT HIM SOME SLACK, STORM.
HE WAS EXPECTING A BOY AND INSTEAD HE GOT ME! AND THEN MY MOTHER...
LET'S HIT THE SHOWERS AND FIND A CANTINA. IF I'M HAVING DINNER WITH DAD TOMORROW, I'D BETTER START PREPARING FOR IT TONIGHT!

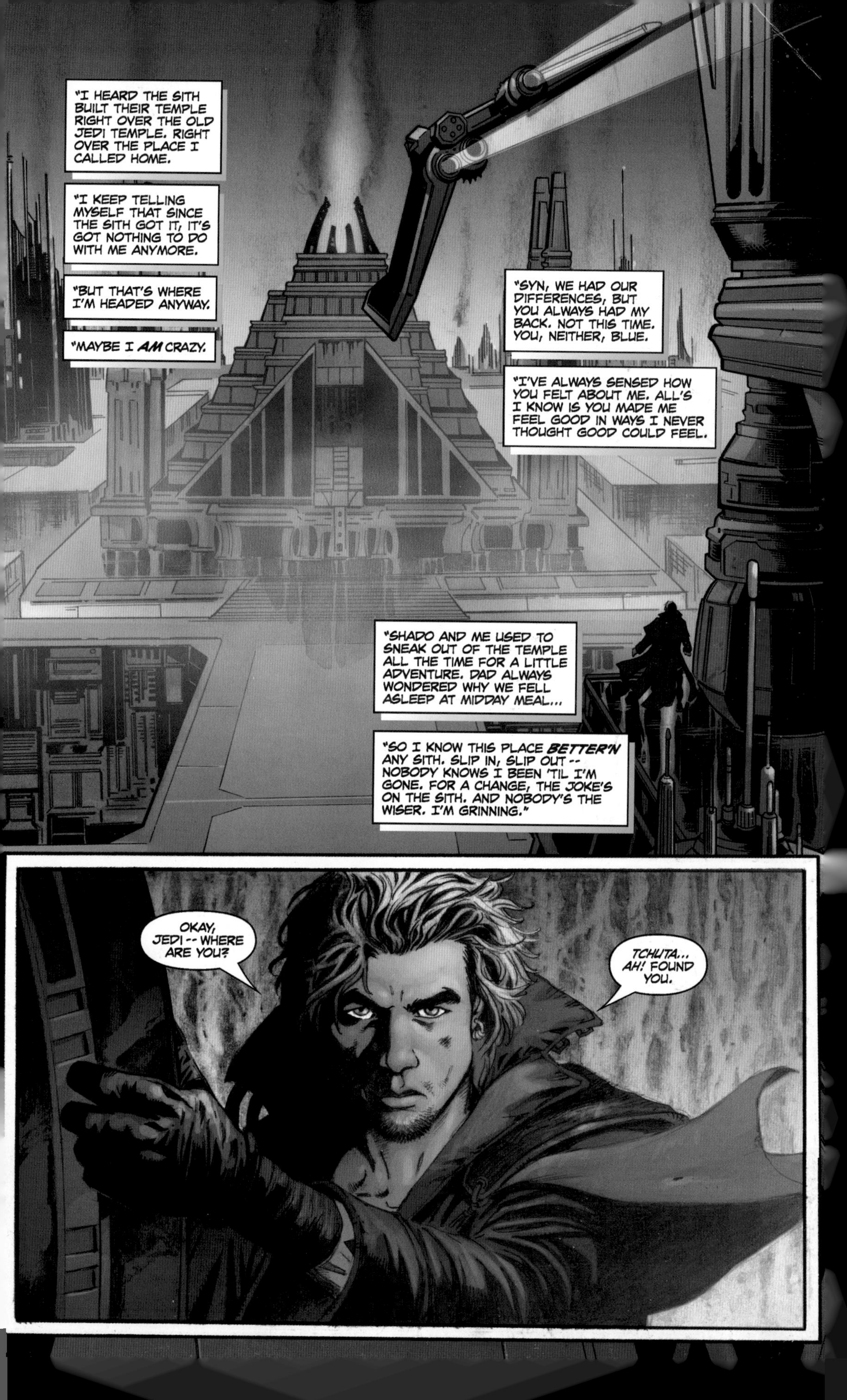
"I HEARD THE SITH BUILT THEIR TEMPLE RIGHT OVER THE OLD JEDI TEMPLE. RIGHT OVER THE PLACE I CALLED HOME.
"I KEEP TELLING MYSELF THAT SINCE THE SITH GOT IT, IT'S GOT NOTHING TO DO WITH ME ANYMORE.
"BUT THAT'S WHERE I'M HEADED ANYWAY.
"MAYBE I *AM* CRAZY.
"SYN, WE HAD OUR DIFFERENCES, BUT YOU ALWAYS HAD MY BACK. NOT THIS TIME. YOU, NEITHER, BLUE.
"I'VE ALWAYS SENSED HOW YOU FELT ABOUT ME. ALL'S I KNOW IS YOU MADE ME FEEL GOOD IN WAYS I NEVER THOUGHT GOOD COULD FEEL.
"SHADO AND ME USED TO SNEAK OUT OF THE TEMPLE ALL THE TIME FOR A LITTLE ADVENTURE. DAD ALWAYS WONDERED WHY WE FELL ASLEEP AT MIDDAY MEAL...
"SO I KNOW THIS PLACE *BETTER'N* ANY SITH. SLIP IN, SLIP OUT -- NOBODY KNOWS I BEEN 'TIL I'M GONE. FOR A CHANGE, THE JOKE'S ON THE SITH. AND NOBODY'S THE WISER. I'M GRINNING."
OKAY, JEDI -- WHERE ARE YOU?
TCHUTA... AH! FOUND YOU.

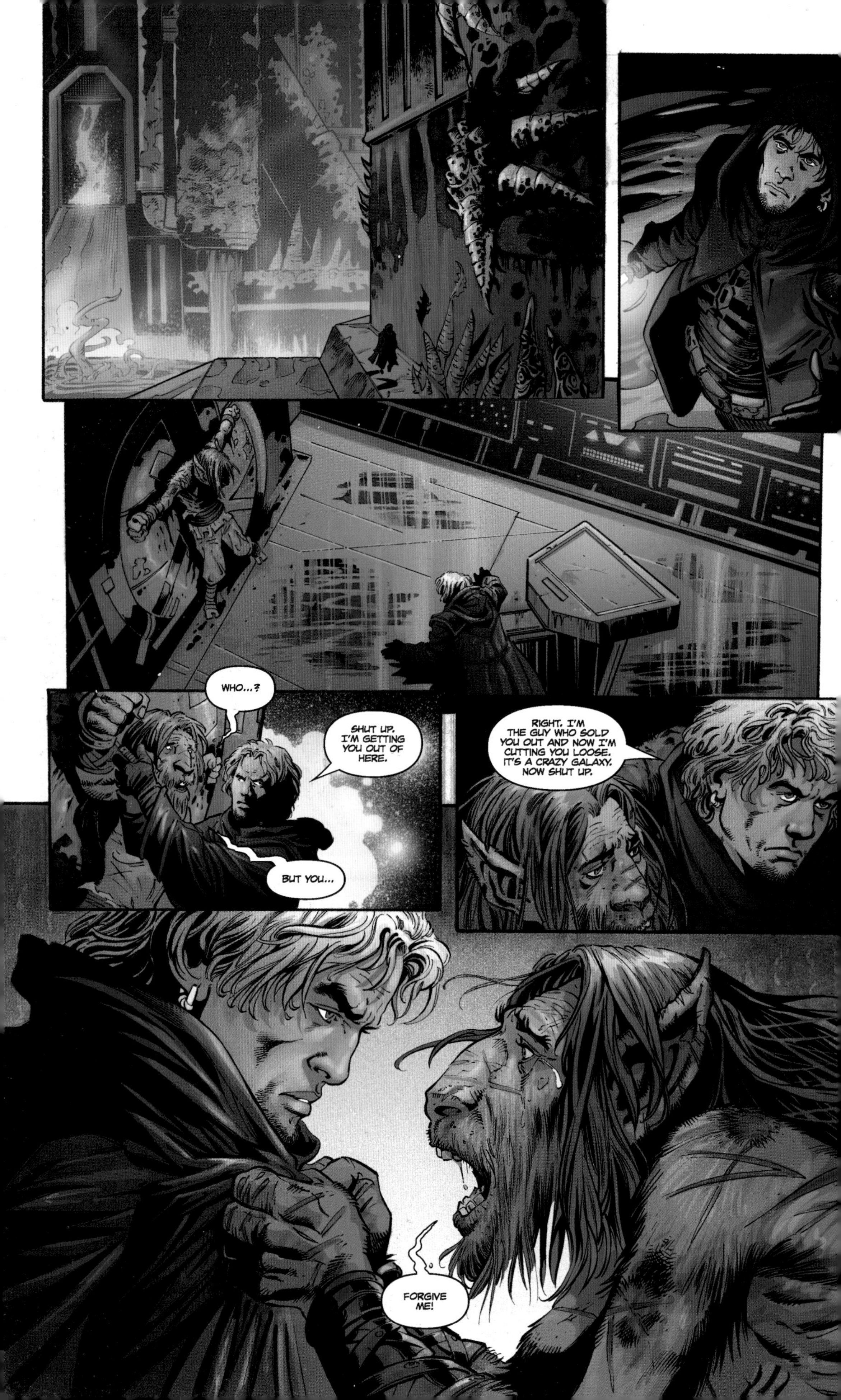
WHO...?
SHUT UP. I'M GETTING YOU OUT OF HERE.
BUT YOU...
RIGHT. I'M THE GUY WHO SOLD YOU OUT AND NOW I'M CUTTING YOU LOOSE. IT'S A CRAZY GALAXY. NOW SHUT UP.
FORGIVE ME!

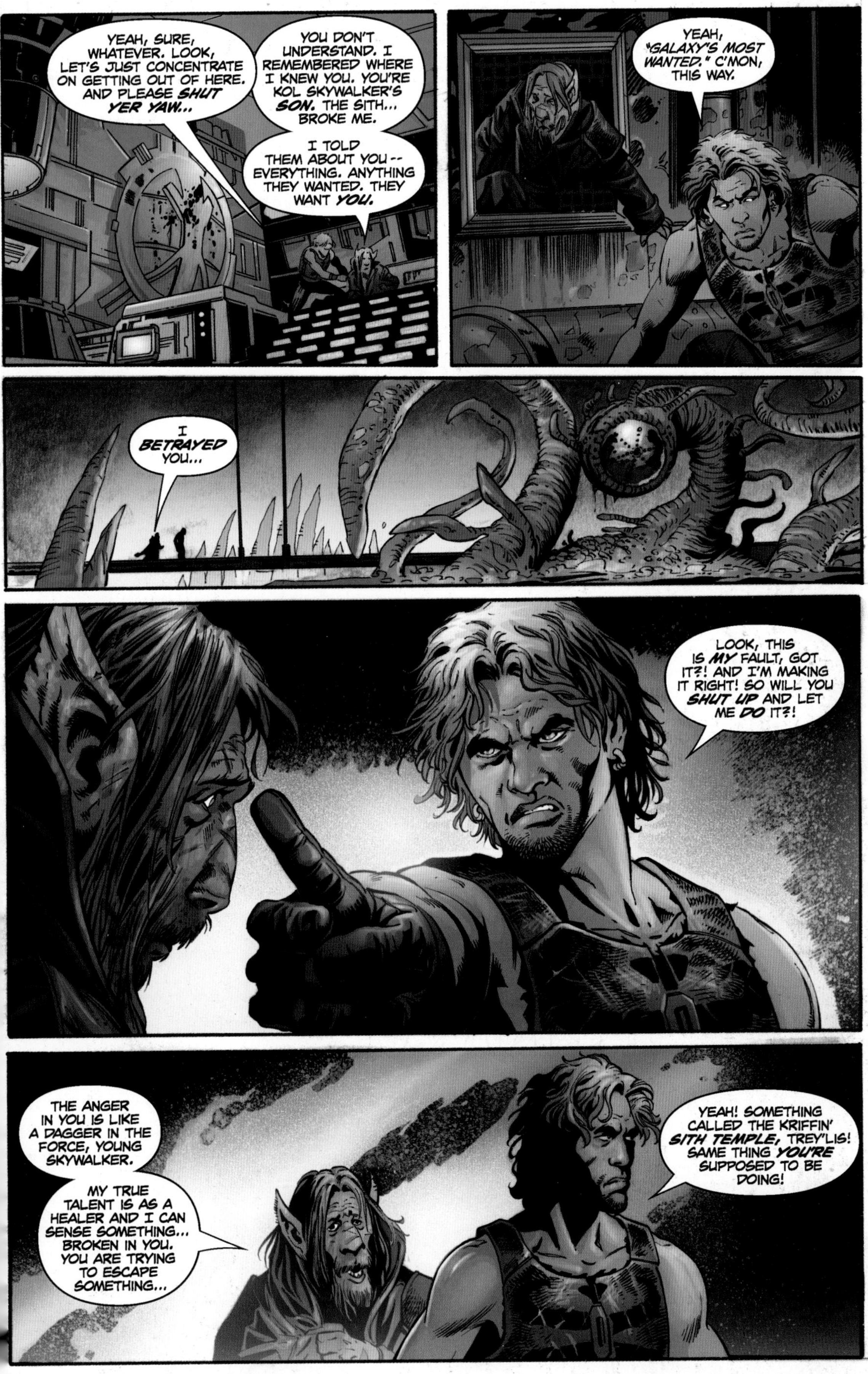
YEAH, SURE, WHATEVER. LOOK, LET'S JUST CONCENTRATE ON GETTING OUT OF HERE. AND PLEASE SHUT YER YAW...
YOU DON'T UNDERSTAND. I REMEMBERED WHERE I KNEW YOU. YOU'RE KOL SKYWALKER'S SON. THE SITH... BROKE ME.
I TOLD THEM ABOUT YOU -- EVERYTHING. ANYTHING THEY WANTED. THEY WANT YOU.
YEAH, "GALAXY'S MOST WANTED." C'MON, THIS WAY.
I BETRAYED YOU...
LOOK, THIS IS MY FAULT, GOT IT?! AND I'M MAKING IT RIGHT! SO WILL YOU SHUT UP AND LET ME DO IT?!
THE ANGER IN YOU IS LIKE A DAGGER IN THE FORCE, YOUNG SKYWALKER.
MY TRUE TALENT IS AS A HEALER AND I CAN SENSE SOMETHING... BROKEN IN YOU. YOU ARE TRYING TO ESCAPE SOMETHING...
YEAH! SOMETHING CALLED THE KRIFFIN' SITH TEMPLE, TREY'LIS! SAME THING YOU'RE SUPPOSED TO BE DOING!

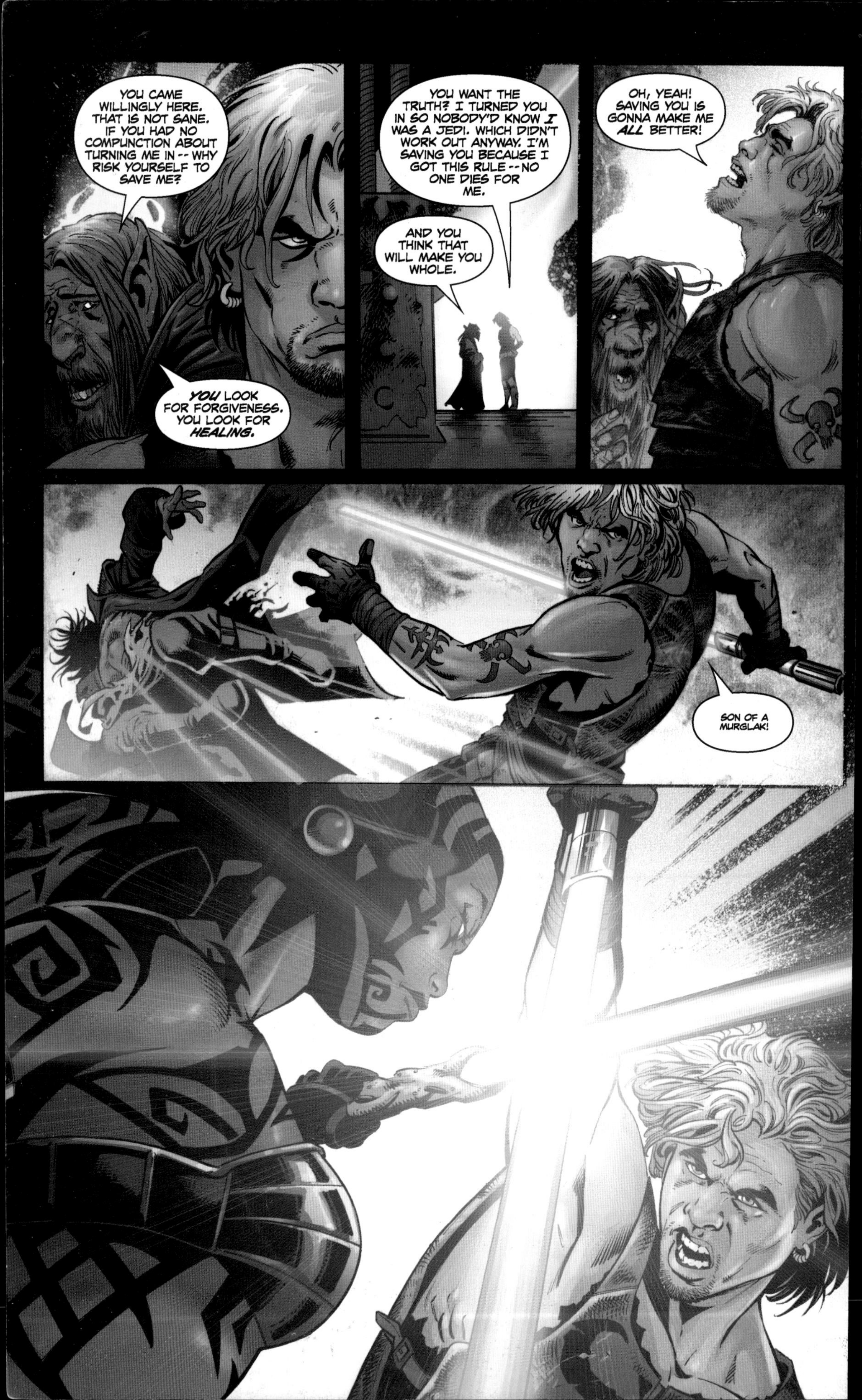

YOU CAME WILLINGLY HERE. THAT IS NOT SANE. IF YOU HAD NO COMPUNCTION ABOUT TURNING ME IN -- WHY RISK YOURSELF TO SAVE ME?
YOU LOOK FOR FORGIVENESS. YOU LOOK FOR HEALING.
YOU WANT THE TRUTH? I TURNED YOU IN SO NOBODY'D KNOW I WAS A JEDI. WHICH DIDN'T WORK OUT ANYWAY. I'M SAVING YOU BECAUSE I GOT THIS RULE -- NO ONE DIES FOR ME.
AND YOU THINK THAT WILL MAKE YOU WHOLE.
OH, YEAH! SAVING YOU IS GONNA MAKE ME ALL BETTER!
SON OF A MURGLAK!

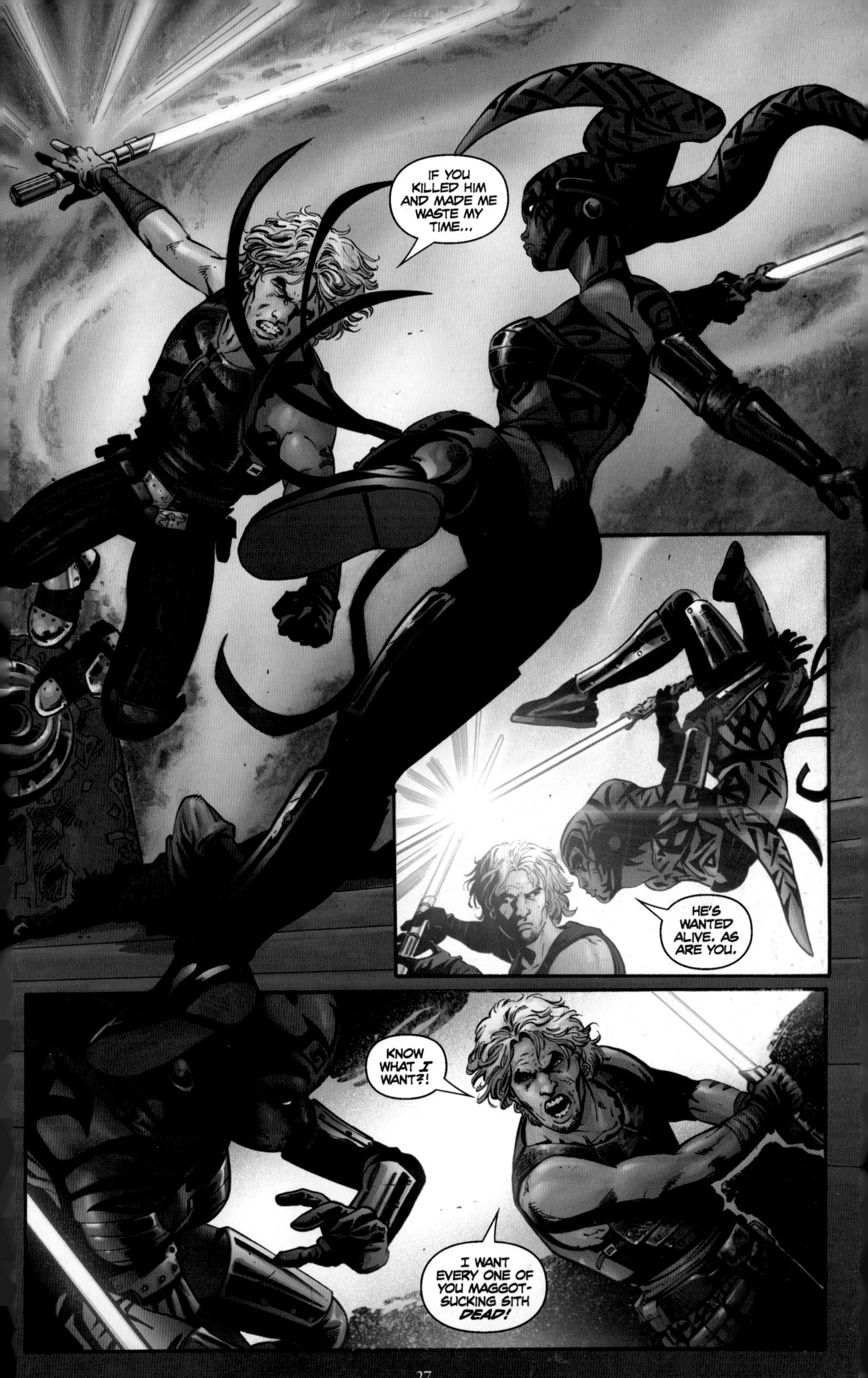
IF YOU KILLED HIM AND MADE ME WASTE MY TIME...
HE'S WANTED ALIVE. AS ARE YOU.
KNOW WHAT *I* WANT?!
I WANT EVERY ONE OF YOU MAGGOT-SUCKING SITH ***DEAD!***

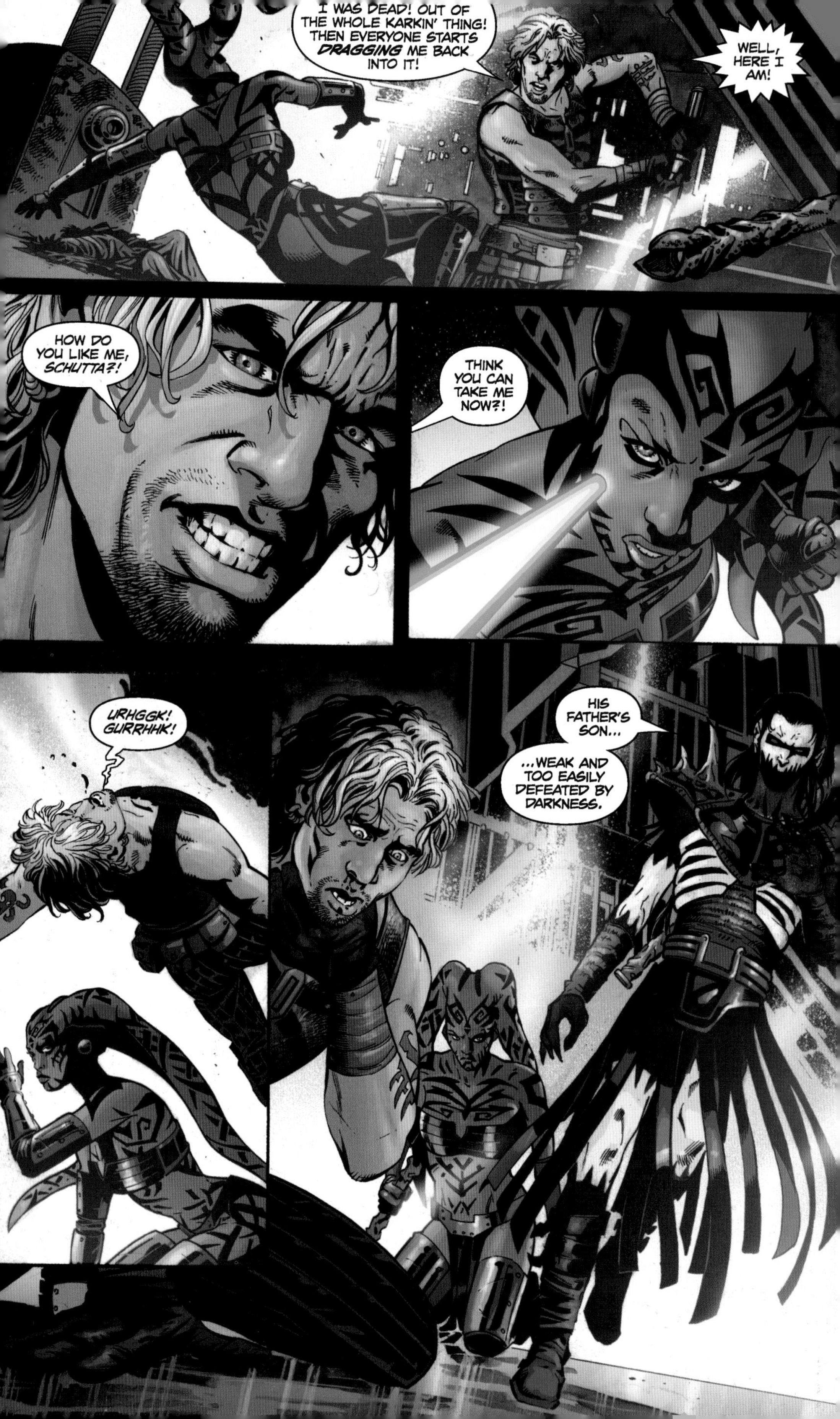
I WAS DEAD! OUT OF THE WHOLE KARKIN' THING! THEN EVERYONE STARTS DRAGGING ME BACK INTO IT!
WELL, HERE I AM!
HOW DO YOU LIKE ME, SCHUTTA?!
THINK YOU CAN TAKE ME NOW?!
URHGGK! GURRHHK!
HIS FATHER'S SON...
...WEAK AND TOO EASILY DEFEATED BY DARKNESS.

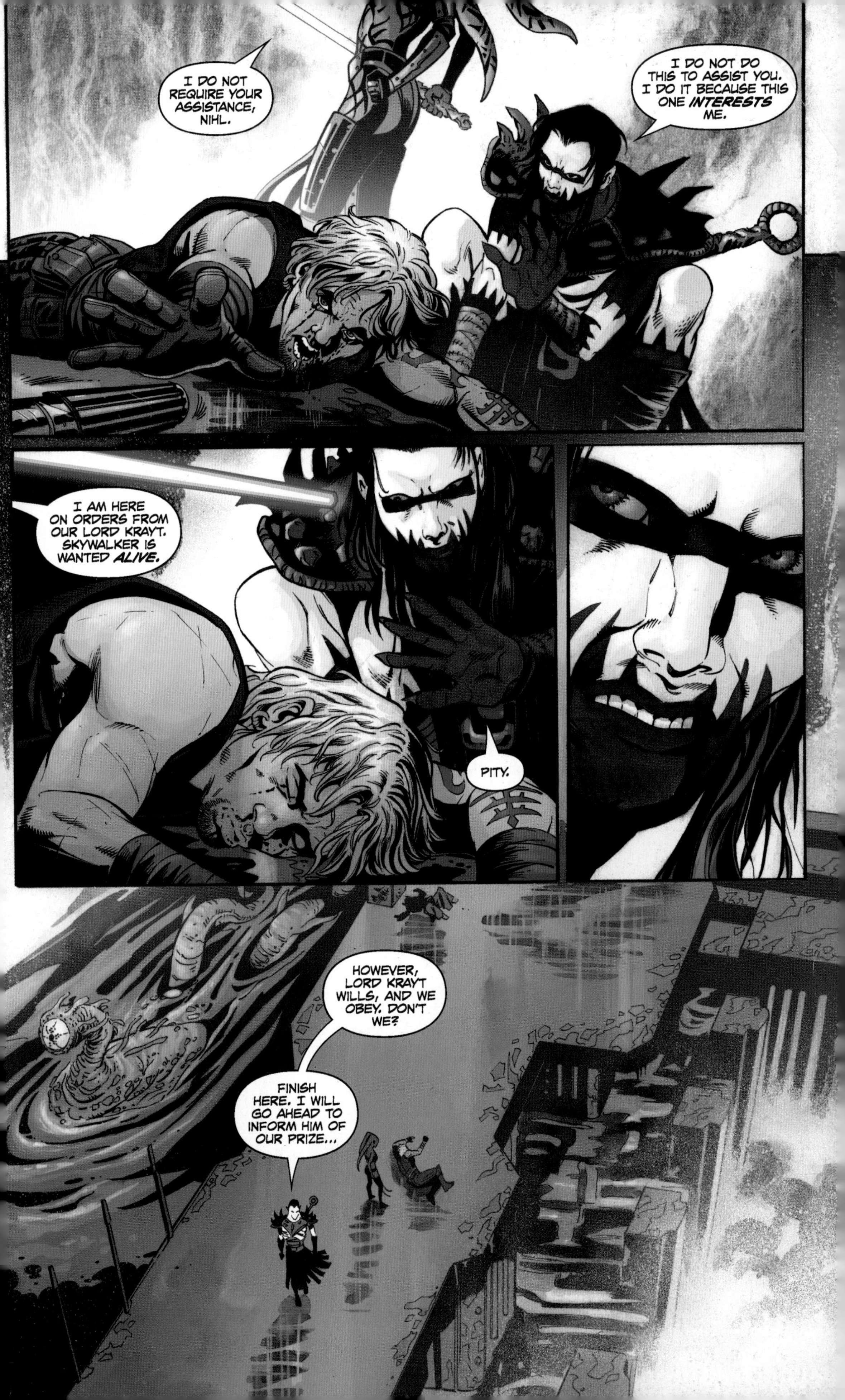
I DO NOT REQUIRE YOUR ASSISTANCE, NIHL.
I DO NOT DO THIS TO ASSIST YOU. I DO IT BECAUSE THIS ONE *INTERESTS* ME.
I AM HERE ON ORDERS FROM OUR LORD KRAYT. SKYWALKER IS WANTED *ALIVE.*
PITY.
HOWEVER, LORD KRAYT WILLS, AND WE OBEY. DON'T WE?
FINISH HERE. I WILL GO AHEAD TO INFORM HIM OF OUR PRIZE...

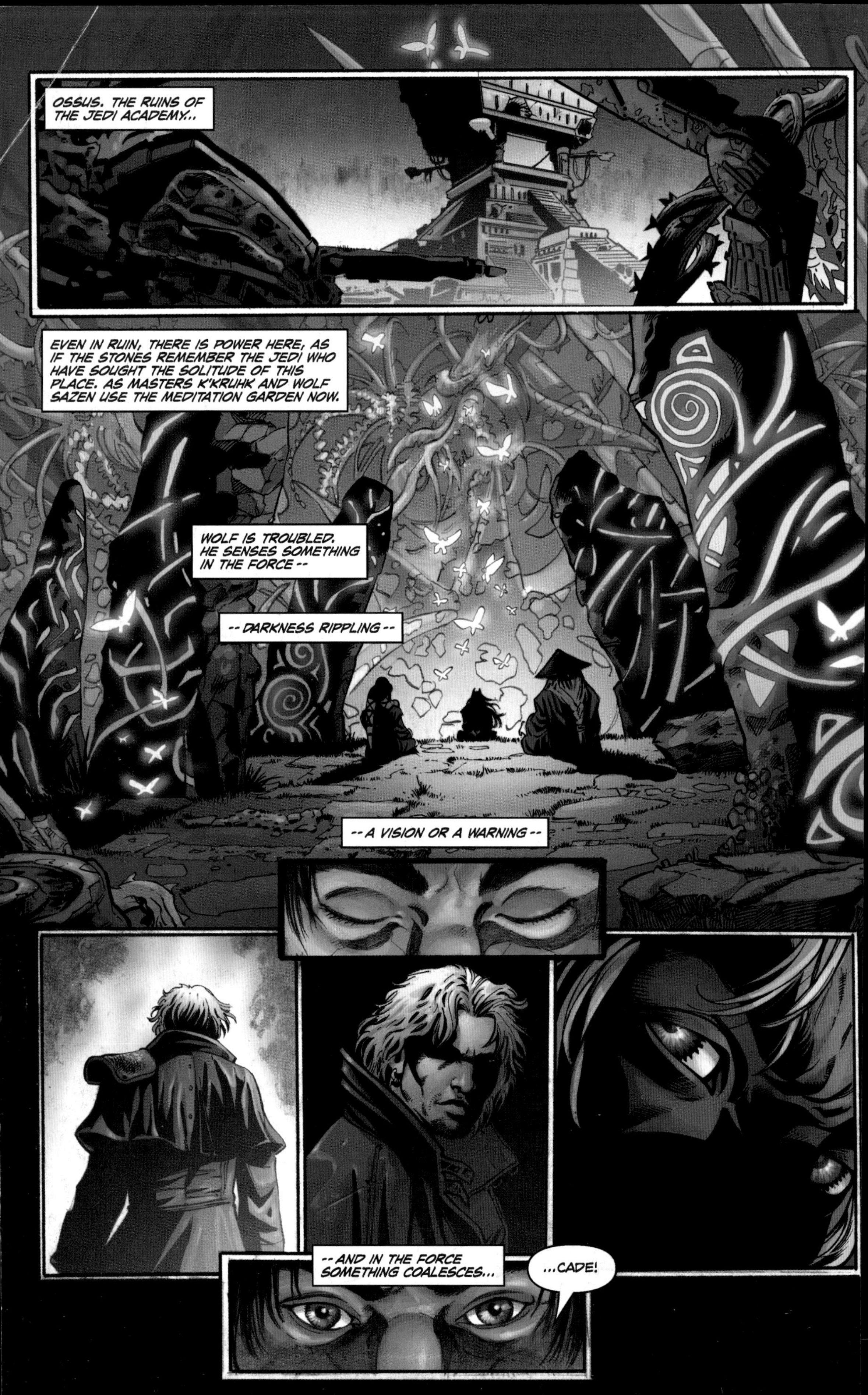
OSSUS. THE RUINS OF THE JEDI ACADEMY...
EVEN IN RUIN, THERE IS POWER HERE, AS IF THE STONES REMEMBER THE JEDI WHO HAVE SOUGHT THE SOLITUDE OF THIS PLACE. AS MASTERS K'KRUHK AND WOLF SAZEN USE THE MEDITATION GARDEN NOW.
WOLF IS TROUBLED. HE SENSES SOMETHING IN THE FORCE --
-- DARKNESS RIPPLING --
-- A VISION OR A WARNING --
-- AND IN THE FORCE SOMETHING COALESCES...
...CADE!

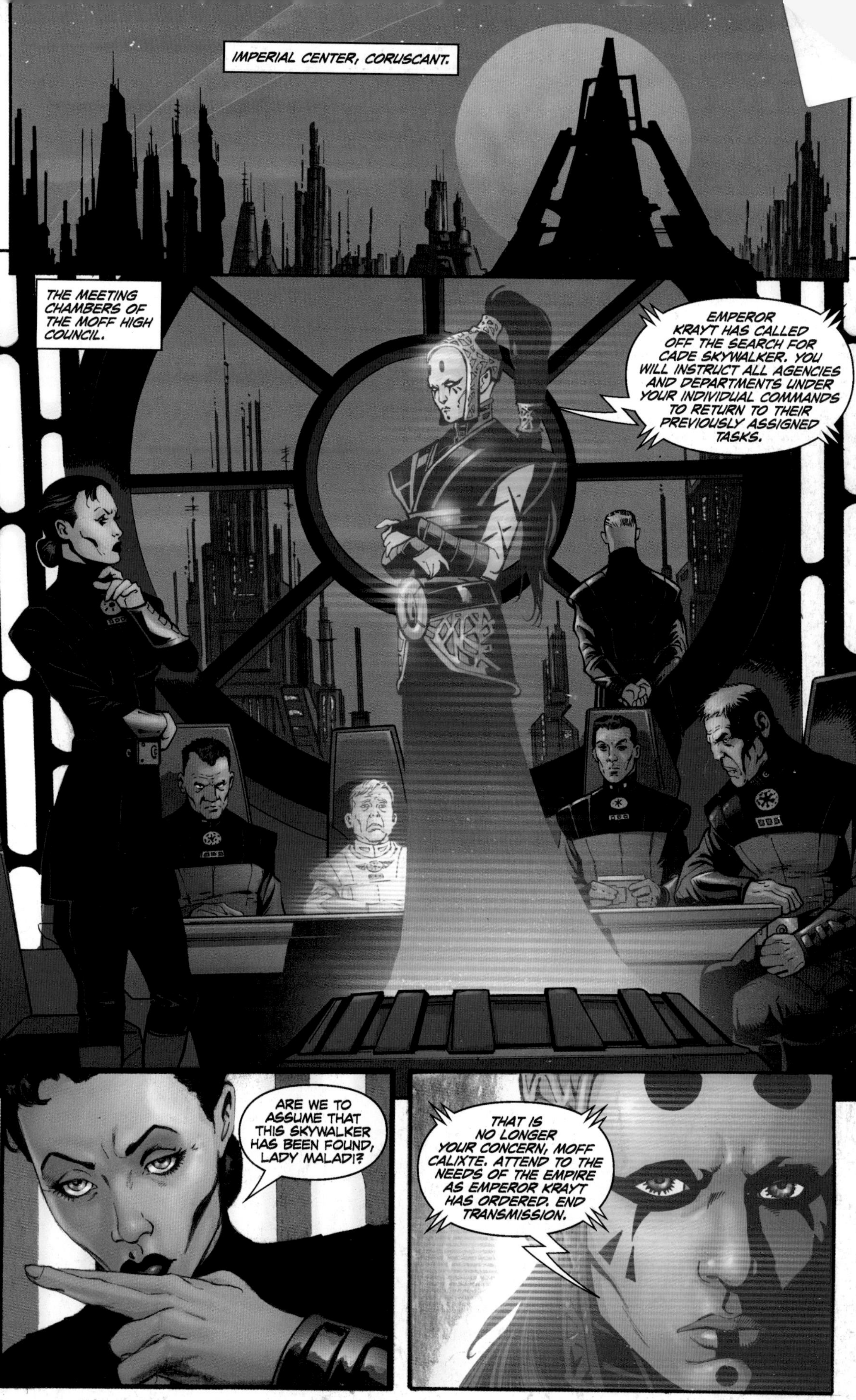

IMPERIAL CENTER, CORUSCANT.
THE MEETING CHAMBERS OF THE MOFF HIGH COUNCIL.
EMPEROR KRAYT HAS CALLED OFF THE SEARCH FOR CADE SKYWALKER. YOU WILL INSTRUCT ALL AGENCIES AND DEPARTMENTS UNDER YOUR INDIVIDUAL COMMANDS TO RETURN TO THEIR PREVIOUSLY ASSIGNED TASKS.
ARE WE TO ASSUME THAT THIS SKYWALKER HAS BEEN FOUND, LADY MALADI?
THAT IS NO LONGER YOUR CONCERN, MOFF CALIXTE. ATTEND TO THE NEEDS OF THE EMPIRE AS EMPEROR KRAYT HAS ORDERED. END TRANSMISSION.

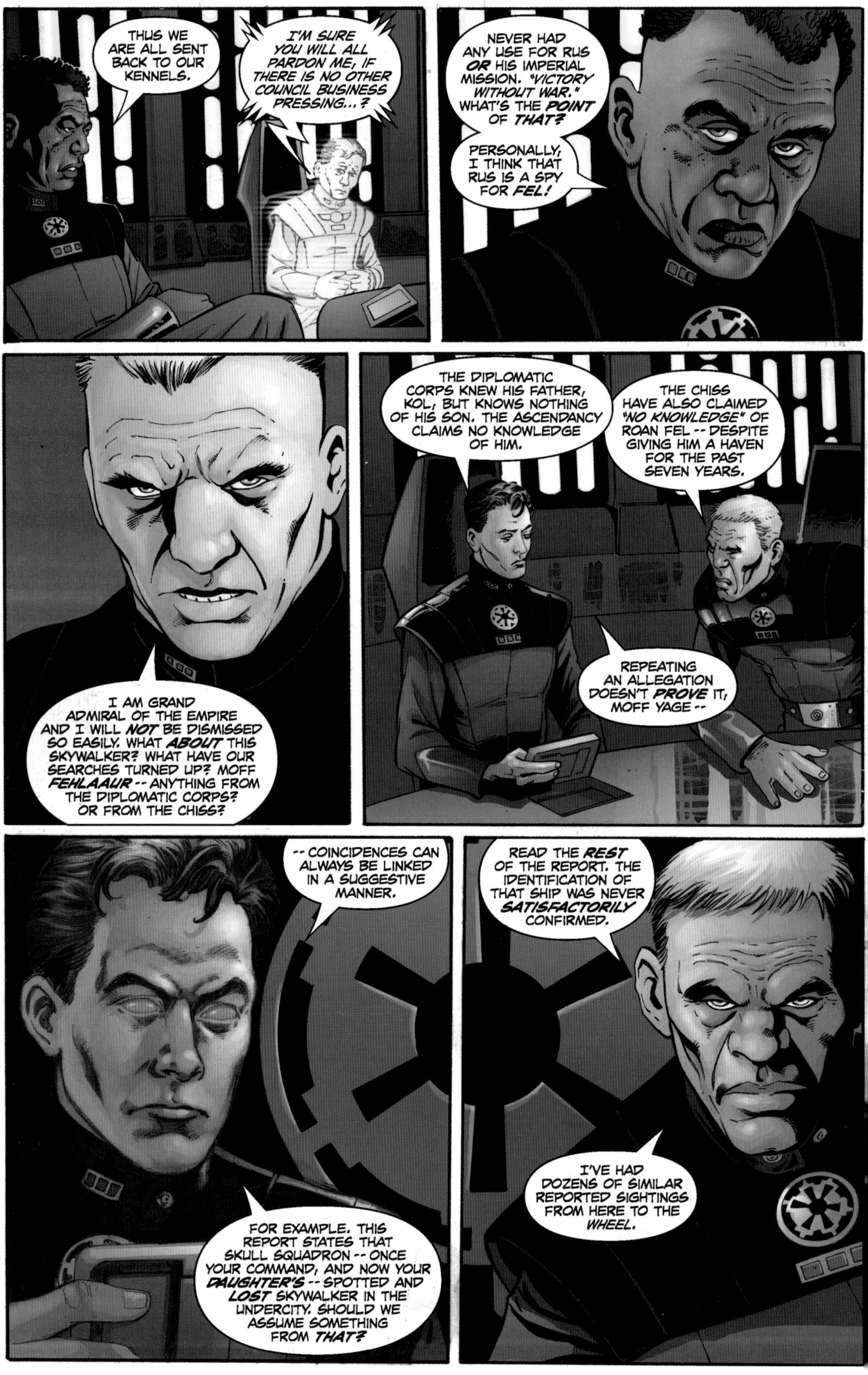
THUS WE ARE ALL SENT BACK TO OUR KENNELS.
I'M SURE YOU WILL ALL PARDON ME, IF THERE IS NO OTHER COUNCIL BUSINESS PRESSING...?
NEVER HAD ANY USE FOR RUS OR HIS IMPERIAL MISSION. "VICTORY WITHOUT WAR." WHAT'S THE POINT OF THAT?
PERSONALLY, I THINK THAT RUS IS A SPY FOR FEL!
I AM GRAND ADMIRAL OF THE EMPIRE AND I WILL NOT BE DISMISSED SO EASILY. WHAT ABOUT THIS SKYWALKER? WHAT HAVE OUR SEARCHES TURNED UP? MOFF FEHLAAUR -- ANYTHING FROM THE DIPLOMATIC CORPS? OR FROM THE CHISS?
THE DIPLOMATIC CORPS KNEW HIS FATHER, KOL, BUT KNOWS NOTHING OF HIS SON. THE ASCENDANCY CLAIMS NO KNOWLEDGE OF HIM.
THE CHISS HAVE ALSO CLAIMED "NO KNOWLEDGE" OF ROAN FEL -- DESPITE GIVING HIM A HAVEN FOR THE PAST SEVEN YEARS.
REPEATING AN ALLEGATION DOESN'T PROVE IT, MOFF YAGE --
-- COINCIDENCES CAN ALWAYS BE LINKED IN A SUGGESTIVE MANNER.
FOR EXAMPLE. THIS REPORT STATES THAT SKULL SQUADRON -- ONCE YOUR COMMAND, AND NOW YOUR DAUGHTER'S -- SPOTTED AND LOST SKYWALKER IN THE UNDERCITY. SHOULD WE ASSUME SOMETHING FROM THAT?
READ THE REST OF THE REPORT. THE IDENTIFICATION OF THAT SHIP WAS NEVER SATISFACTORILY CONFIRMED.
I'VE HAD DOZENS OF SIMILAR REPORTED SIGHTINGS FROM HERE TO THE WHEEL.

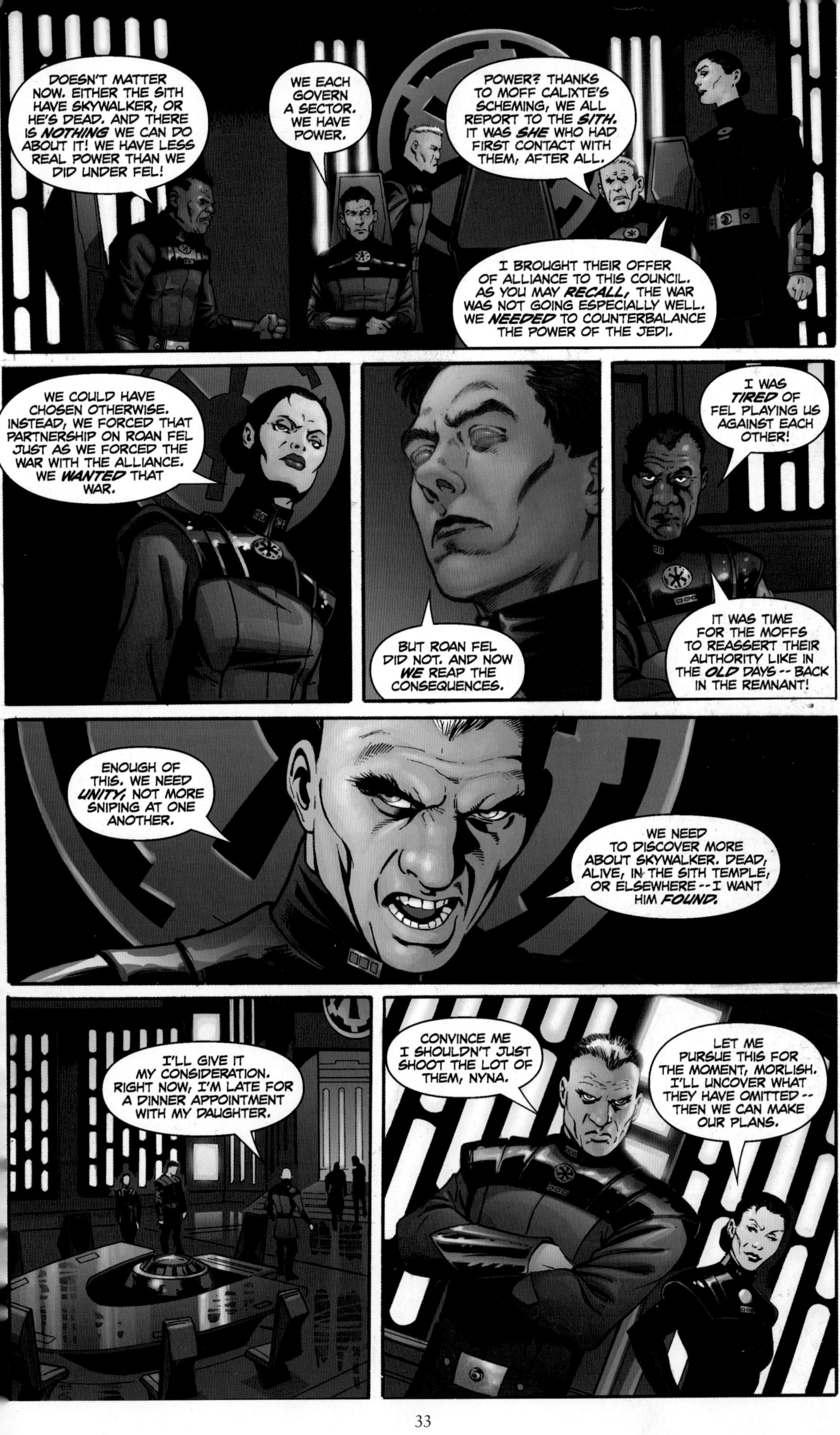
DOESN'T MATTER NOW. EITHER THE SITH HAVE SKYWALKER, OR HE'S DEAD. AND THERE IS NOTHING WE CAN DO ABOUT IT! WE HAVE LESS REAL POWER THAN WE DID UNDER FEL!
WE EACH GOVERN A SECTOR. WE HAVE POWER.
POWER? THANKS TO MOFF CALIXTE'S SCHEMING, WE ALL REPORT TO THE SITH. IT WAS SHE WHO HAD FIRST CONTACT WITH THEM, AFTER ALL.
I BROUGHT THEIR OFFER OF ALLIANCE TO THIS COUNCIL. AS YOU MAY RECALL, THE WAR WAS NOT GOING ESPECIALLY WELL. WE NEEDED TO COUNTERBALANCE THE POWER OF THE JEDI.
WE COULD HAVE CHOSEN OTHERWISE. INSTEAD, WE FORCED THAT PARTNERSHIP ON ROAN FEL JUST AS WE FORCED THE WAR WITH THE ALLIANCE. WE WANTED THAT WAR.
BUT ROAN FEL DID NOT. AND NOW WE REAP THE CONSEQUENCES.
I WAS TIRED OF FEL PLAYING US AGAINST EACH OTHER!
IT WAS TIME FOR THE MOFFS TO REASSERT THEIR AUTHORITY LIKE IN THE OLD DAYS -- BACK IN THE REMNANT!
ENOUGH OF THIS. WE NEED UNITY, NOT MORE SNIPING AT ONE ANOTHER.
WE NEED TO DISCOVER MORE ABOUT SKYWALKER. DEAD, ALIVE, IN THE SITH TEMPLE, OR ELSEWHERE -- I WANT HIM FOUND.
I'LL GIVE IT MY CONSIDERATION. RIGHT NOW, I'M LATE FOR A DINNER APPOINTMENT WITH MY DAUGHTER.
CONVINCE ME I SHOULDN'T JUST SHOOT THE LOT OF THEM, NYNA.
LET ME PURSUE THIS FOR THE MOMENT, MORLISH. I'LL UNCOVER WHAT THEY HAVE OMITTED -- THEN WE CAN MAKE OUR PLANS.

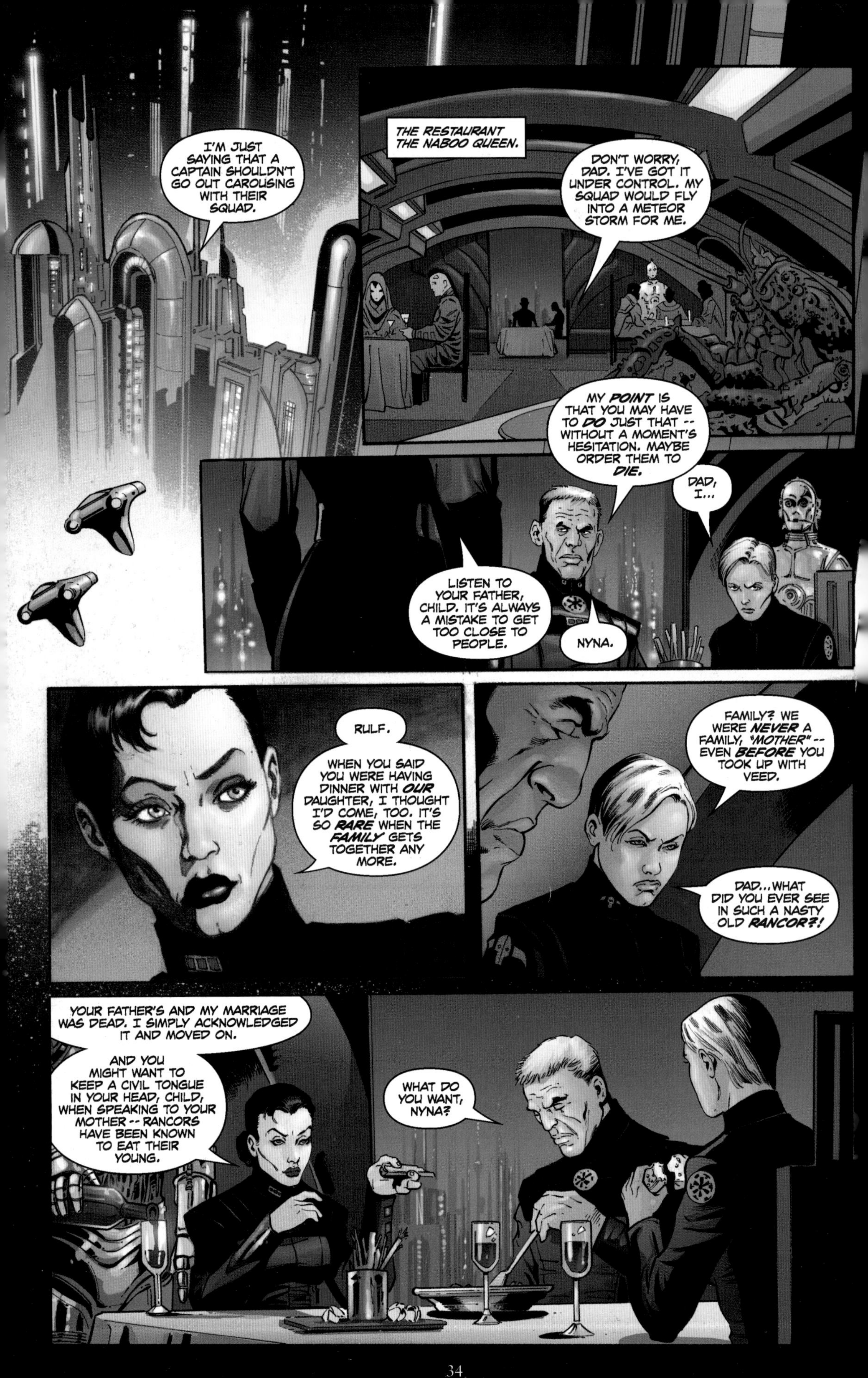
I'M JUST SAYING THAT A CAPTAIN SHOULDN'T GO OUT CAROUSING WITH THEIR SQUAD.
THE RESTAURANT THE NABOO QUEEN.
DON'T WORRY, DAD. I'VE GOT IT UNDER CONTROL. MY SQUAD WOULD FLY INTO A METEOR STORM FOR ME.
MY POINT IS THAT YOU MAY HAVE TO DO JUST THAT -- WITHOUT A MOMENT'S HESITATION. MAYBE ORDER THEM TO DIE.
DAD, I...
LISTEN TO YOUR FATHER, CHILD. IT'S ALWAYS A MISTAKE TO GET TOO CLOSE TO PEOPLE.
NYNA.
RULF.
WHEN YOU SAID YOU WERE HAVING DINNER WITH OUR DAUGHTER, I THOUGHT I'D COME, TOO. IT'S SO RARE WHEN THE FAMILY GETS TOGETHER ANY MORE.
FAMILY? WE WERE NEVER A FAMILY, "MOTHER" -- EVEN BEFORE YOU TOOK UP WITH VEED.
DAD...WHAT DID YOU EVER SEE IN SUCH A NASTY OLD RANCOR?!
YOUR FATHER'S AND MY MARRIAGE WAS DEAD. I SIMPLY ACKNOWLEDGED IT AND MOVED ON.
AND YOU MIGHT WANT TO KEEP A CIVIL TONGUE IN YOUR HEAD, CHILD, WHEN SPEAKING TO YOUR MOTHER -- RANCORS HAVE BEEN KNOWN TO EAT THEIR YOUNG.
WHAT DO YOU WANT, NYNA?

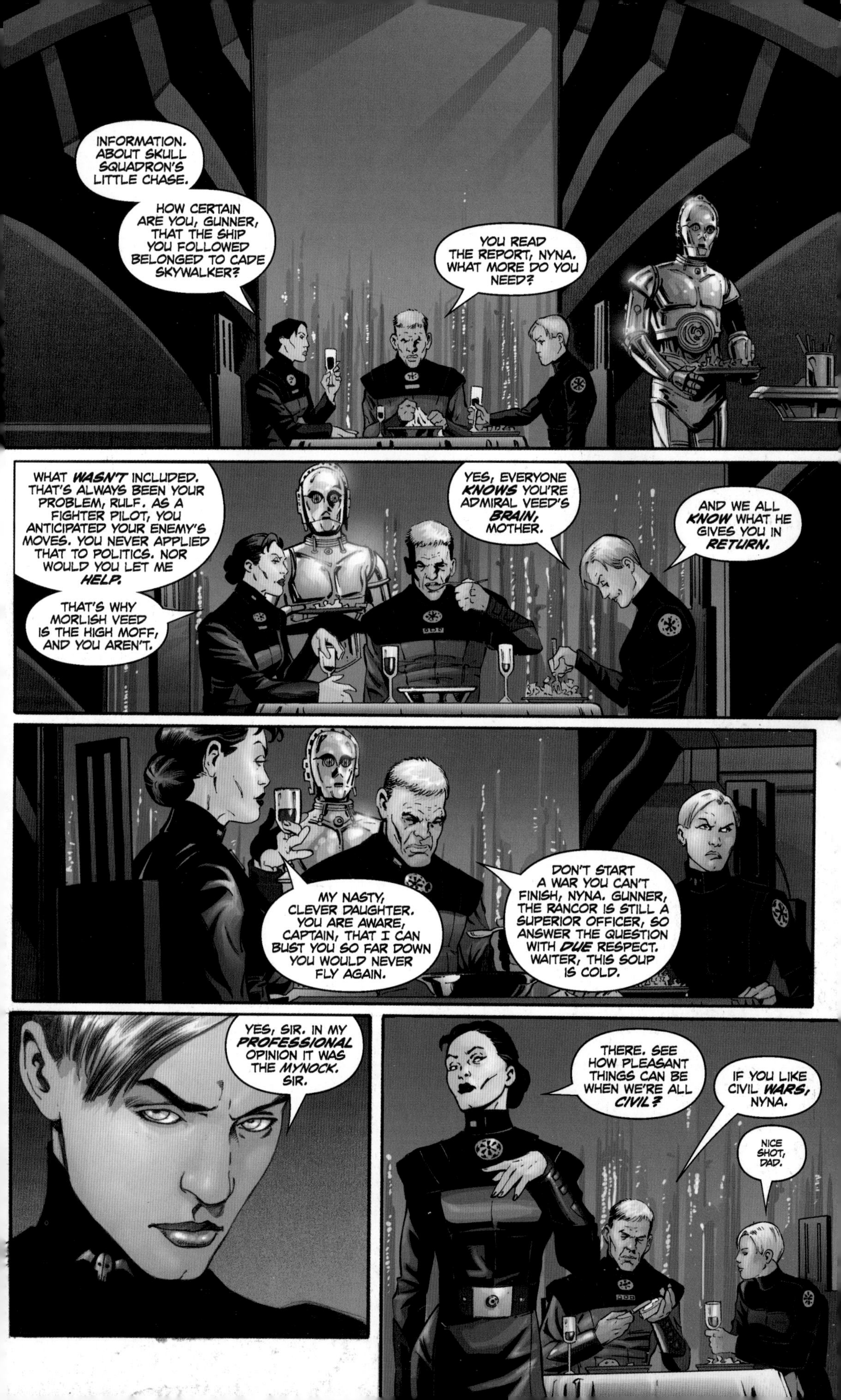

INFORMATION. ABOUT SKULL SQUADRON'S LITTLE CHASE.
HOW CERTAIN ARE YOU, GUNNER, THAT THE SHIP YOU FOLLOWED BELONGED TO CADE SKYWALKER?
YOU READ THE REPORT, NYNA. WHAT MORE DO YOU NEED?
WHAT *WASN'T* INCLUDED. THAT'S ALWAYS BEEN YOUR PROBLEM, RULF. AS A FIGHTER PILOT, YOU ANTICIPATED YOUR ENEMY'S MOVES. YOU NEVER APPLIED THAT TO POLITICS. NOR WOULD YOU LET ME *HELP.*
THAT'S WHY MORLISH VEED IS THE HIGH MOFF, AND YOU AREN'T.
YES, EVERYONE *KNOWS* YOU'RE ADMIRAL VEED'S *BRAIN,* MOTHER.
AND WE ALL *KNOW* WHAT HE GIVES YOU IN *RETURN.*
MY NASTY, CLEVER DAUGHTER. YOU ARE AWARE, CAPTAIN, THAT I CAN BUST YOU SO FAR DOWN YOU WOULD NEVER FLY AGAIN.
DON'T START A WAR YOU CAN'T FINISH, NYNA. GUNNER, THE RANCOR IS STILL A SUPERIOR OFFICER, SO ANSWER THE QUESTION WITH *DUE* RESPECT. WAITER, THIS SOUP IS COLD.
YES, SIR. IN MY *PROFESSIONAL* OPINION IT WAS THE *MYNOCK.* SIR.
THERE. SEE HOW PLEASANT THINGS CAN BE WHEN WE'RE ALL *CIVIL?*
IF YOU LIKE CIVIL *WARS,* NYNA.
NICE SHOT, DAD.

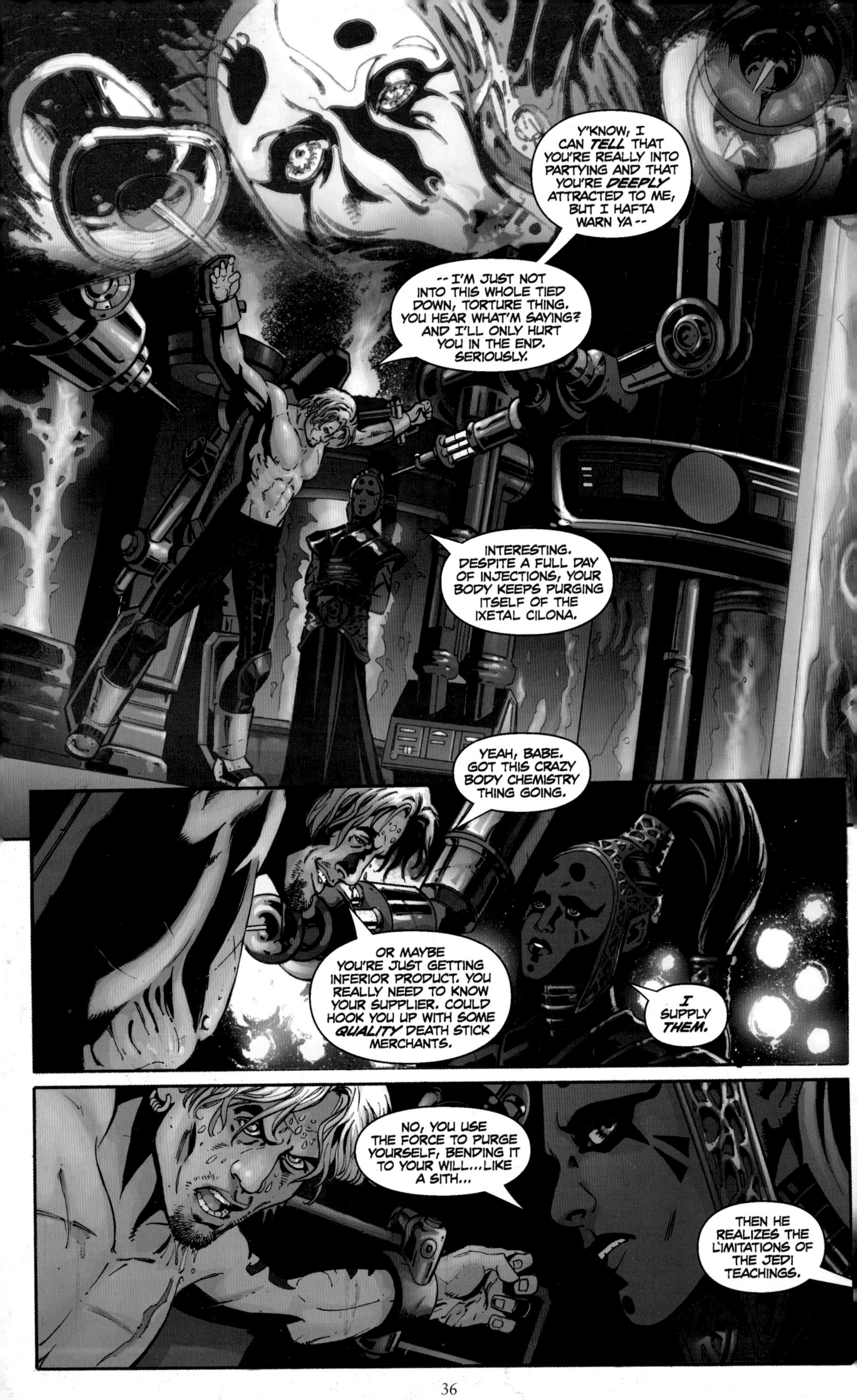
Y'KNOW, I CAN TELL THAT YOU'RE REALLY INTO PARTYING AND THAT YOU'RE DEEPLY ATTRACTED TO ME, BUT I HAFTA WARN YA --
-- I'M JUST NOT INTO THIS WHOLE TIED DOWN, TORTURE THING. YOU HEAR WHAT'M SAYING? AND I'LL ONLY HURT YOU IN THE END. SERIOUSLY.
INTERESTING. DESPITE A FULL DAY OF INJECTIONS, YOUR BODY KEEPS PURGING ITSELF OF THE IXETAL CILONA.
YEAH, BABE. GOT THIS CRAZY BODY CHEMISTRY THING GOING.
OR MAYBE YOU'RE JUST GETTING INFERIOR PRODUCT. YOU REALLY NEED TO KNOW YOUR SUPPLIER. COULD HOOK YOU UP WITH SOME QUALITY DEATH STICK MERCHANTS.
I SUPPLY THEM.
NO, YOU USE THE FORCE TO PURGE YOURSELF, BENDING IT TO YOUR WILL...LIKE A SITH...
THEN HE REALIZES THE LIMITATIONS OF THE JEDI TEACHINGS.

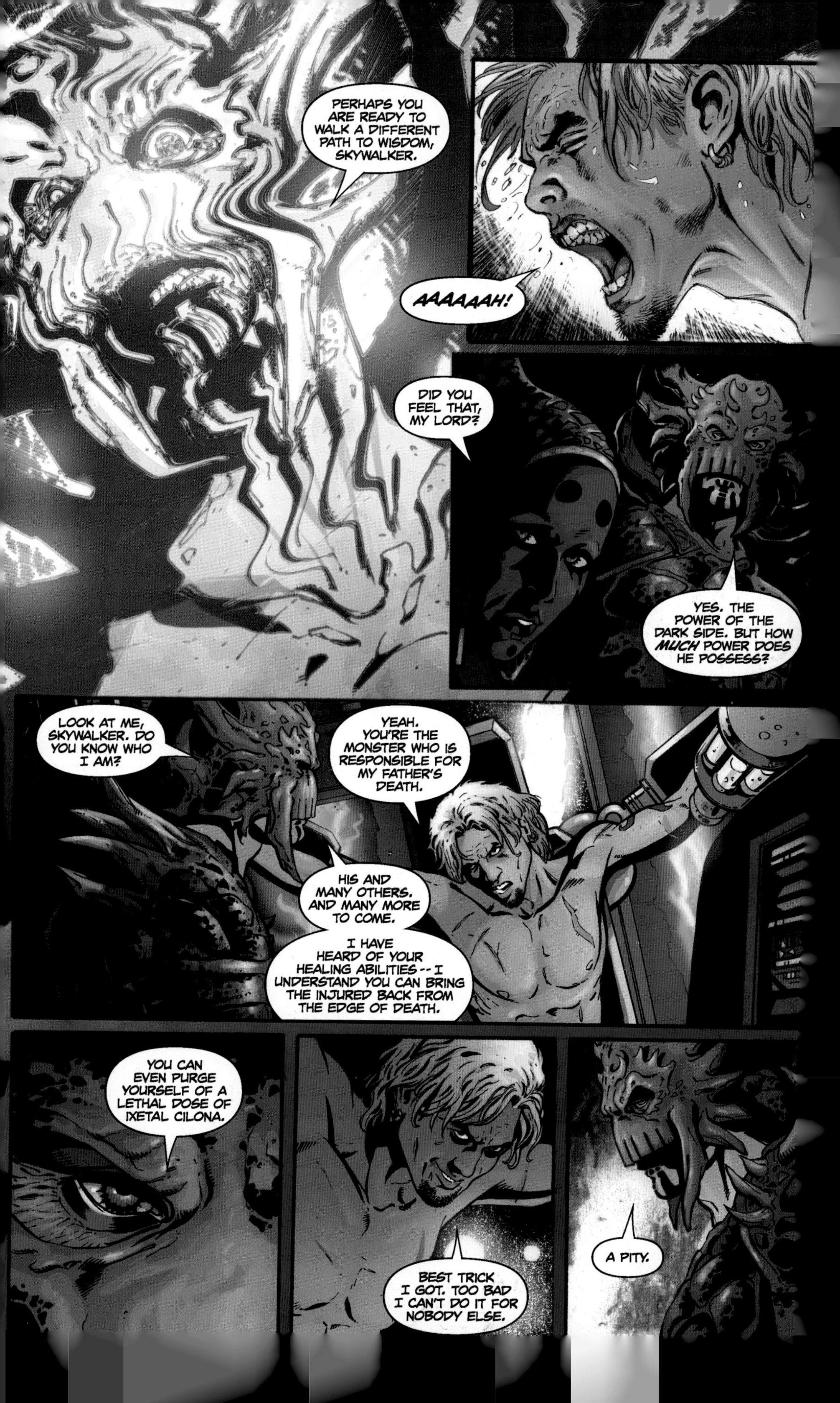
PERHAPS YOU ARE READY TO WALK A DIFFERENT PATH TO WISDOM, SKYWALKER.
AAAAAAH!
DID YOU FEEL THAT, MY LORD?
YES. THE POWER OF THE DARK SIDE. BUT HOW *MUCH* POWER DOES HE POSSESS?
LOOK AT ME, SKYWALKER. DO YOU KNOW WHO I AM?
YEAH. YOU'RE THE MONSTER WHO IS RESPONSIBLE FOR MY FATHER'S DEATH.
HIS AND MANY OTHERS. AND MANY MORE TO COME.
I HAVE HEARD OF YOUR HEALING ABILITIES -- I UNDERSTAND YOU CAN BRING THE INJURED BACK FROM THE EDGE OF DEATH.
YOU CAN EVEN PURGE YOURSELF OF A LETHAL DOSE OF IXETAL CILONA.
BEST TRICK I GOT. TOO BAD I CAN'T DO IT FOR NOBODY ELSE.
A PITY.

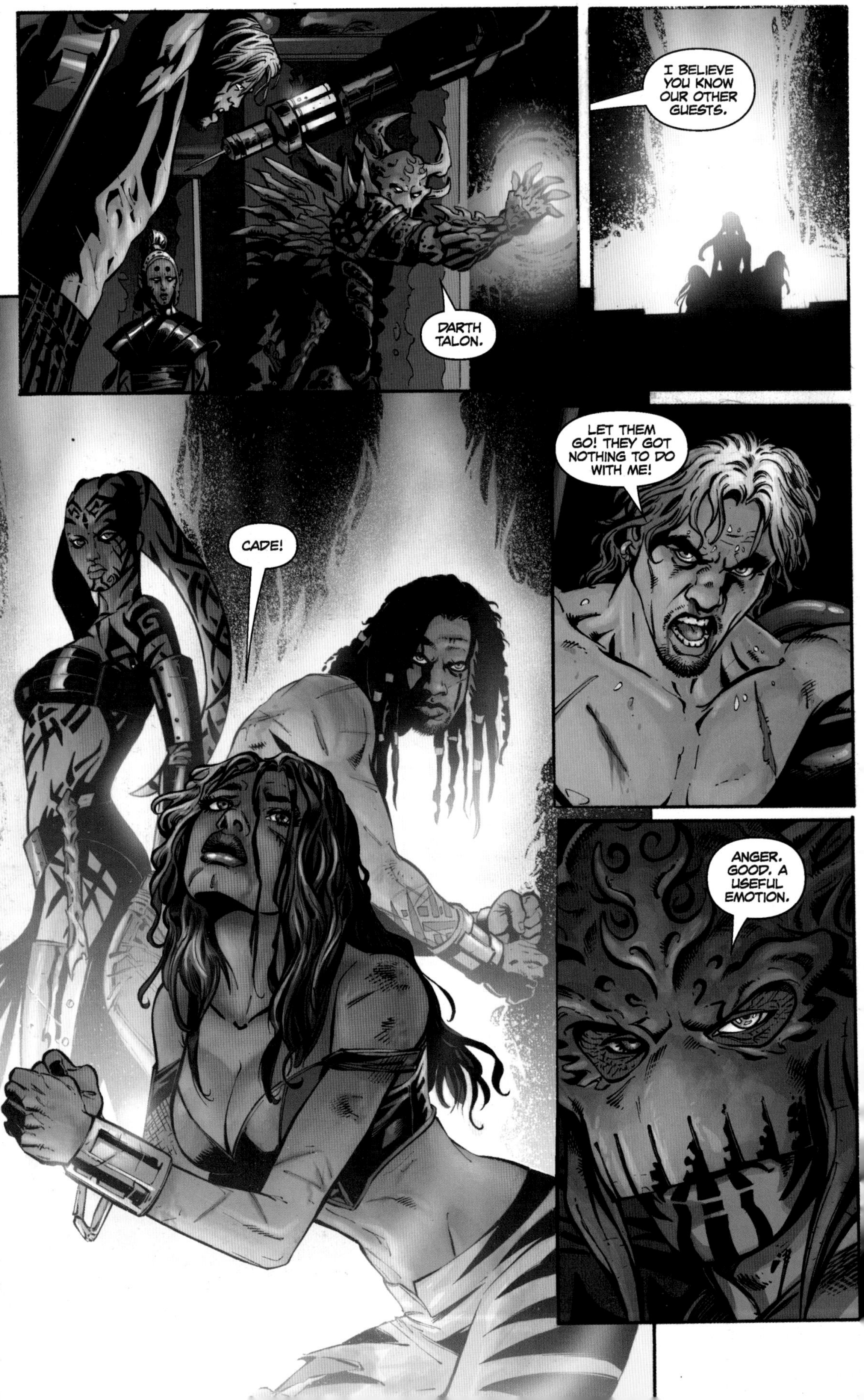
DARTH
TALON.
I BELIEVE
YOU KNOW
OUR OTHER
GUESTS.
CADE!
LET THEM
GO! THEY GOT
NOTHING TO DO
WITH ME!
ANGER.
GOOD. A
USEFUL
EMOTION.

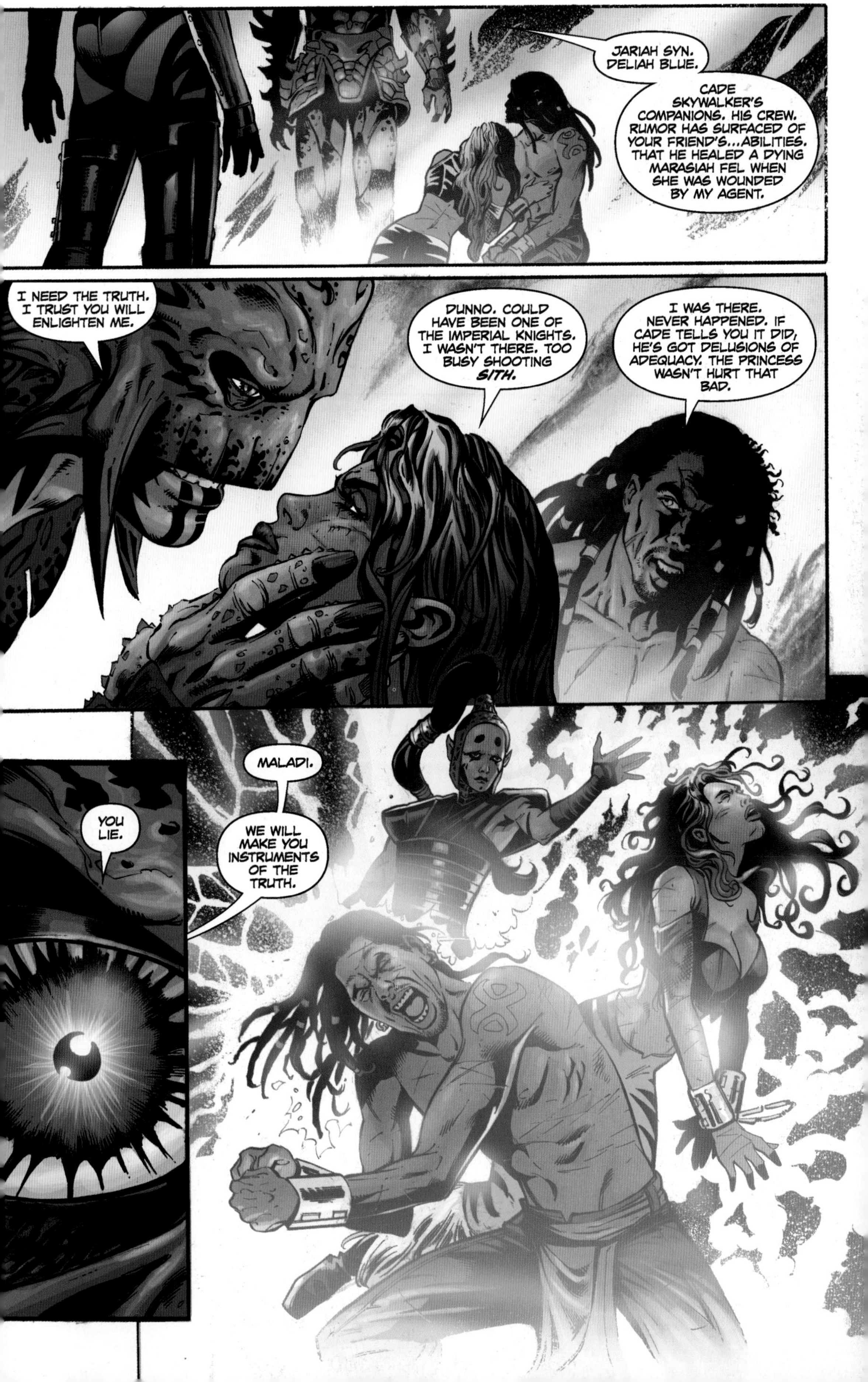
JARIAH SYN. DELIAH BLUE.
CADE SKYWALKER'S COMPANIONS. HIS CREW. RUMOR HAS SURFACED OF YOUR FRIEND'S...ABILITIES. THAT HE HEALED A DYING MARASIAH FEL WHEN SHE WAS WOUNDED BY MY AGENT.
I NEED THE TRUTH. I TRUST YOU WILL ENLIGHTEN ME.
DUNNO. COULD HAVE BEEN ONE OF THE IMPERIAL KNIGHTS. I WASN'T THERE. TOO BUSY SHOOTING SITH.
I WAS THERE. NEVER HAPPENED. IF CADE TELLS YOU IT DID, HE'S GOT DELUSIONS OF ADEQUACY. THE PRINCESS WASN'T HURT THAT BAD.
YOU LIE.
MALADI.
WE WILL MAKE YOU INSTRUMENTS OF THE TRUTH.

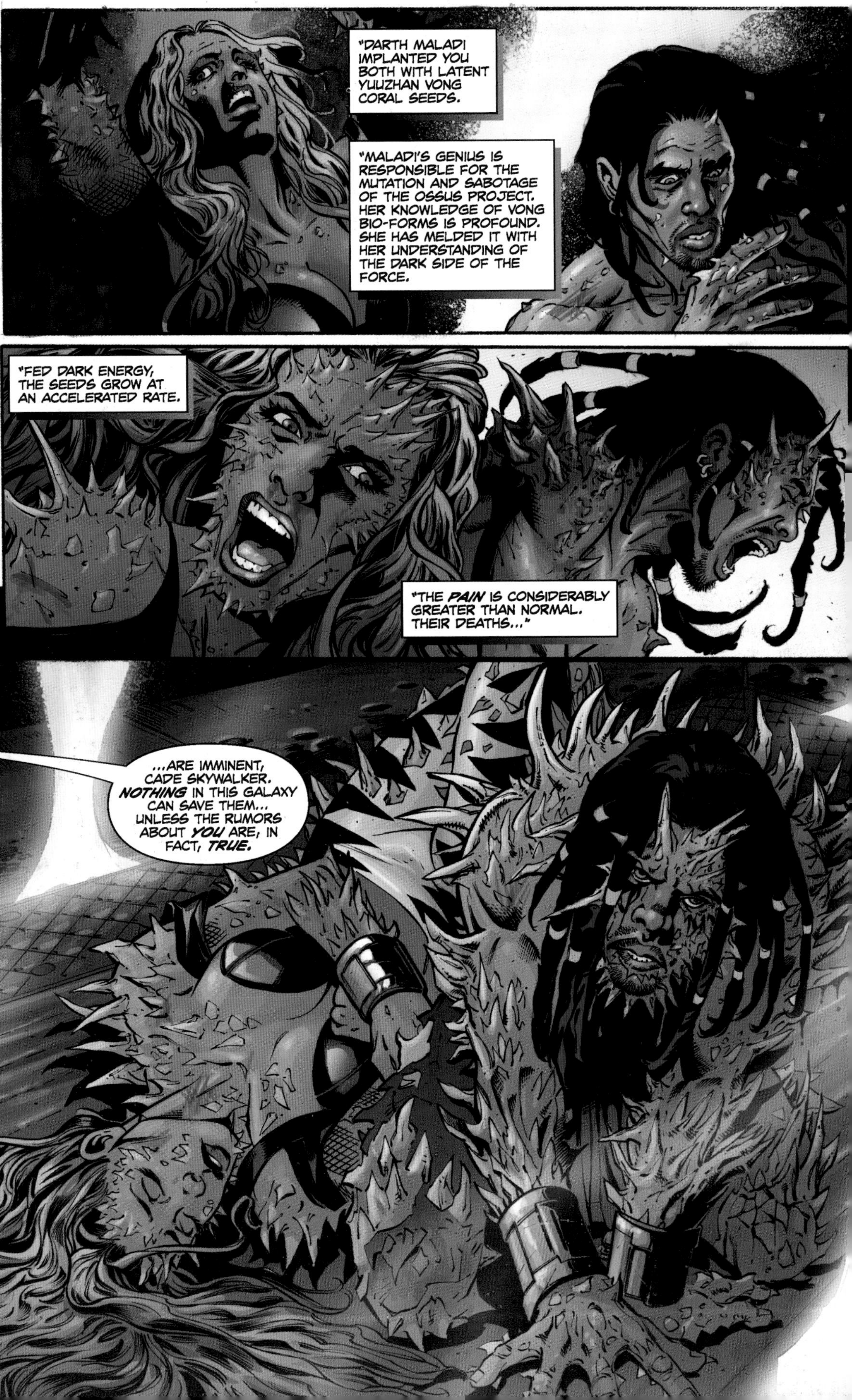
"DARTH MALADI IMPLANTED YOU BOTH WITH LATENT YUUZHAN VONG CORAL SEEDS.
"MALADI'S GENIUS IS RESPONSIBLE FOR THE MUTATION AND SABOTAGE OF THE OSSUS PROJECT. HER KNOWLEDGE OF VONG BIO-FORMS IS PROFOUND. SHE HAS MELDED IT WITH HER UNDERSTANDING OF THE DARK SIDE OF THE FORCE.
"FED DARK ENERGY, THE SEEDS GROW AT AN ACCELERATED RATE.
"THE *PAIN* IS CONSIDERABLY GREATER THAN NORMAL. THEIR DEATHS..."
...ARE IMMINENT, CADE SKYWALKER. ***NOTHING*** IN THIS GALAXY CAN SAVE THEM... UNLESS THE RUMORS ABOUT ***YOU*** ARE, IN FACT, ***TRUE.***

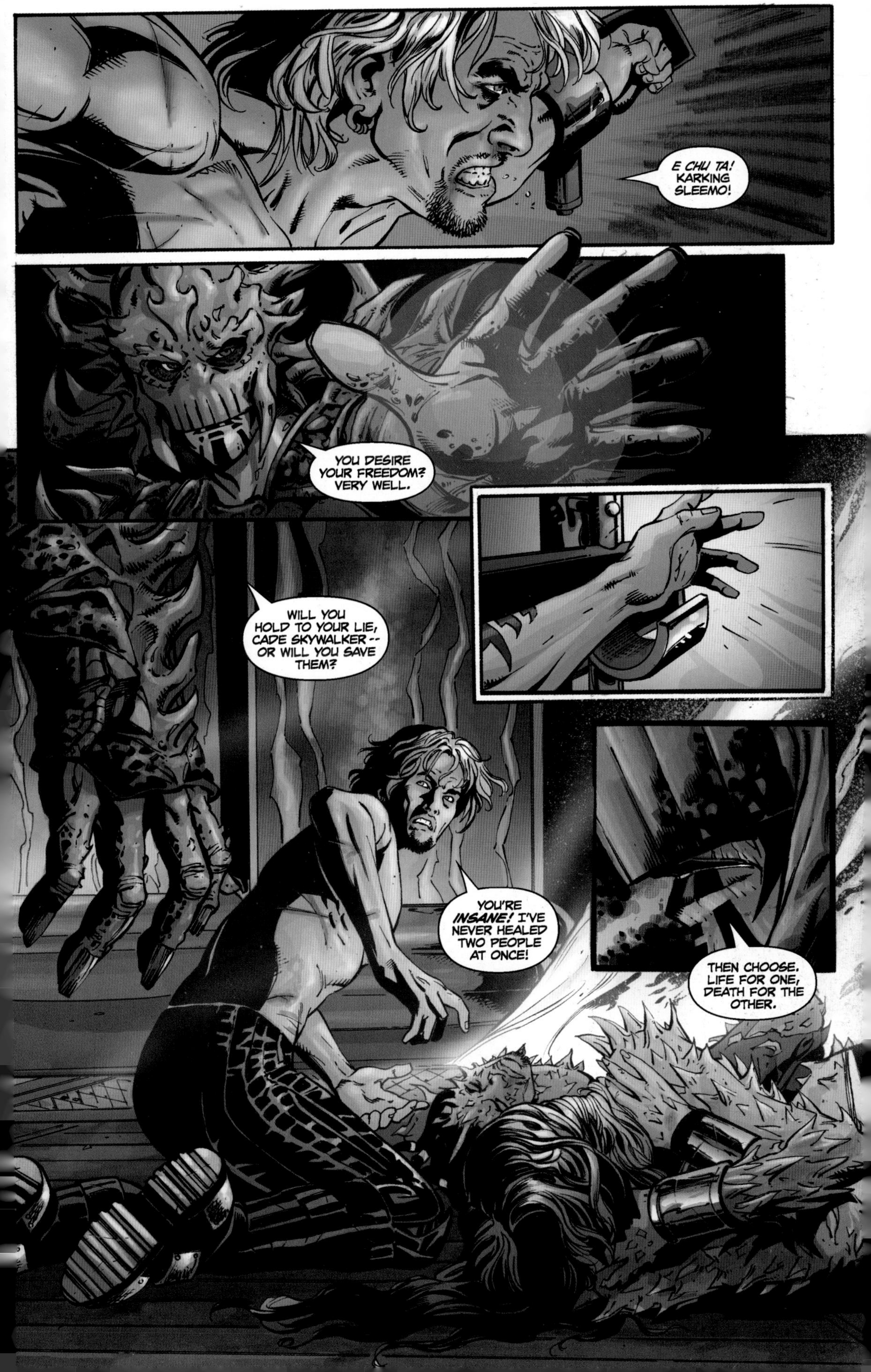
E CHU TA! KARKING SLEEMO!
YOU DESIRE YOUR FREEDOM? VERY WELL.
WILL YOU HOLD TO YOUR LIE, CADE SKYWALKER -- OR WILL YOU SAVE THEM?
YOU'RE *INSANE!* I'VE NEVER HEALED TWO PEOPLE AT ONCE!
THEN CHOOSE. LIFE FOR ONE, DEATH FOR THE OTHER.

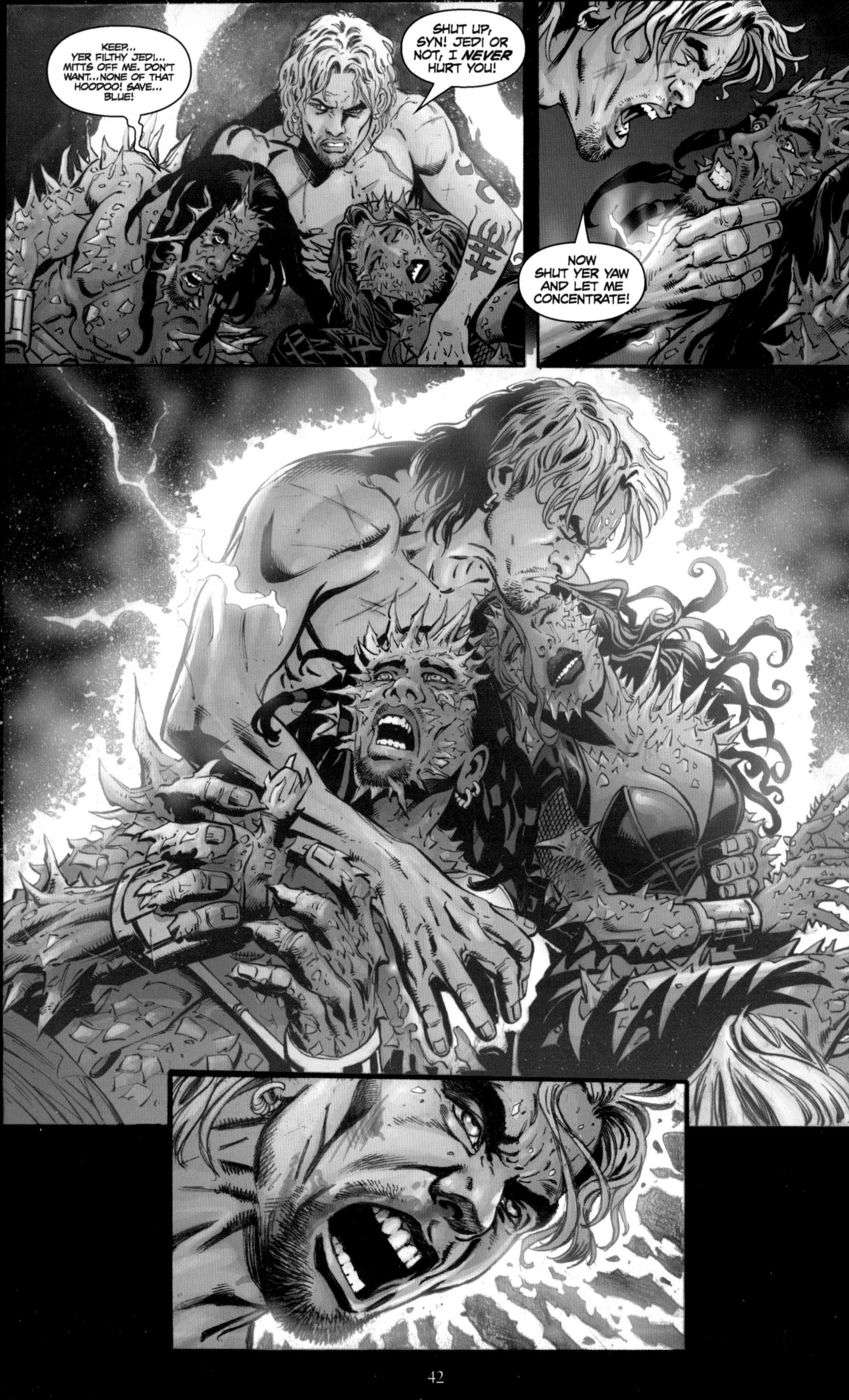
KEEP... YER FILTHY JEDI... MITTS OFF ME. DON'T WANT...NONE OF THAT HOODOO! SAVE... BLUE!
SHUT UP, SYN! JEDI OR NOT, I NEVER HURT YOU!
NOW SHUT YER YAW AND LET ME CONCENTRATE!

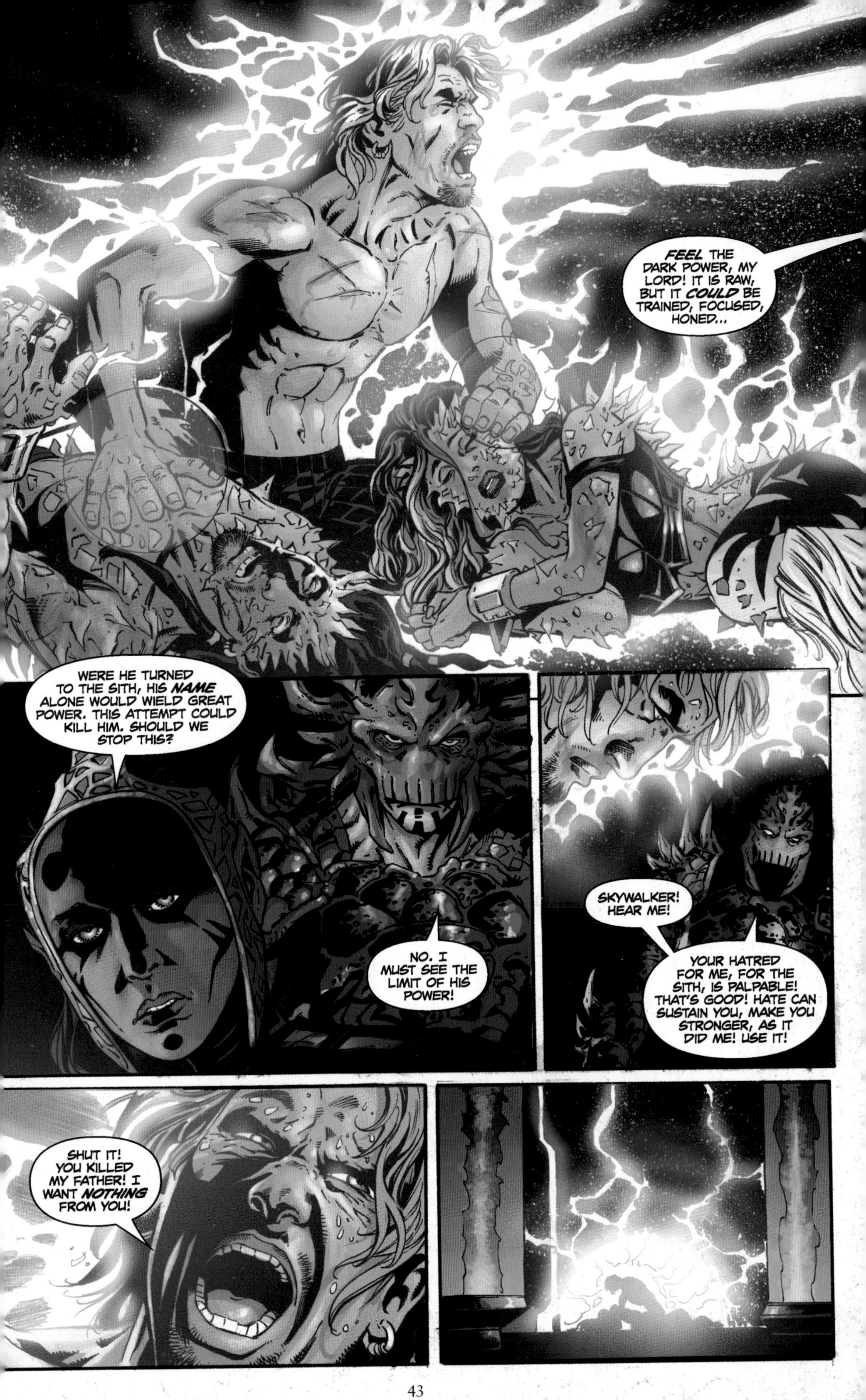
FEEL THE DARK POWER, MY LORD! IT IS RAW, BUT IT COULD BE TRAINED, FOCUSED, HONED...
WERE HE TURNED TO THE SITH, HIS NAME ALONE WOULD WIELD GREAT POWER. THIS ATTEMPT COULD KILL HIM. SHOULD WE STOP THIS?
NO. I MUST SEE THE LIMIT OF HIS POWER!
SKYWALKER! HEAR ME!
YOUR HATRED FOR ME, FOR THE SITH, IS PALPABLE! THAT'S GOOD! HATE CAN SUSTAIN YOU, MAKE YOU STRONGER, AS IT DID ME! USE IT!
SHUT IT! YOU KILLED MY FATHER! I WANT NOTHING FROM YOU!

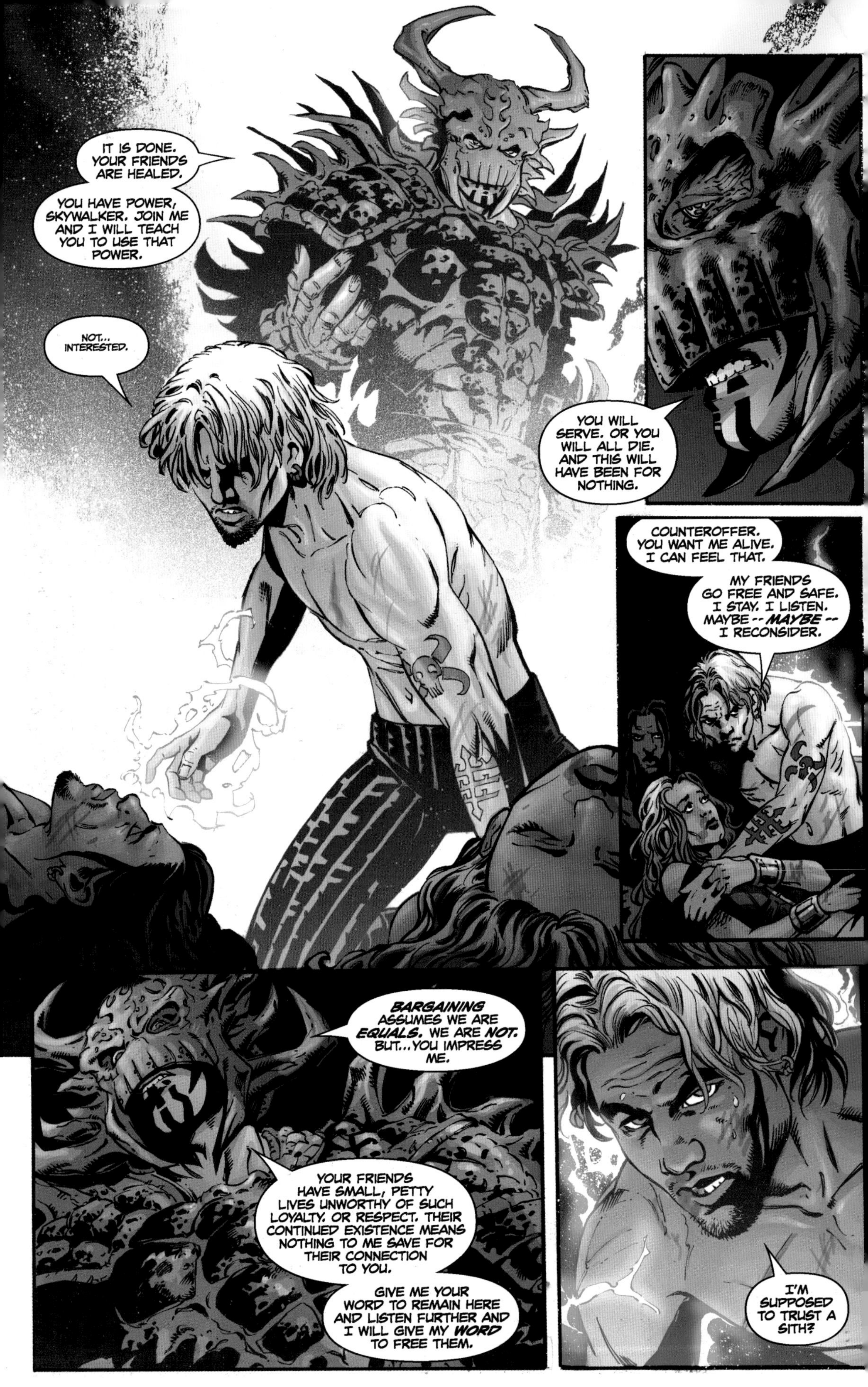
IT IS DONE. YOUR FRIENDS ARE HEALED.
YOU HAVE POWER, SKYWALKER. JOIN ME AND I WILL TEACH YOU TO USE THAT POWER.
NOT... INTERESTED.
YOU WILL SERVE. OR YOU WILL ALL DIE. AND THIS WILL HAVE BEEN FOR NOTHING.
COUNTEROFFER. YOU WANT ME ALIVE. I CAN FEEL THAT.
MY FRIENDS GO FREE AND SAFE. I STAY. I LISTEN. MAYBE -- *MAYBE* -- I RECONSIDER.
BARGAINING ASSUMES WE ARE *EQUALS.* WE ARE *NOT.* BUT...YOU IMPRESS ME.
YOUR FRIENDS HAVE SMALL, PETTY LIVES UNWORTHY OF SUCH LOYALTY. OR RESPECT. THEIR CONTINUED EXISTENCE MEANS NOTHING TO ME SAVE FOR THEIR CONNECTION TO YOU.
GIVE ME YOUR WORD TO REMAIN HERE AND LISTEN FURTHER AND I WILL GIVE MY *WORD* TO FREE THEM.
I'M SUPPOSED TO TRUST A SITH?

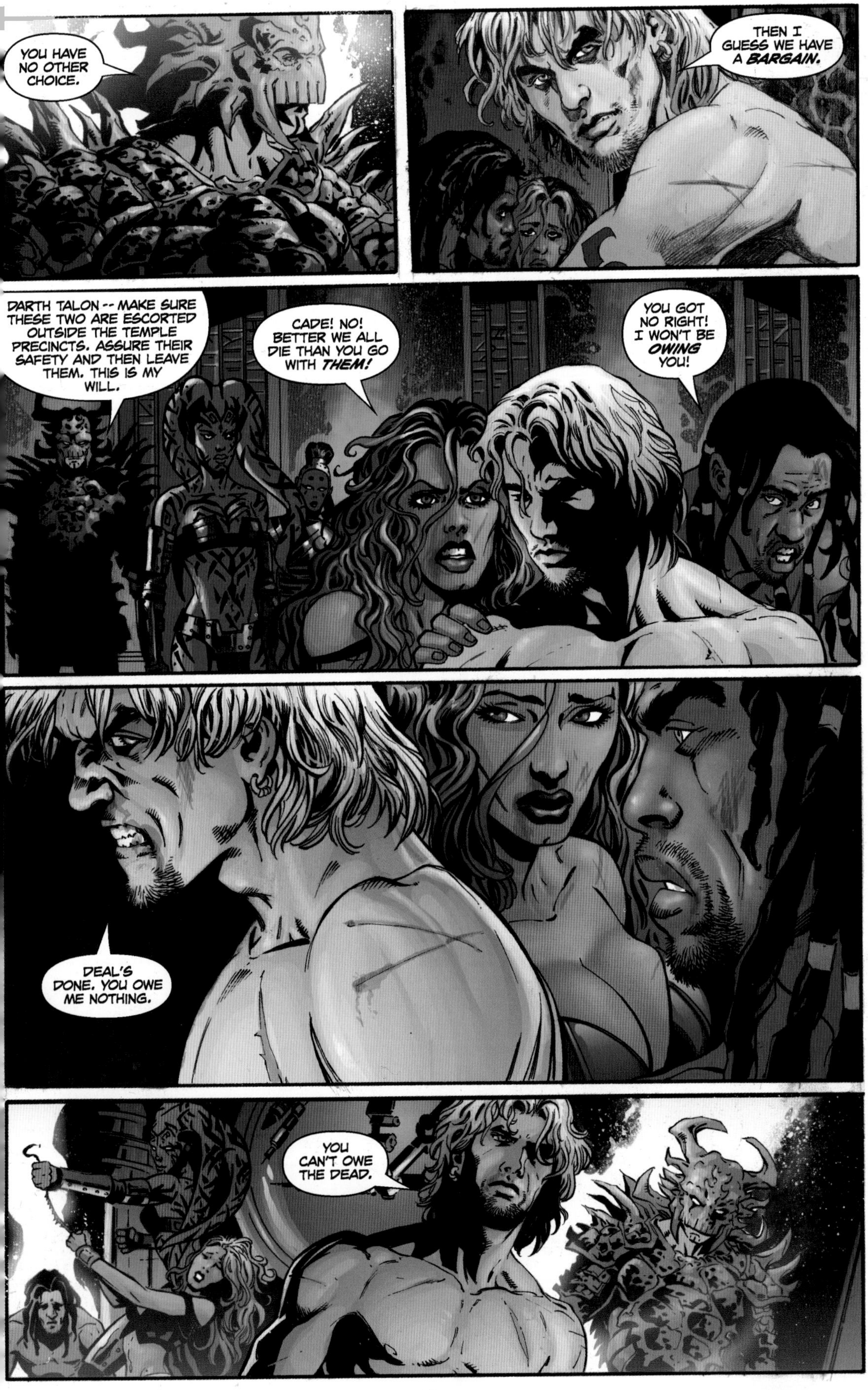
YOU HAVE NO OTHER CHOICE.
THEN I GUESS WE HAVE A BARGAIN.
DARTH TALON -- MAKE SURE THESE TWO ARE ESCORTED OUTSIDE THE TEMPLE PRECINCTS. ASSURE THEIR SAFETY AND THEN LEAVE THEM. THIS IS MY WILL.
CADE! NO! BETTER WE ALL DIE THAN YOU GO WITH THEM!
YOU GOT NO RIGHT! I WON'T BE OWING YOU!
DEAL'S DONE. YOU OWE ME NOTHING.
YOU CAN'T OWE THE DEAD.

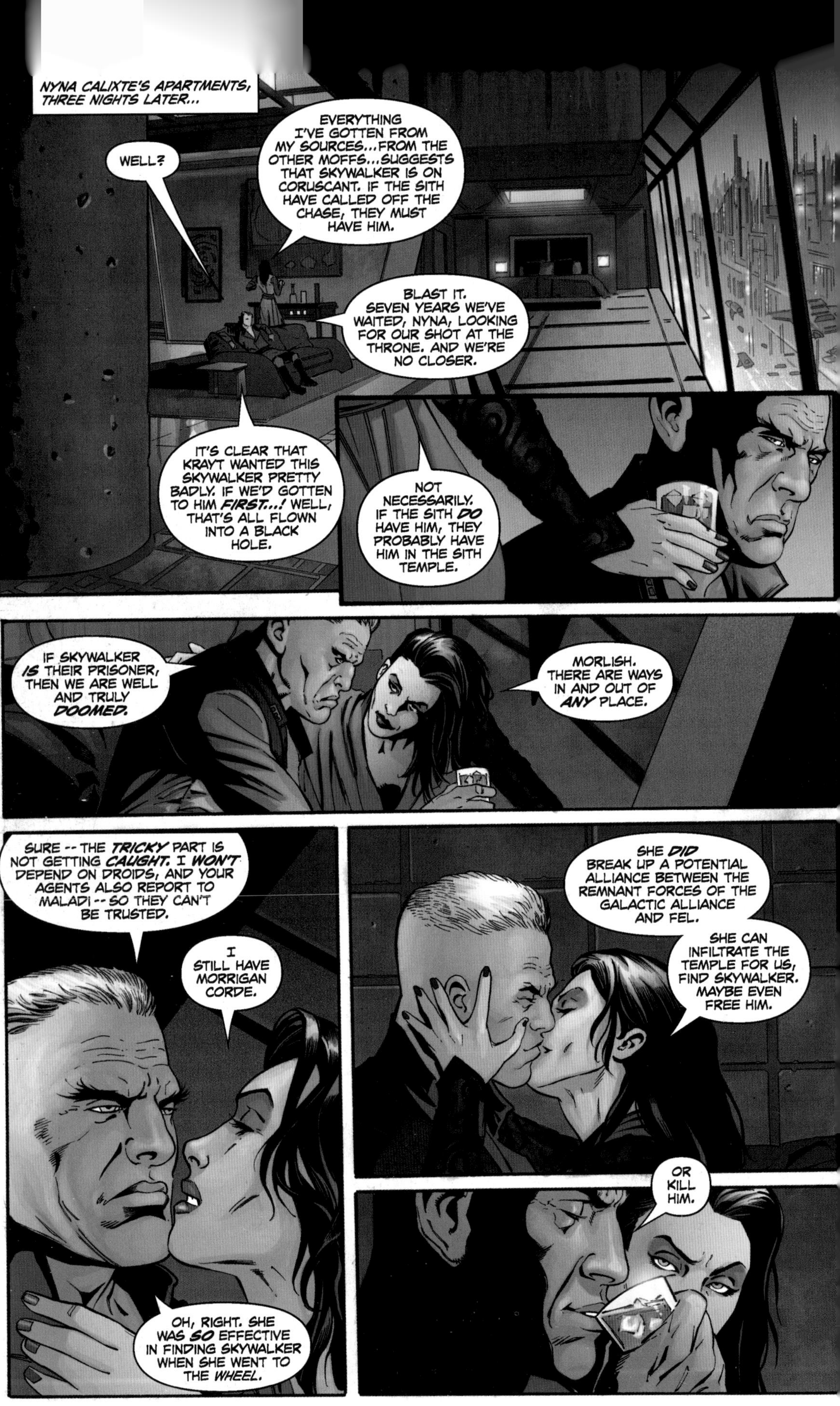
NYNA CALIXTE'S APARTMENTS, THREE NIGHTS LATER...
WELL?
EVERYTHING I'VE GOTTEN FROM MY SOURCES...FROM THE OTHER MOFFS...SUGGESTS THAT SKYWALKER IS ON CORUSCANT. IF THE SITH HAVE CALLED OFF THE CHASE, THEY MUST HAVE HIM.
BLAST IT. SEVEN YEARS WE'VE WAITED, NYNA, LOOKING FOR OUR SHOT AT THE THRONE. AND WE'RE NO CLOSER.
IT'S CLEAR THAT KRAYT WANTED THIS SKYWALKER PRETTY BADLY. IF WE'D GOTTEN TO HIM FIRST...! WELL, THAT'S ALL FLOWN INTO A BLACK HOLE.
NOT NECESSARILY. IF THE SITH DO HAVE HIM, THEY PROBABLY HAVE HIM IN THE SITH TEMPLE.
IF SKYWALKER IS THEIR PRISONER, THEN WE ARE WELL AND TRULY DOOMED.
MORLISH. THERE ARE WAYS IN AND OUT OF ANY PLACE.
SURE -- THE TRICKY PART IS NOT GETTING CAUGHT. I WON'T DEPEND ON DROIDS, AND YOUR AGENTS ALSO REPORT TO MALADI -- SO THEY CAN'T BE TRUSTED.
I STILL HAVE MORRIGAN CORDE.
OH, RIGHT. SHE WAS SO EFFECTIVE IN FINDING SKYWALKER WHEN SHE WENT TO THE WHEEL.
SHE DID BREAK UP A POTENTIAL ALLIANCE BETWEEN THE REMNANT FORCES OF THE GALACTIC ALLIANCE AND FEL.
SHE CAN INFILTRATE THE TEMPLE FOR US, FIND SKYWALKER. MAYBE EVEN FREE HIM.
OR KILL HIM.

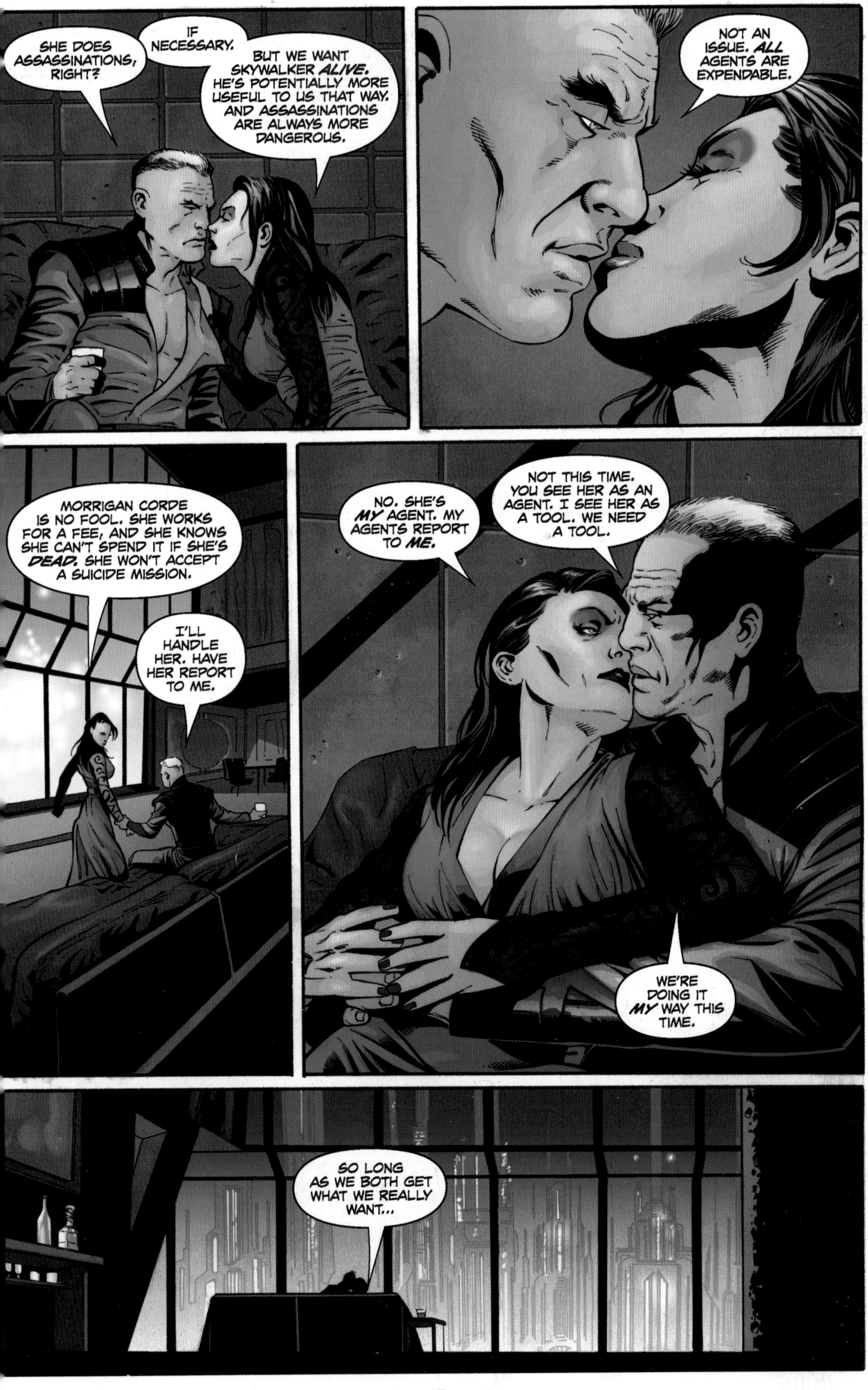
SHE DOES ASSASSINATIONS, RIGHT?
IF NECESSARY.
BUT WE WANT SKYWALKER ALIVE. HE'S POTENTIALLY MORE USEFUL TO US THAT WAY. AND ASSASSINATIONS ARE ALWAYS MORE DANGEROUS.
NOT AN ISSUE. ALL AGENTS ARE EXPENDABLE.
MORRIGAN CORDE IS NO FOOL. SHE WORKS FOR A FEE, AND SHE KNOWS SHE CAN'T SPEND IT IF SHE'S DEAD. SHE WON'T ACCEPT A SUICIDE MISSION.
I'LL HANDLE HER. HAVE HER REPORT TO ME.
NO. SHE'S MY AGENT. MY AGENTS REPORT TO ME.
NOT THIS TIME. YOU SEE HER AS AN AGENT. I SEE HER AS A TOOL. WE NEED A TOOL.
WE'RE DOING IT MY WAY THIS TIME.
SO LONG AS WE BOTH GET WHAT WE REALLY WANT...

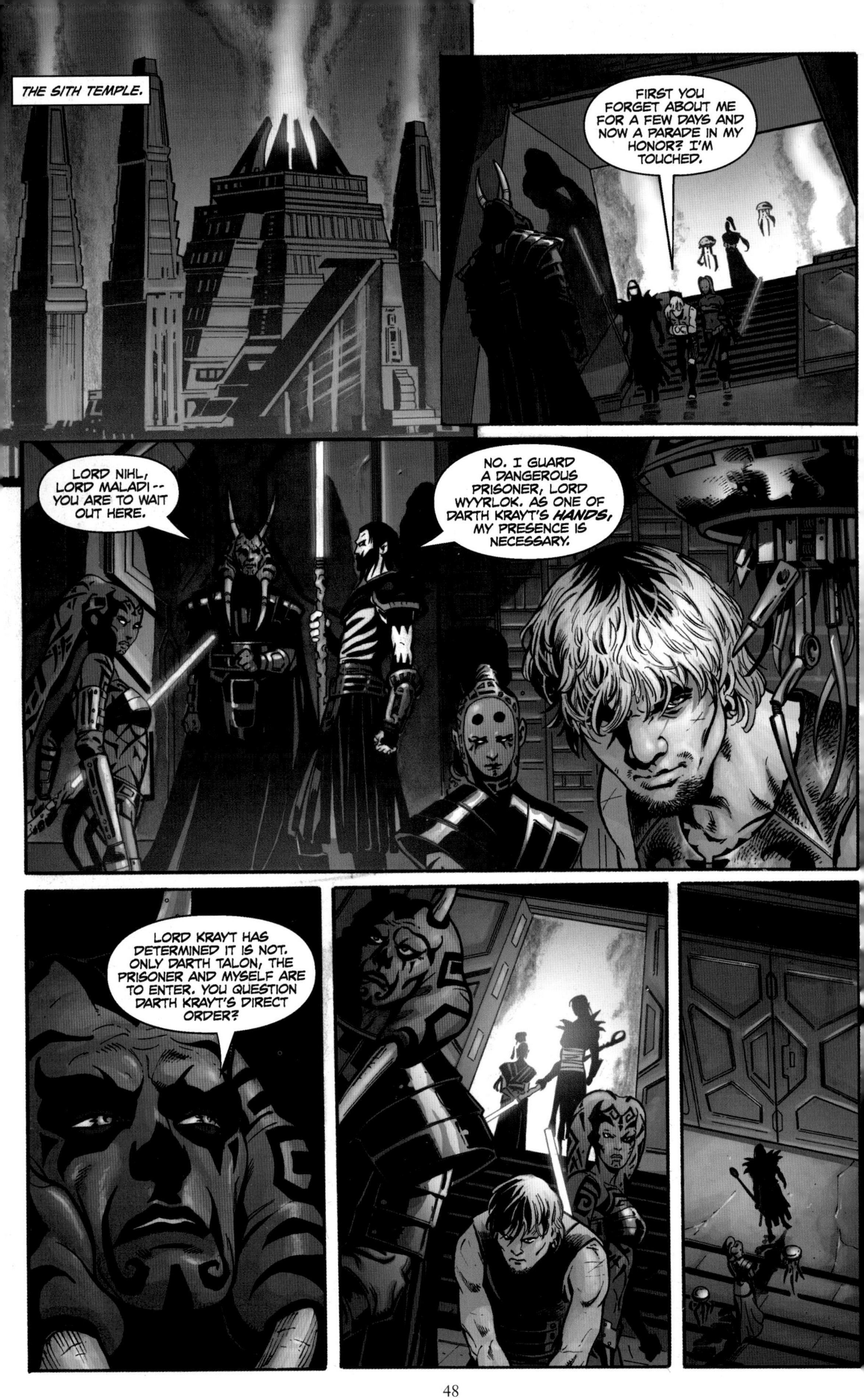
THE SITH TEMPLE.
FIRST YOU FORGET ABOUT ME FOR A FEW DAYS AND NOW A PARADE IN MY HONOR? I'M TOUCHED.
LORD NIHL, LORD MALADI -- YOU ARE TO WAIT OUT HERE.
NO. I GUARD A DANGEROUS PRISONER, LORD WYYRLOK. AS ONE OF DARTH KRAYT'S *HANDS*, MY PRESENCE IS NECESSARY.
LORD KRAYT HAS DETERMINED IT IS NOT. ONLY DARTH TALON, THE PRISONER AND MYSELF ARE TO ENTER. YOU QUESTION DARTH KRAYT'S DIRECT ORDER?

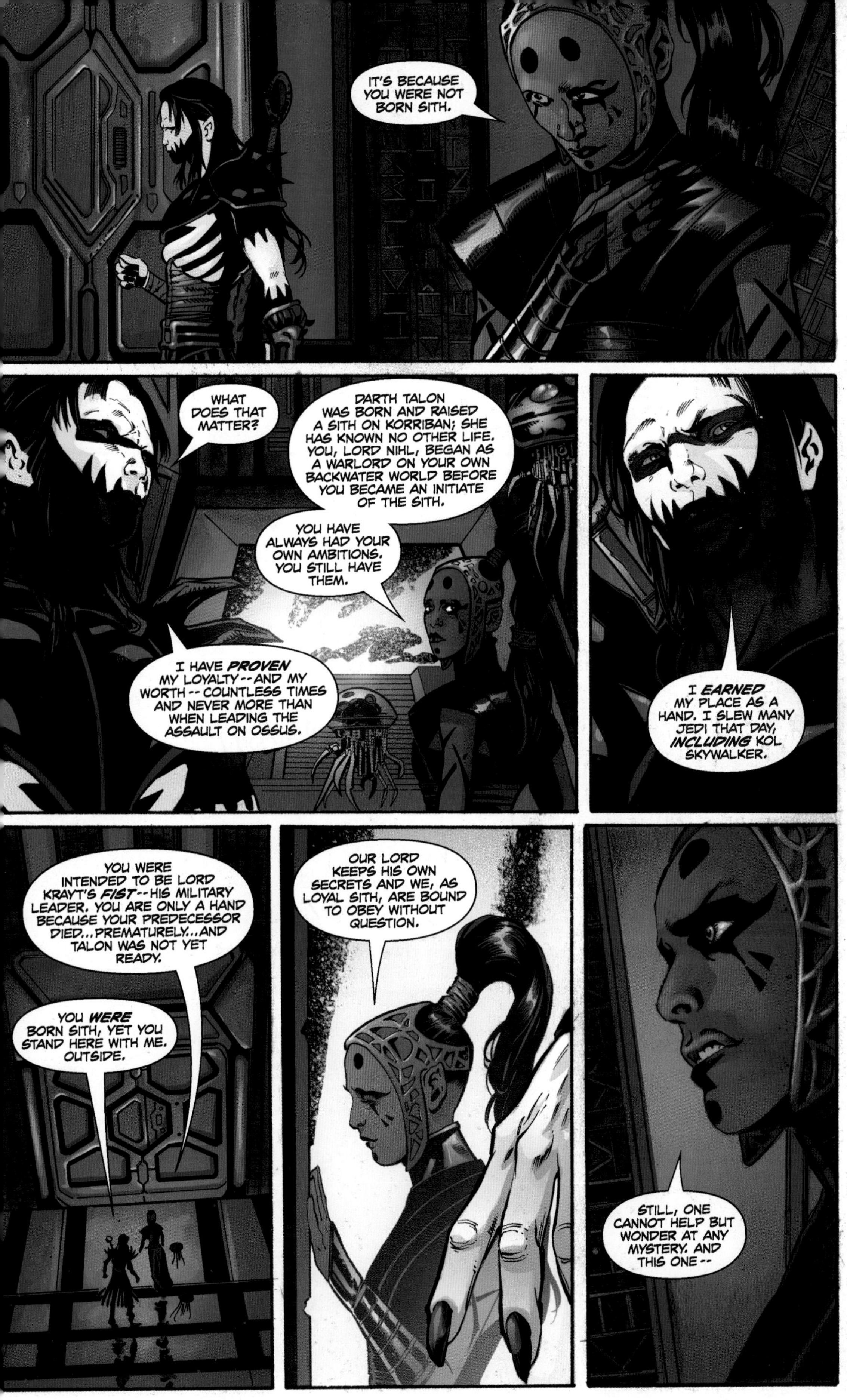

IT'S BECAUSE YOU WERE NOT BORN SITH.
WHAT DOES THAT MATTER?
DARTH TALON WAS BORN AND RAISED A SITH ON KORRIBAN; SHE HAS KNOWN NO OTHER LIFE. YOU, LORD NIHL, BEGAN AS A WARLORD ON YOUR OWN BACKWATER WORLD BEFORE YOU BECAME AN INITIATE OF THE SITH.
YOU HAVE ALWAYS HAD YOUR OWN AMBITIONS. YOU STILL HAVE THEM.
I HAVE PROVEN MY LOYALTY--AND MY WORTH--COUNTLESS TIMES AND NEVER MORE THAN WHEN LEADING THE ASSAULT ON OSSUS.
I EARNED MY PLACE AS A HAND. I SLEW MANY JEDI THAT DAY, INCLUDING KOL SKYWALKER.
YOU WERE INTENDED TO BE LORD KRAYT'S FIST--HIS MILITARY LEADER. YOU ARE ONLY A HAND BECAUSE YOUR PREDECESSOR DIED...PREMATURELY...AND TALON WAS NOT YET READY.
YOU WERE BORN SITH, YET YOU STAND HERE WITH ME. OUTSIDE.
OUR LORD KEEPS HIS OWN SECRETS AND WE, AS LOYAL SITH, ARE BOUND TO OBEY WITHOUT QUESTION.
STILL, ONE CANNOT HELP BUT WONDER AT ANY MYSTERY. AND THIS ONE--

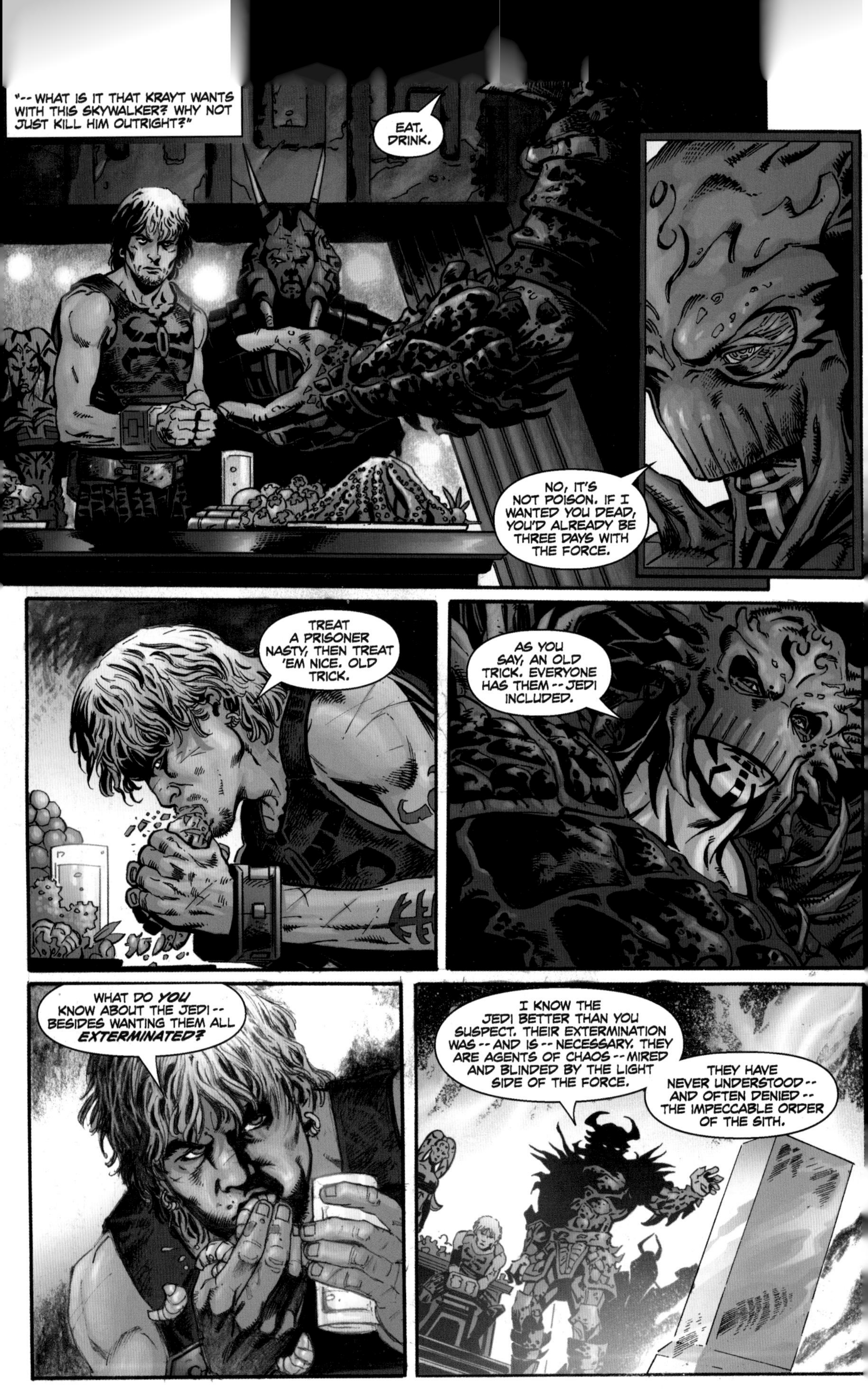
"-- WHAT IS IT THAT KRAYT WANTS WITH THIS SKYWALKER? WHY NOT JUST KILL HIM OUTRIGHT?"
EAT. DRINK.
NO, IT'S NOT POISON. IF I WANTED YOU DEAD, YOU'D ALREADY BE THREE DAYS WITH THE FORCE.
TREAT A PRISONER NASTY, THEN TREAT 'EM NICE. OLD TRICK.
AS YOU SAY, AN OLD TRICK. EVERYONE HAS THEM -- JEDI INCLUDED.
WHAT DO *YOU* KNOW ABOUT THE JEDI -- BESIDES WANTING THEM ALL ***EXTERMINATED?***
I KNOW THE JEDI BETTER THAN YOU SUSPECT. THEIR EXTERMINATION WAS -- AND IS -- NECESSARY. THEY ARE AGENTS OF CHAOS -- MIRED AND BLINDED BY THE LIGHT SIDE OF THE FORCE.
THEY HAVE NEVER UNDERSTOOD -- AND OFTEN DENIED -- THE IMPECCABLE ORDER OF THE SITH.

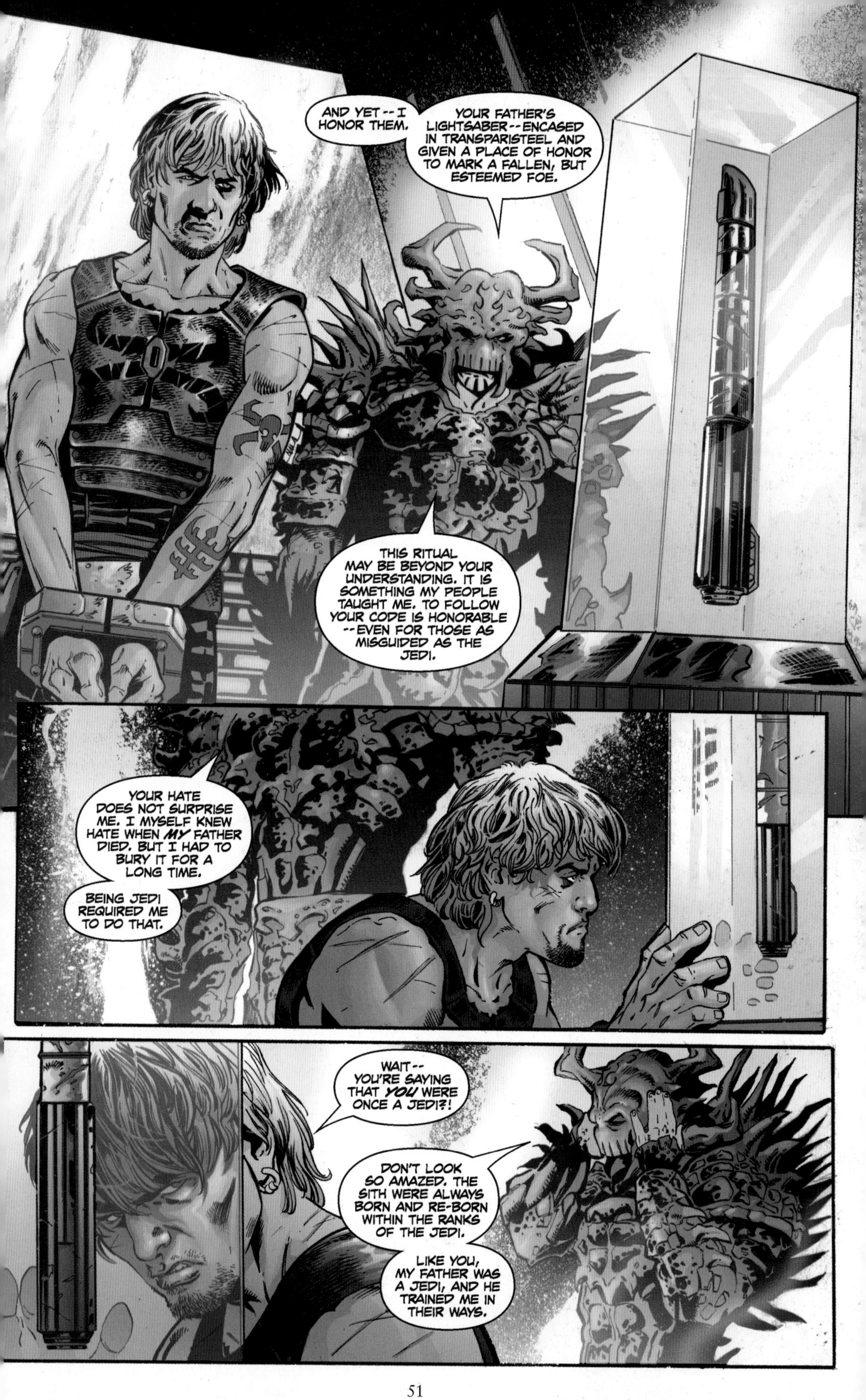
AND YET -- I HONOR THEM.
YOUR FATHER'S LIGHTSABER -- ENCASED IN TRANSPARISTEEL AND GIVEN A PLACE OF HONOR TO MARK A FALLEN, BUT ESTEEMED FOE.
THIS RITUAL MAY BE BEYOND YOUR UNDERSTANDING. IT IS SOMETHING MY PEOPLE TAUGHT ME. TO FOLLOW YOUR CODE IS HONORABLE -- EVEN FOR THOSE AS MISGUIDED AS THE JEDI.
YOUR HATE DOES NOT SURPRISE ME. I MYSELF KNEW HATE WHEN MY FATHER DIED. BUT I HAD TO BURY IT FOR A LONG TIME.
BEING JEDI REQUIRED ME TO DO THAT.
WAIT -- YOU'RE SAYING THAT YOU WERE ONCE A JEDI?!
DON'T LOOK SO AMAZED. THE SITH WERE ALWAYS BORN AND RE-BORN WITHIN THE RANKS OF THE JEDI.
LIKE YOU, MY FATHER WAS A JEDI, AND HE TRAINED ME IN THEIR WAYS.

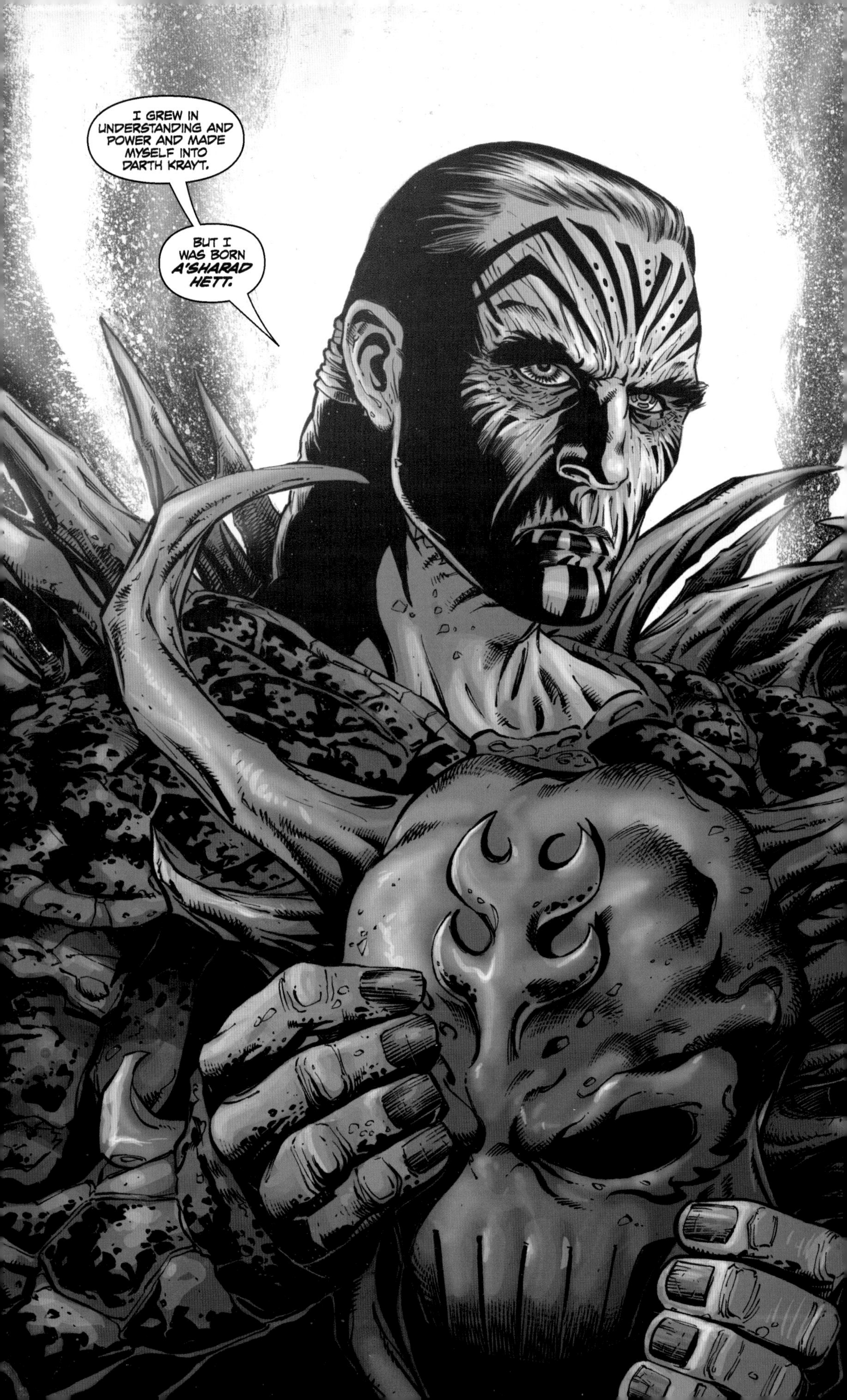
I GREW IN UNDERSTANDING AND POWER AND MADE MYSELF INTO DARTH KRAYT.
BUT I WAS BORN *A'SHARAD HETT.*

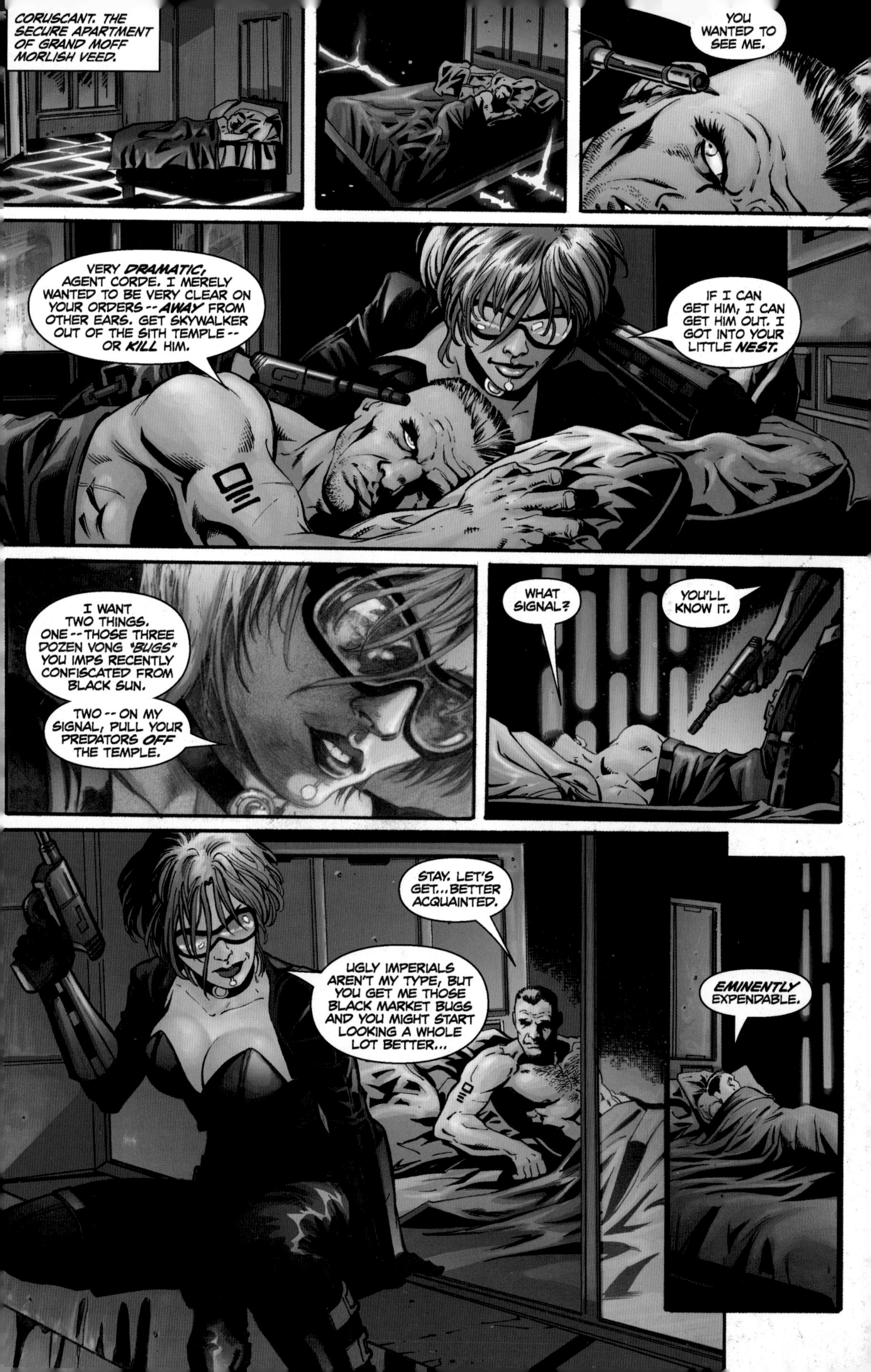
CORUSCANT. THE SECURE APARTMENT OF GRAND MOFF MORLISH VEED.
YOU WANTED TO SEE ME.
VERY DRAMATIC, AGENT CORDE. I MERELY WANTED TO BE VERY CLEAR ON YOUR ORDERS -- AWAY FROM OTHER EARS. GET SKYWALKER OUT OF THE SITH TEMPLE -- OR KILL HIM.
IF I CAN GET HIM, I CAN GET HIM OUT. I GOT INTO YOUR LITTLE NEST.
I WANT TWO THINGS. ONE -- THOSE THREE DOZEN VONG "BUGS" YOU IMPS RECENTLY CONFISCATED FROM BLACK SUN.
TWO -- ON MY SIGNAL, PULL YOUR PREDATORS OFF THE TEMPLE.
WHAT SIGNAL?
YOU'LL KNOW IT.
STAY. LET'S GET... BETTER ACQUAINTED.
UGLY IMPERIALS AREN'T MY TYPE, BUT YOU GET ME THOSE BLACK MARKET BUGS AND YOU MIGHT START LOOKING A WHOLE LOT BETTER...
EMINENTLY EXPENDABLE.

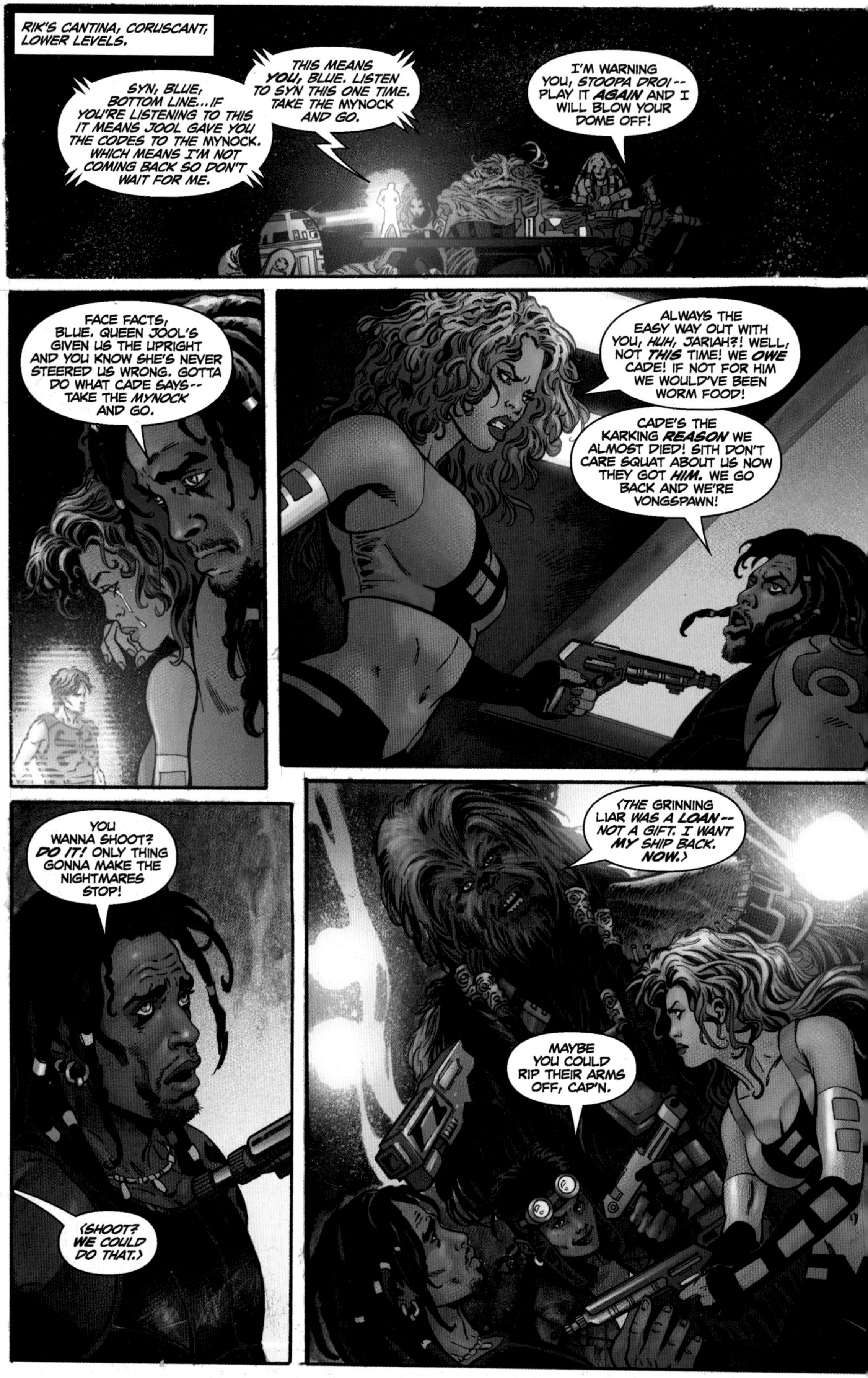
RIK'S CANTINA, CORUSCANT, LOWER LEVELS.
SYN, BLUE, BOTTOM LINE...IF YOU'RE LISTENING TO THIS IT MEANS JOOL GAVE YOU THE CODES TO THE MYNOCK. WHICH MEANS I'M NOT COMING BACK SO DON'T WAIT FOR ME.
THIS MEANS YOU, BLUE. LISTEN TO SYN THIS ONE TIME. TAKE THE MYNOCK AND GO.
I'M WARNING YOU, STOOPA DROI-- PLAY IT AGAIN AND I WILL BLOW YOUR DOME OFF!
FACE FACTS, BLUE. QUEEN JOOL'S GIVEN US THE UPRIGHT AND YOU KNOW SHE'S NEVER STEERED US WRONG. GOTTA DO WHAT CADE SAYS-- TAKE THE MYNOCK AND GO.
ALWAYS THE EASY WAY OUT WITH YOU, HUH, JARIAH?! WELL, NOT THIS TIME! WE OWE CADE! IF NOT FOR HIM WE WOULD'VE BEEN WORM FOOD!
CADE'S THE KARKING REASON WE ALMOST DIED! SITH DON'T CARE SQUAT ABOUT US NOW THEY GOT HIM. WE GO BACK AND WE'RE VONGSPAWN!
YOU WANNA SHOOT? DO IT! ONLY THING GONNA MAKE THE NIGHTMARES STOP!
‹SHOOT? WE COULD DO THAT.›
‹THE GRINNING LIAR WAS A LOAN-- NOT A GIFT. I WANT MY SHIP BACK. NOW.›
MAYBE YOU COULD RIP THEIR ARMS OFF, CAP'N.

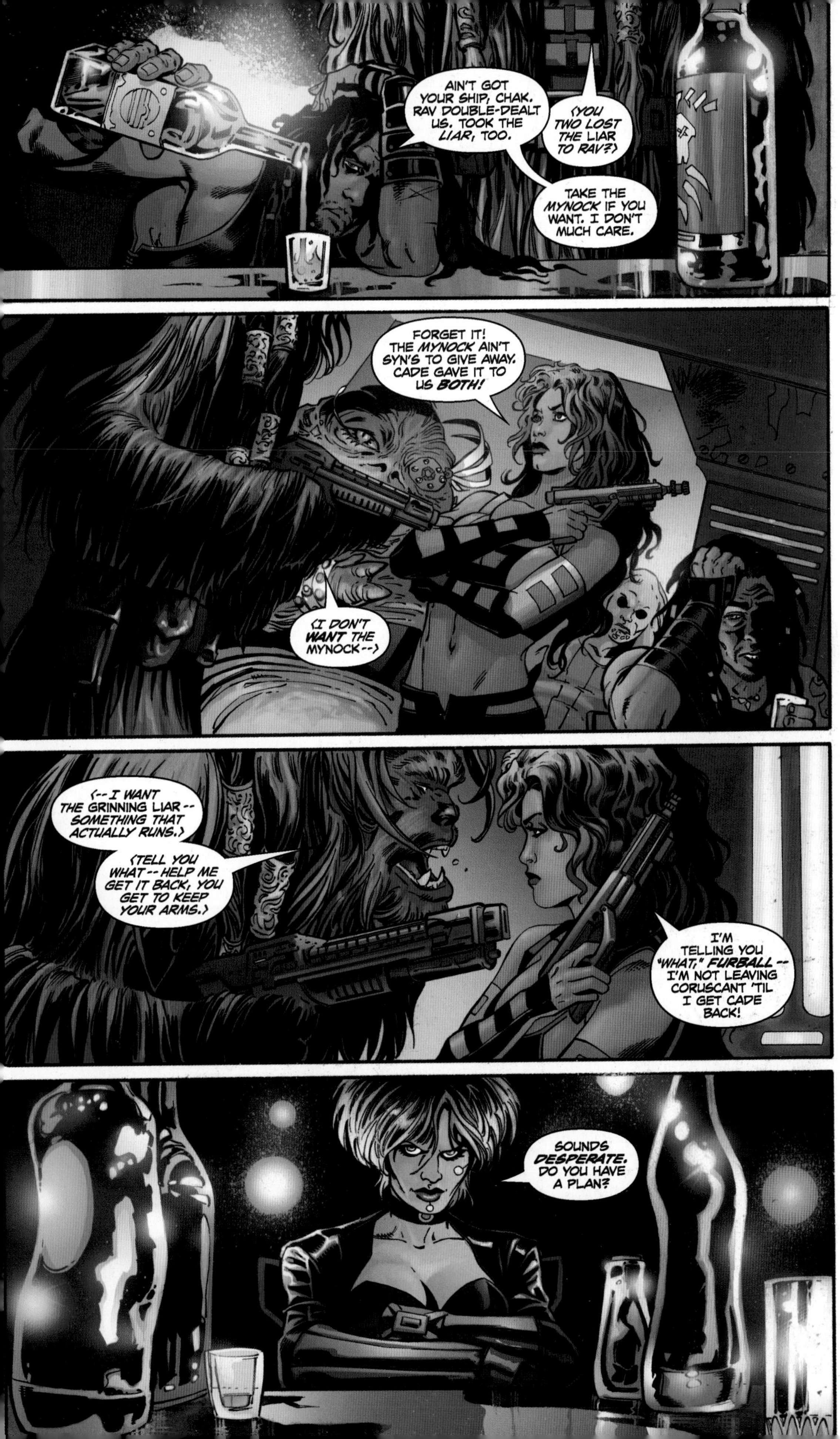
AIN'T GOT YOUR SHIP, CHAK. RAV DOUBLE-DEALT US. TOOK THE LIAR, TOO.
‹YOU TWO LOST THE LIAR TO RAV?›
TAKE THE MYNOCK IF YOU WANT. I DON'T MUCH CARE.
FORGET IT! THE MYNOCK AIN'T SYN'S TO GIVE AWAY. CADE GAVE IT TO US BOTH!
‹I DON'T WANT THE MYNOCK--›
‹--I WANT THE GRINNING LIAR--SOMETHING THAT ACTUALLY RUNS.›
‹TELL YOU WHAT--HELP ME GET IT BACK, YOU GET TO KEEP YOUR ARMS.›
I'M TELLING YOU "WHAT," FURBALL--I'M NOT LEAVING CORUSCANT 'TIL I GET CADE BACK!
SOUNDS DESPERATE. DO YOU HAVE A PLAN?

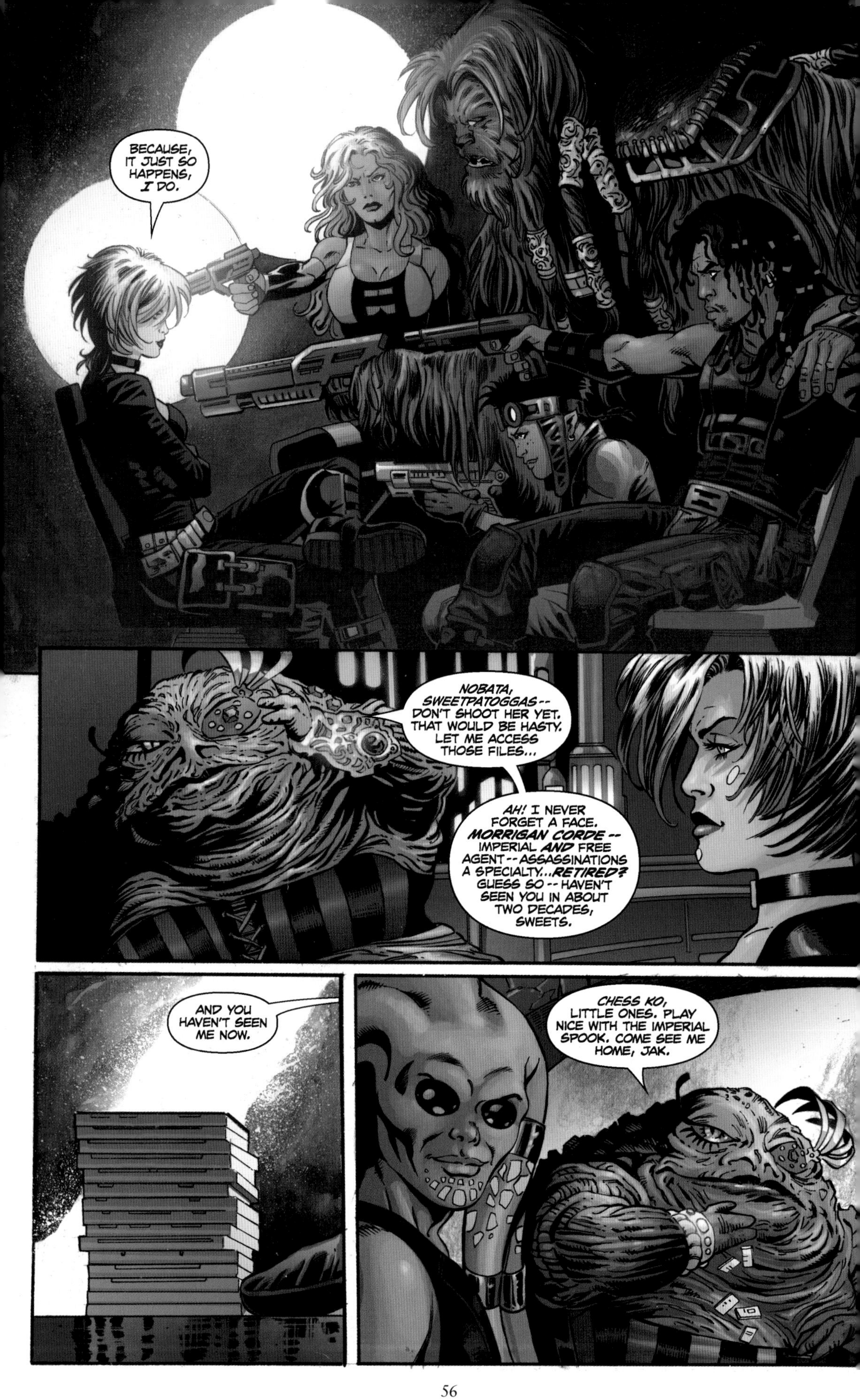
BECAUSE, IT JUST SO HAPPENS, I DO.
NOBATA, SWEETPATOGGAS-- DON'T SHOOT HER YET. THAT WOULD BE HASTY. LET ME ACCESS THOSE FILES...
AH! I NEVER FORGET A FACE. MORRIGAN CORDE-- IMPERIAL AND FREE AGENT--ASSASSINATIONS A SPECIALTY...RETIRED? GUESS SO--HAVEN'T SEEN YOU IN ABOUT TWO DECADES, SWEETS.
AND YOU HAVEN'T SEEN ME NOW.
CHESS KO, LITTLE ONES. PLAY NICE WITH THE IMPERIAL SPOOK. COME SEE ME HOME, JAK.

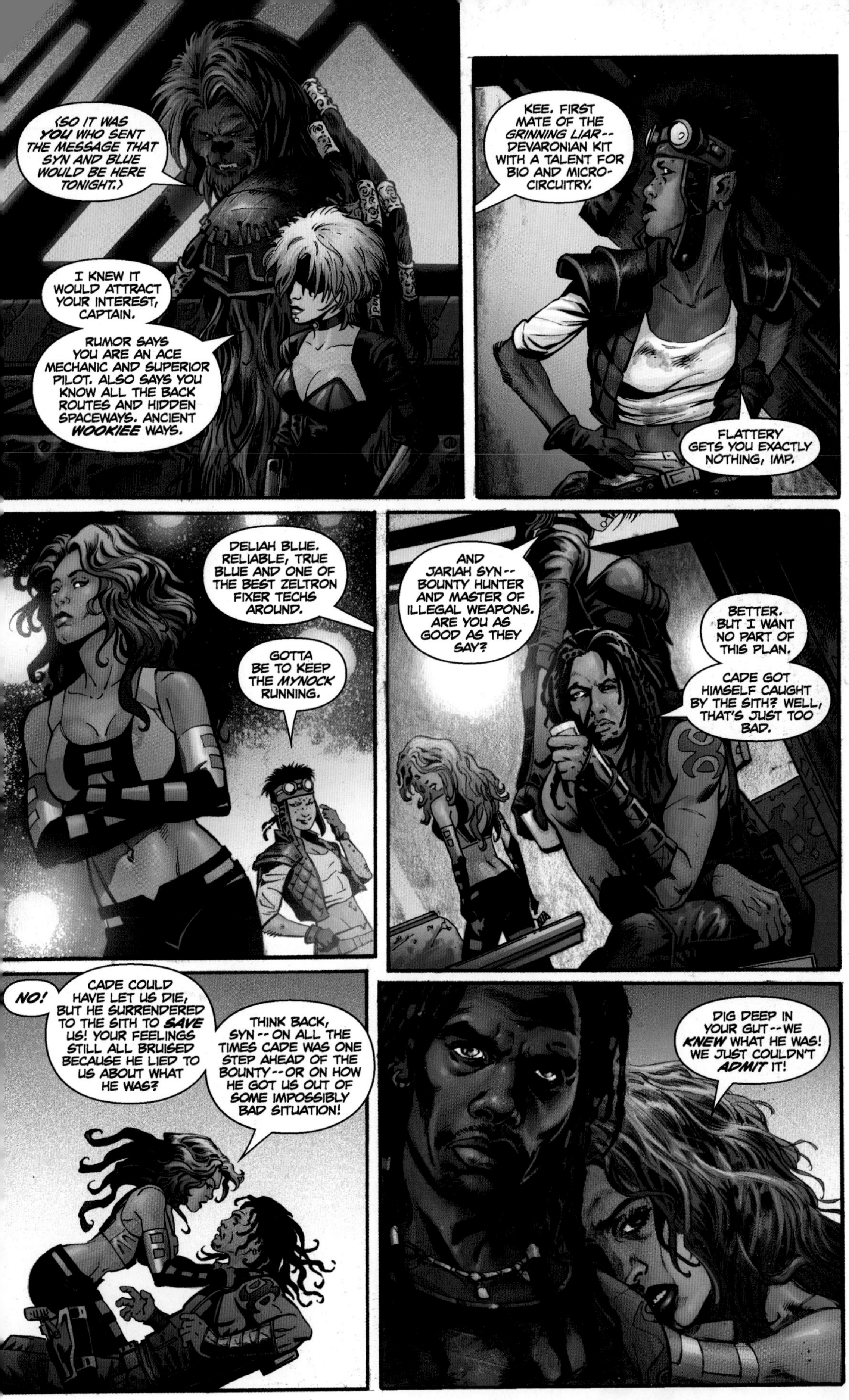

<SO IT WAS YOU WHO SENT THE MESSAGE THAT SYN AND BLUE WOULD BE HERE TONIGHT.>
I KNEW IT WOULD ATTRACT YOUR INTEREST, CAPTAIN.
RUMOR SAYS YOU ARE AN ACE MECHANIC AND SUPERIOR PILOT. ALSO SAYS YOU KNOW ALL THE BACK ROUTES AND HIDDEN SPACEWAYS. ANCIENT WOOKIEE WAYS.
KEE. FIRST MATE OF THE GRINNING LIAR-- DEVARONIAN KIT WITH A TALENT FOR BIO AND MICRO-CIRCUITRY.
FLATTERY GETS YOU EXACTLY NOTHING, IMP.
DELIAH BLUE. RELIABLE, TRUE BLUE AND ONE OF THE BEST ZELTRON FIXER TECHS AROUND.
GOTTA BE TO KEEP THE MYNOCK RUNNING.
AND JARIAH SYN-- BOUNTY HUNTER AND MASTER OF ILLEGAL WEAPONS. ARE YOU AS GOOD AS THEY SAY?
BETTER. BUT I WANT NO PART OF THIS PLAN.
CADE GOT HIMSELF CAUGHT BY THE SITH? WELL, THAT'S JUST TOO BAD.
NO!
CADE COULD HAVE LET US DIE, BUT HE SURRENDERED TO THE SITH TO SAVE US! YOUR FEELINGS STILL ALL BRUISED BECAUSE HE LIED TO US ABOUT WHAT HE WAS?
THINK BACK, SYN-- ON ALL THE TIMES CADE WAS ONE STEP AHEAD OF THE BOUNTY--OR ON HOW HE GOT US OUT OF SOME IMPOSSIBLY BAD SITUATION!
DIG DEEP IN YOUR GUT--WE KNEW WHAT HE WAS! WE JUST COULDN'T ADMIT IT!

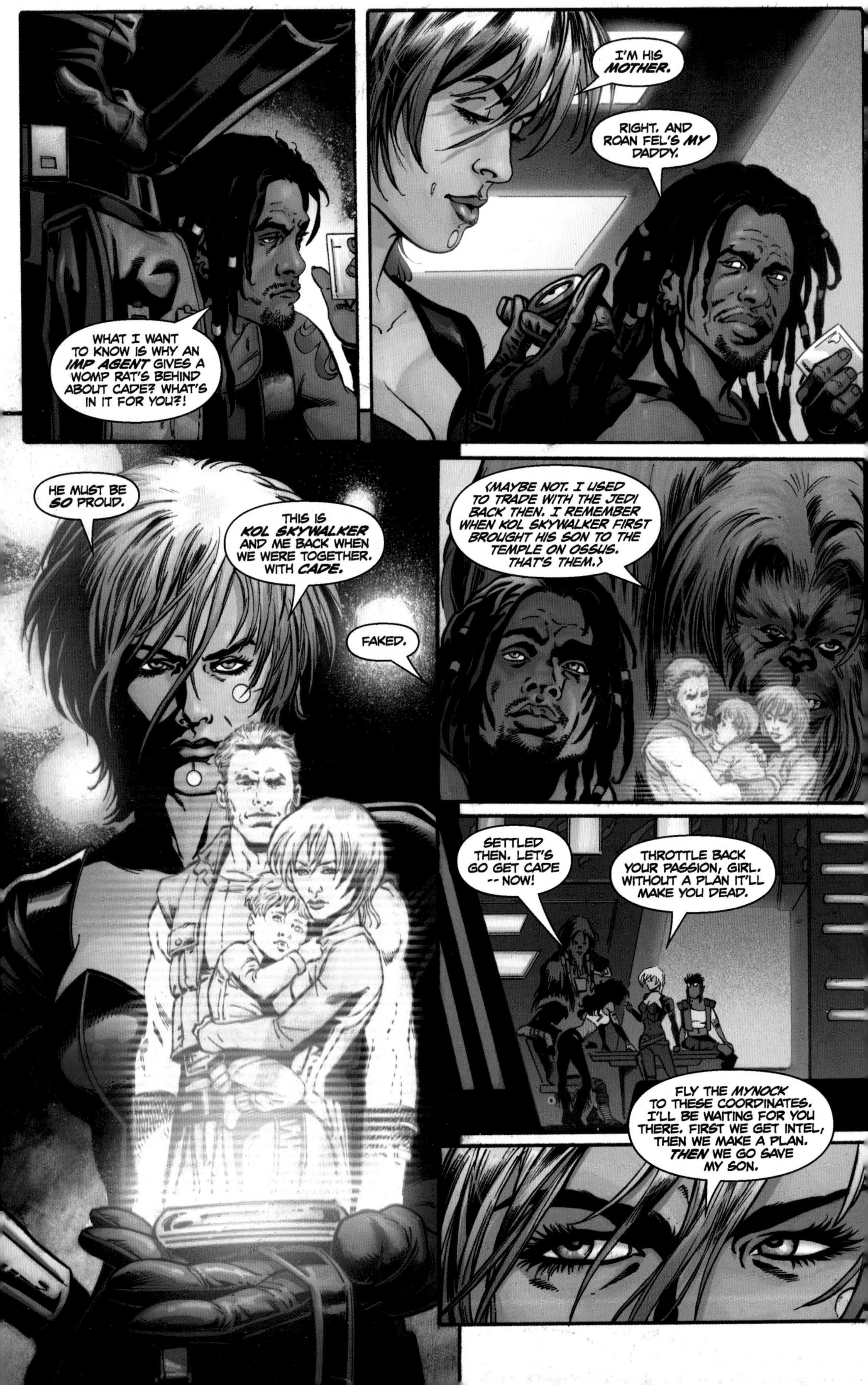
WHAT I WANT TO KNOW IS WHY AN IMP AGENT GIVES A WOMP RAT'S BEHIND ABOUT CADE? WHAT'S IN IT FOR YOU?!
I'M HIS MOTHER.
RIGHT. AND ROAN FEL'S MY DADDY.
HE MUST BE SO PROUD.
THIS IS KOL SKYWALKER AND ME BACK WHEN WE WERE TOGETHER. WITH CADE.
FAKED.
(MAYBE NOT. I USED TO TRADE WITH THE JEDI BACK THEN. I REMEMBER WHEN KOL SKYWALKER FIRST BROUGHT HIS SON TO THE TEMPLE ON OSSUS. THAT'S THEM.)
SETTLED THEN. LET'S GO GET CADE -- NOW!
THROTTLE BACK YOUR PASSION, GIRL. WITHOUT A PLAN IT'LL MAKE YOU DEAD.
FLY THE MYNOCK TO THESE COORDINATES. I'LL BE WAITING FOR YOU THERE. FIRST WE GET INTEL, THEN WE MAKE A PLAN. THEN WE GO SAVE MY SON.

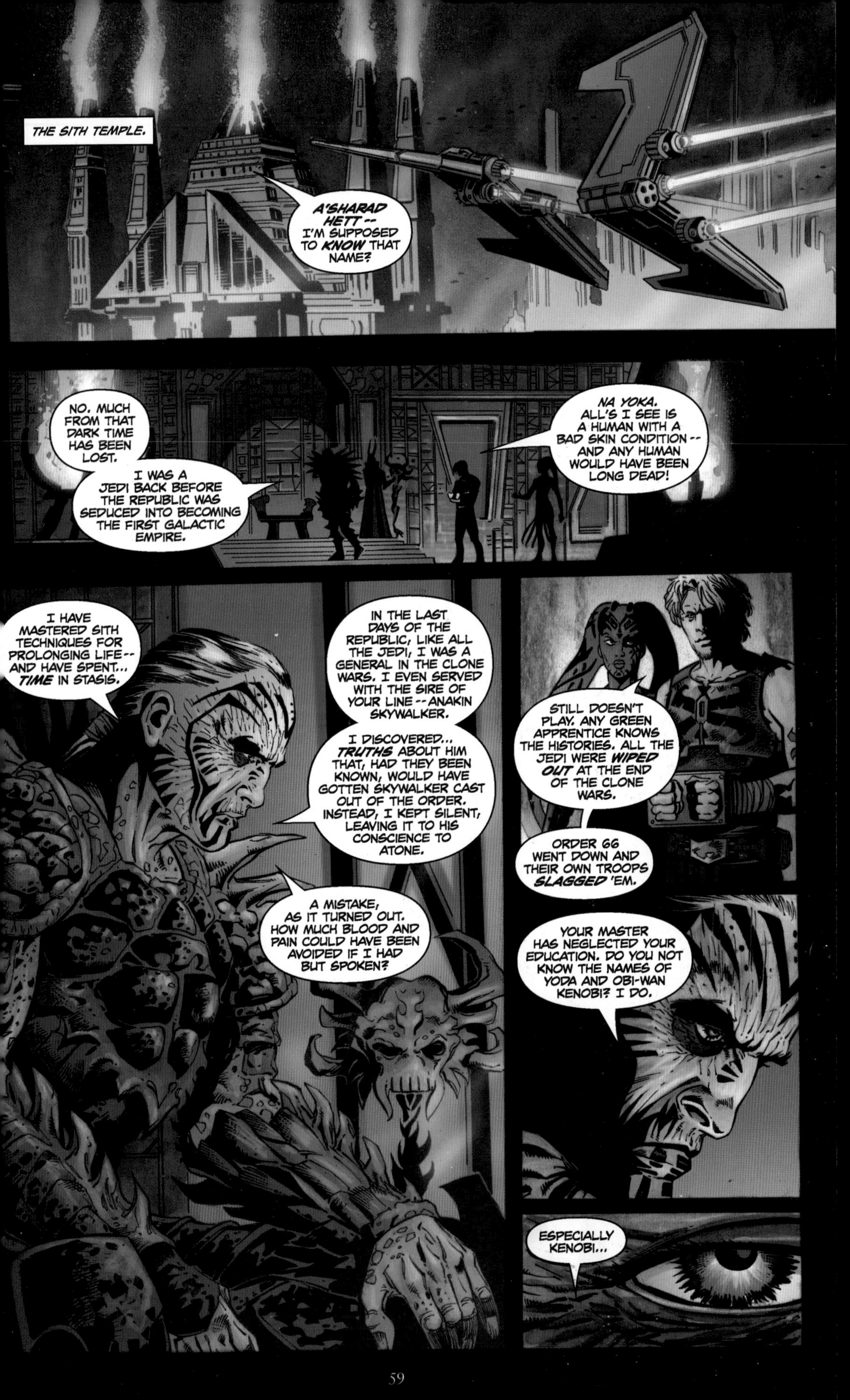
THE SITH TEMPLE.
A'SHARAD HETT -- I'M SUPPOSED TO KNOW THAT NAME?
NO. MUCH FROM THAT DARK TIME HAS BEEN LOST.
I WAS A JEDI BACK BEFORE THE REPUBLIC WAS SEDUCED INTO BECOMING THE FIRST GALACTIC EMPIRE.
NA YOKA. ALL'S I SEE IS A HUMAN WITH A BAD SKIN CONDITION -- AND ANY HUMAN WOULD HAVE BEEN LONG DEAD!
I HAVE MASTERED SITH TECHNIQUES FOR PROLONGING LIFE -- AND HAVE SPENT... TIME IN STASIS.
IN THE LAST DAYS OF THE REPUBLIC, LIKE ALL THE JEDI, I WAS A GENERAL IN THE CLONE WARS. I EVEN SERVED WITH THE SIRE OF YOUR LINE -- ANAKIN SKYWALKER.
I DISCOVERED... TRUTHS ABOUT HIM THAT, HAD THEY BEEN KNOWN, WOULD HAVE GOTTEN SKYWALKER CAST OUT OF THE ORDER. INSTEAD, I KEPT SILENT, LEAVING IT TO HIS CONSCIENCE TO ATONE.
A MISTAKE, AS IT TURNED OUT. HOW MUCH BLOOD AND PAIN COULD HAVE BEEN AVOIDED IF I HAD BUT SPOKEN?
STILL DOESN'T PLAY. ANY GREEN APPRENTICE KNOWS THE HISTORIES. ALL THE JEDI WERE WIPED OUT AT THE END OF THE CLONE WARS.
ORDER 66 WENT DOWN AND THEIR OWN TROOPS SLAGGED 'EM.
YOUR MASTER HAS NEGLECTED YOUR EDUCATION. DO YOU NOT KNOW THE NAMES OF YODA AND OBI-WAN KENOBI? I DO.
ESPECIALLY KENOBI...

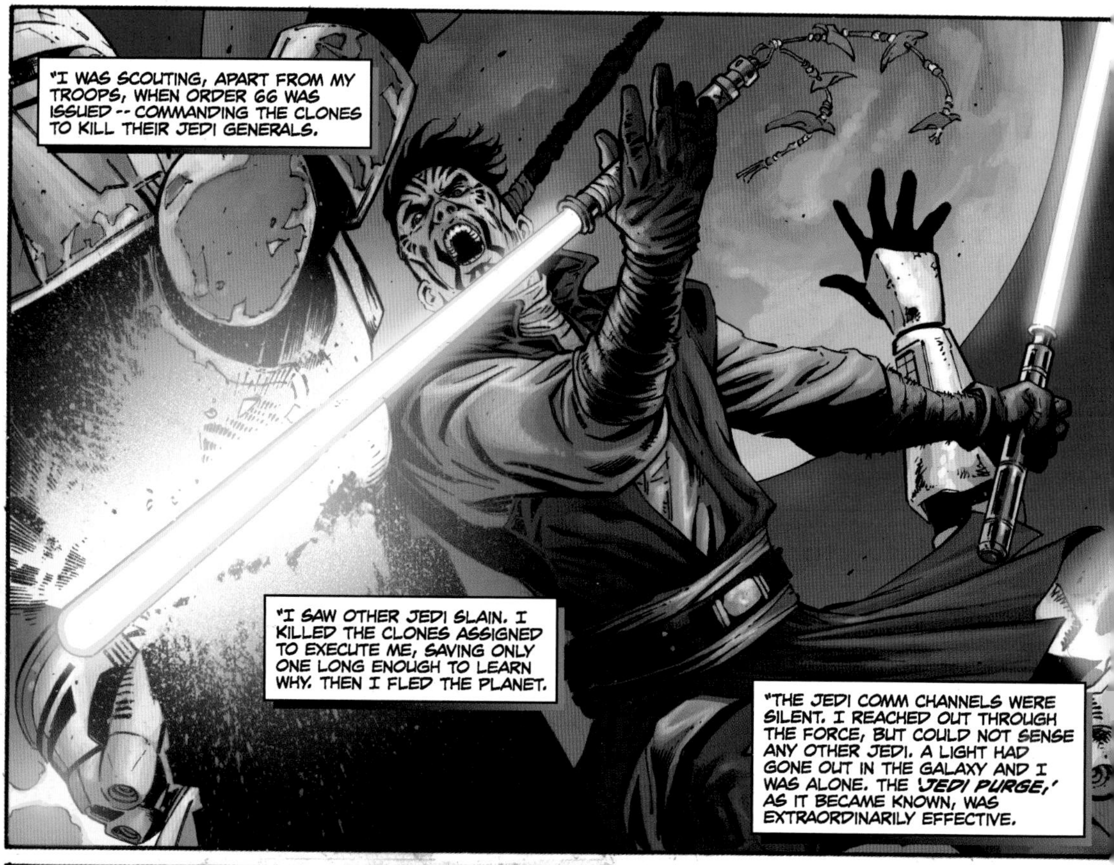
"I WAS SCOUTING, APART FROM MY TROOPS, WHEN ORDER 66 WAS ISSUED -- COMMANDING THE CLONES TO KILL THEIR JEDI GENERALS.
"I SAW OTHER JEDI SLAIN. I KILLED THE CLONES ASSIGNED TO EXECUTE ME, SAVING ONLY ONE LONG ENOUGH TO LEARN WHY. THEN I FLED THE PLANET.
"THE JEDI COMM CHANNELS WERE SILENT. I REACHED OUT THROUGH THE FORCE, BUT COULD NOT SENSE ANY OTHER JEDI. A LIGHT HAD GONE OUT IN THE GALAXY AND I WAS ALONE. THE 'JEDI PURGE,' AS IT BECAME KNOWN, WAS EXTRAORDINARILY EFFECTIVE.

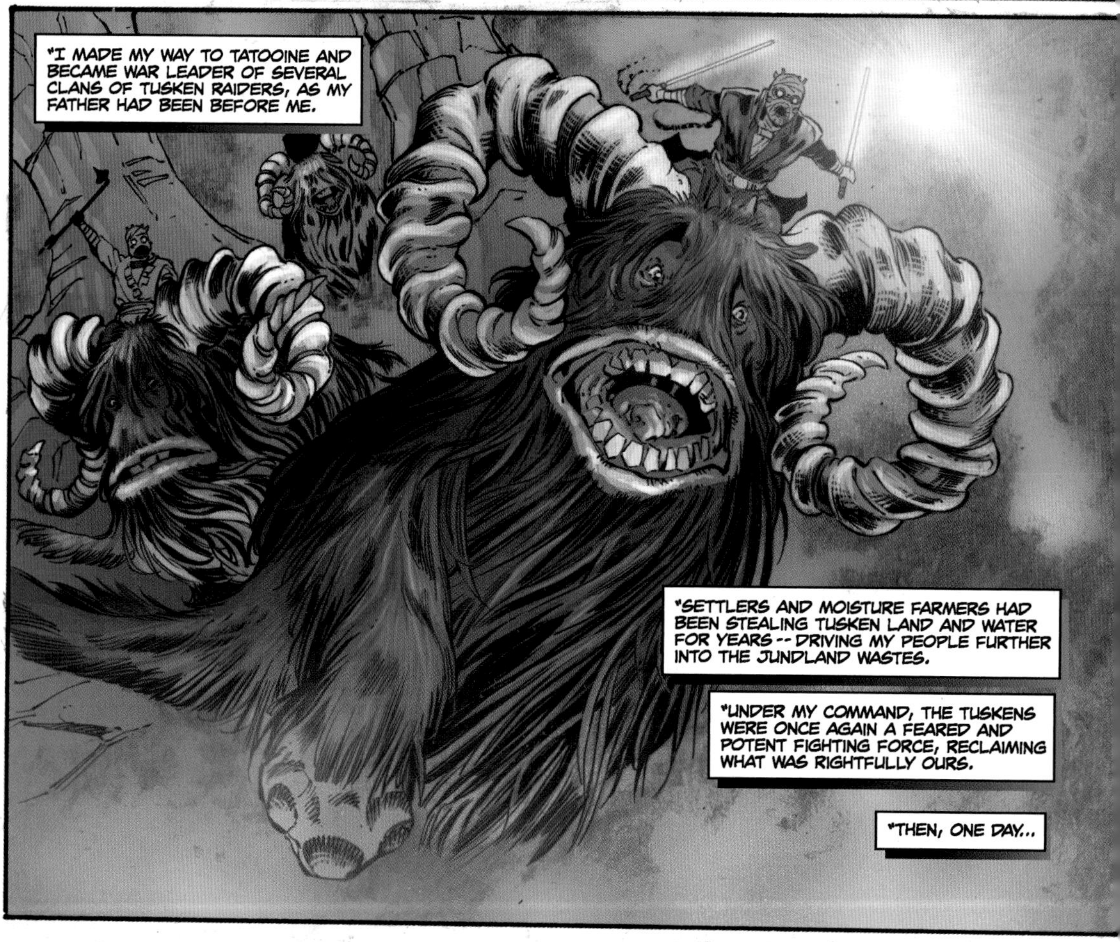
"I MADE MY WAY TO TATOOINE AND BECAME WAR LEADER OF SEVERAL CLANS OF TUSKEN RAIDERS, AS MY FATHER HAD BEEN BEFORE ME.
"SETTLERS AND MOISTURE FARMERS HAD BEEN STEALING TUSKEN LAND AND WATER FOR YEARS -- DRIVING MY PEOPLE FURTHER INTO THE JUNDLAND WASTES.
"UNDER MY COMMAND, THE TUSKENS WERE ONCE AGAIN A FEARED AND POTENT FIGHTING FORCE, RECLAIMING WHAT WAS RIGHTFULLY OURS.
"THEN, ONE DAY...

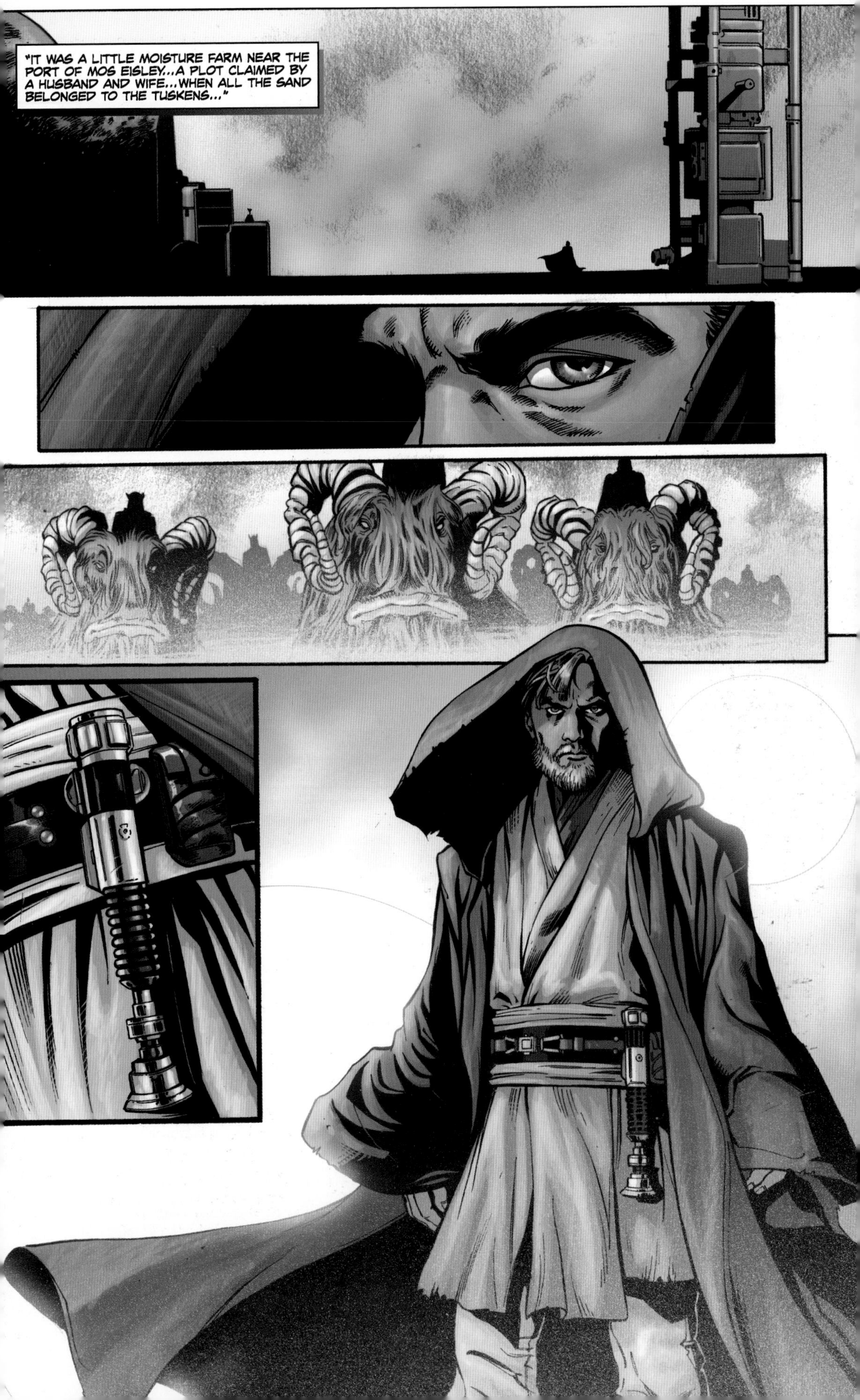
"IT WAS A LITTLE MOISTURE FARM NEAR THE PORT OF MOS EISLEY...A PLOT CLAIMED BY A HUSBAND AND WIFE...WHEN ALL THE SAND BELONGED TO THE TUSKENS..."

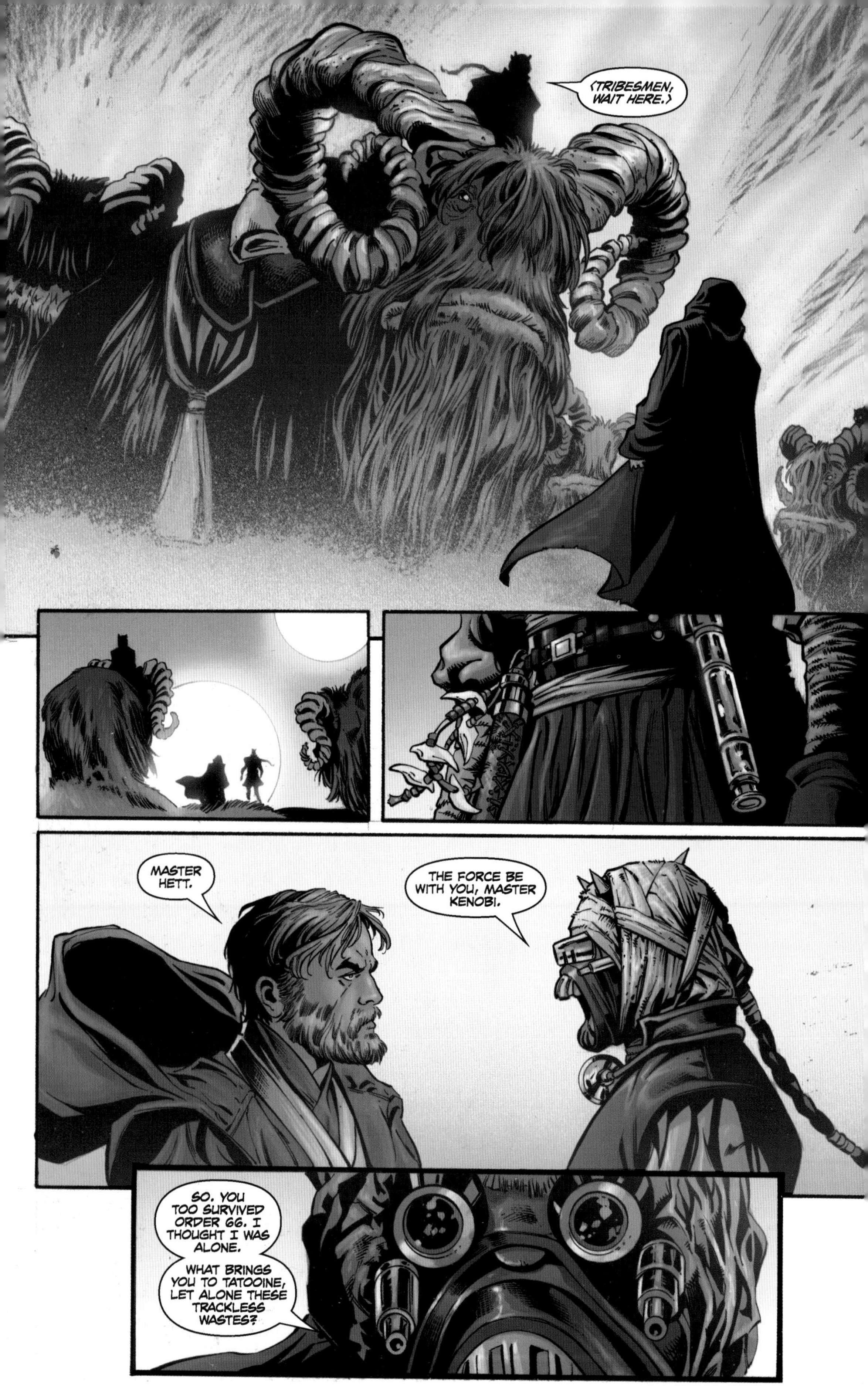

‹TRIBESMEN, WAIT HERE.›
MASTER HETT.
THE FORCE BE WITH YOU, MASTER KENOBI.
SO. YOU TOO SURVIVED ORDER 66. I THOUGHT I WAS ALONE.
WHAT BRINGS YOU TO TATOOINE, LET ALONE THESE TRACKLESS WASTES?

PAST MISTAKES DO NOT JUSTIFY CURRENT ONES. THE DANGER IS IN BECOMING WHAT YOU FIGHT. IT WAS THE TRAP THAT THE JEDI FELL INTO. IT IS THE TRAP THAT TAKES YOU NOW.

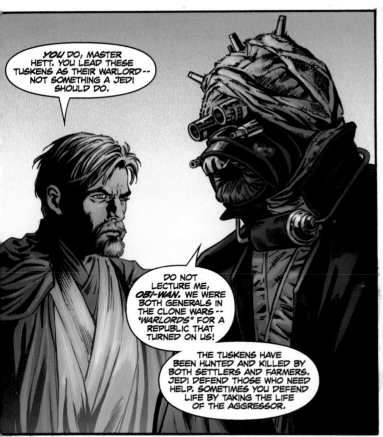

YOU DO, MASTER HETT. YOU LEAD THESE TUSKENS AS THEIR WARLORD-- NOT SOMETHING A JEDI SHOULD DO.

DO NOT LECTURE ME, OBI-WAN. WE WERE BOTH GENERALS IN THE CLONE WARS -- "WARLORDS" FOR A REPUBLIC THAT TURNED ON US!

THE TUSKENS HAVE BEEN HUNTED AND KILLED BY BOTH SETTLERS AND FARMERS. JEDI DEFEND THOSE WHO NEED HELP. SOMETIMES YOU DEFEND LIFE BY TAKING THE LIFE OF THE AGGRESSOR.

IT MUST STOP. YOU MUST SEE THAT, A'SHARAD HETT.

I DO NOT. I WAS RAISED TO MANHOOD AMONGST THE TUSKENS BY MY FATHER, SHARAD HETT, THE GREATEST JEDI OF HIS AGE. HE TAUGHT ME TO THINK AND ACT AS A TUSKEN.

THESE ARE MY PEOPLE! WILL THE SETTLERS STOP KILLING TUSKENS? THEN BLOOD CALLS FOR BLOOD! THE SETTLERS WILL BE FORCED TO ABANDON THE LAND -- OR BE BURIED BENEATH IT!

I CANNOT PERMIT THAT.

YOU WERE A GREAT JEDI, HETT, AND THE SON OF A GREAT JEDI. BUT YOU HAVE GIVEN YOURSELF OVER TO REVENGE. IT STOPS HERE.

YOU WILL HAVE A JEDI FUNERAL, MASTER KENOBI. THAT I PROMISE.

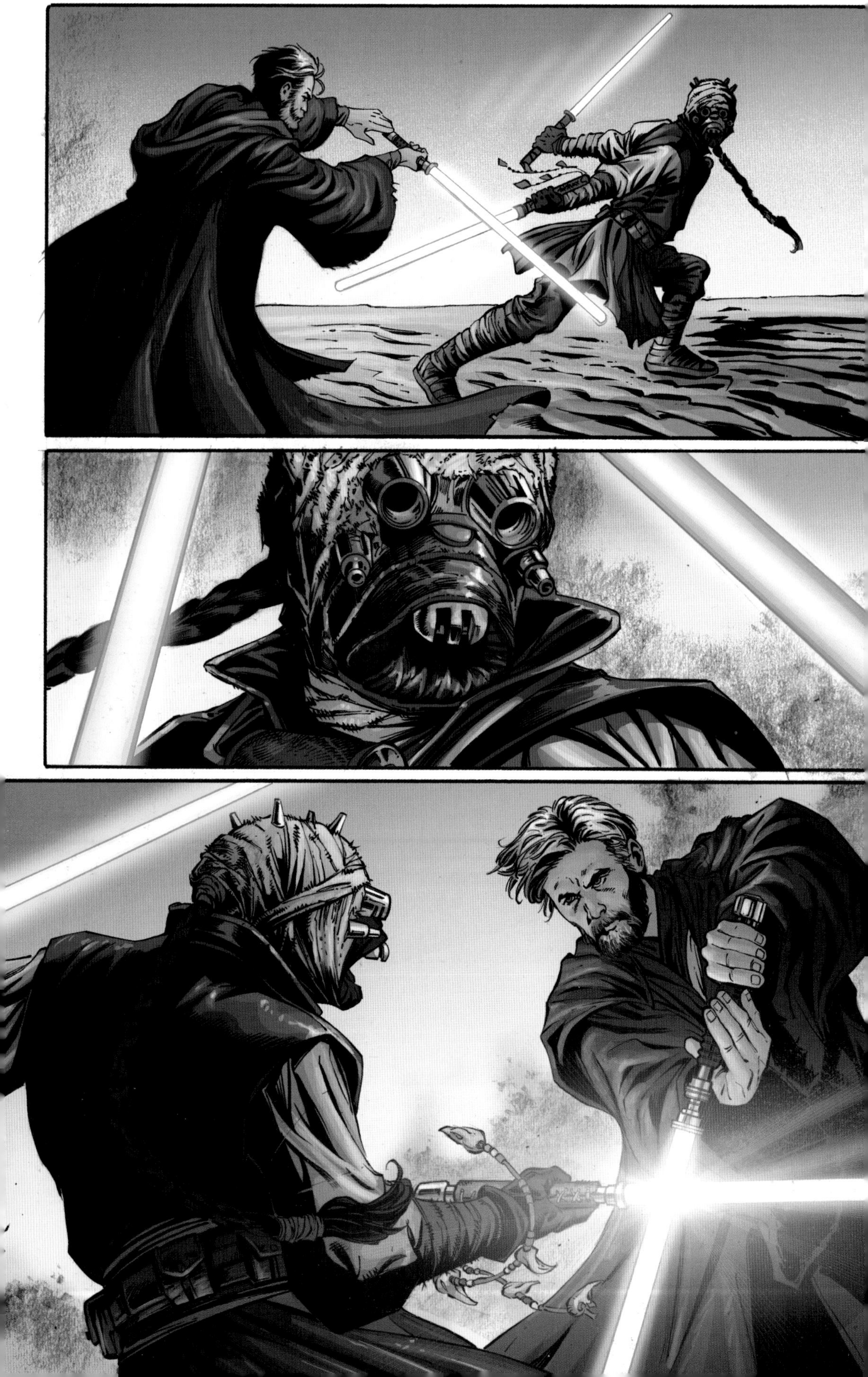

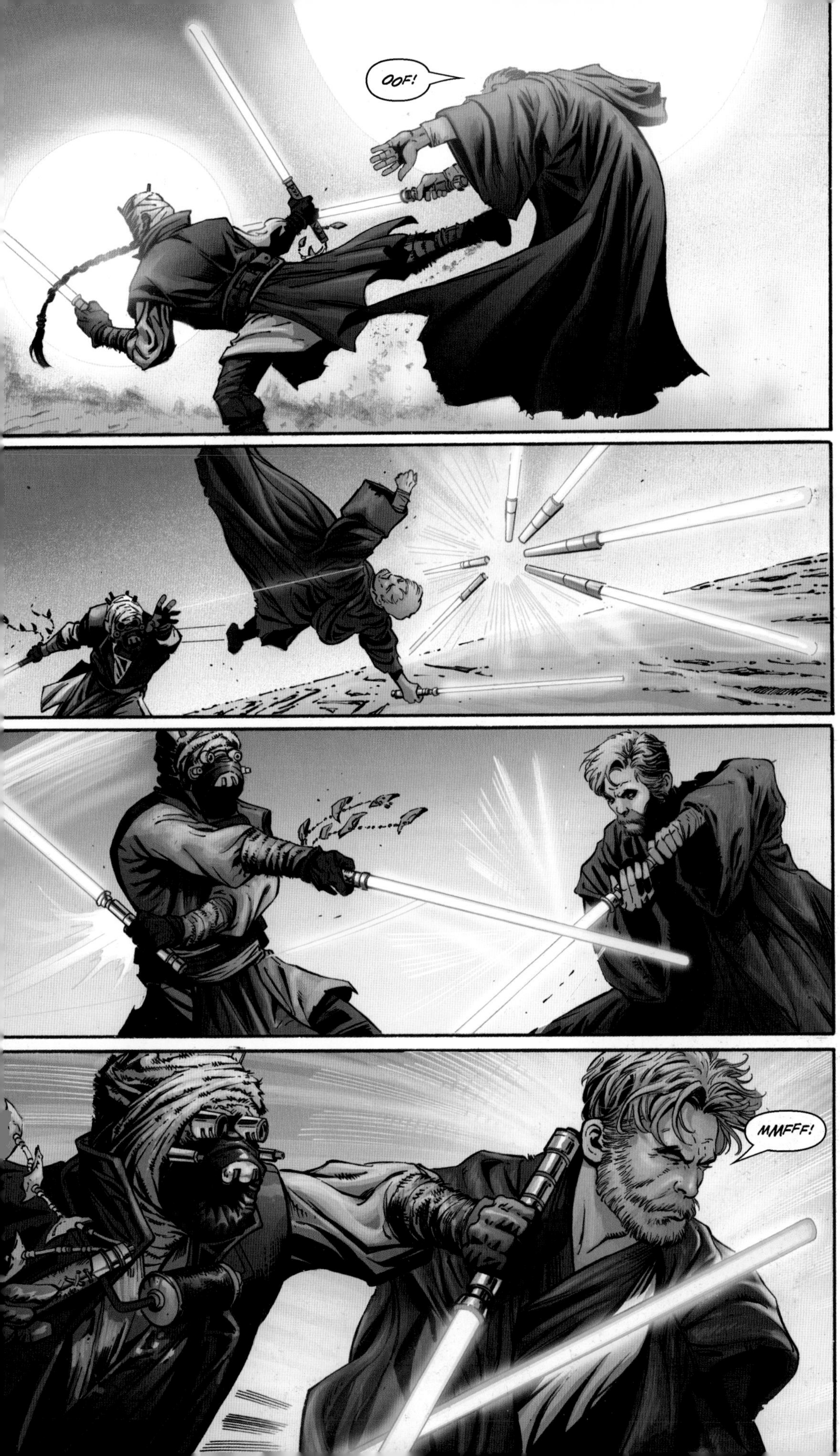
OOF!
MMFFF!

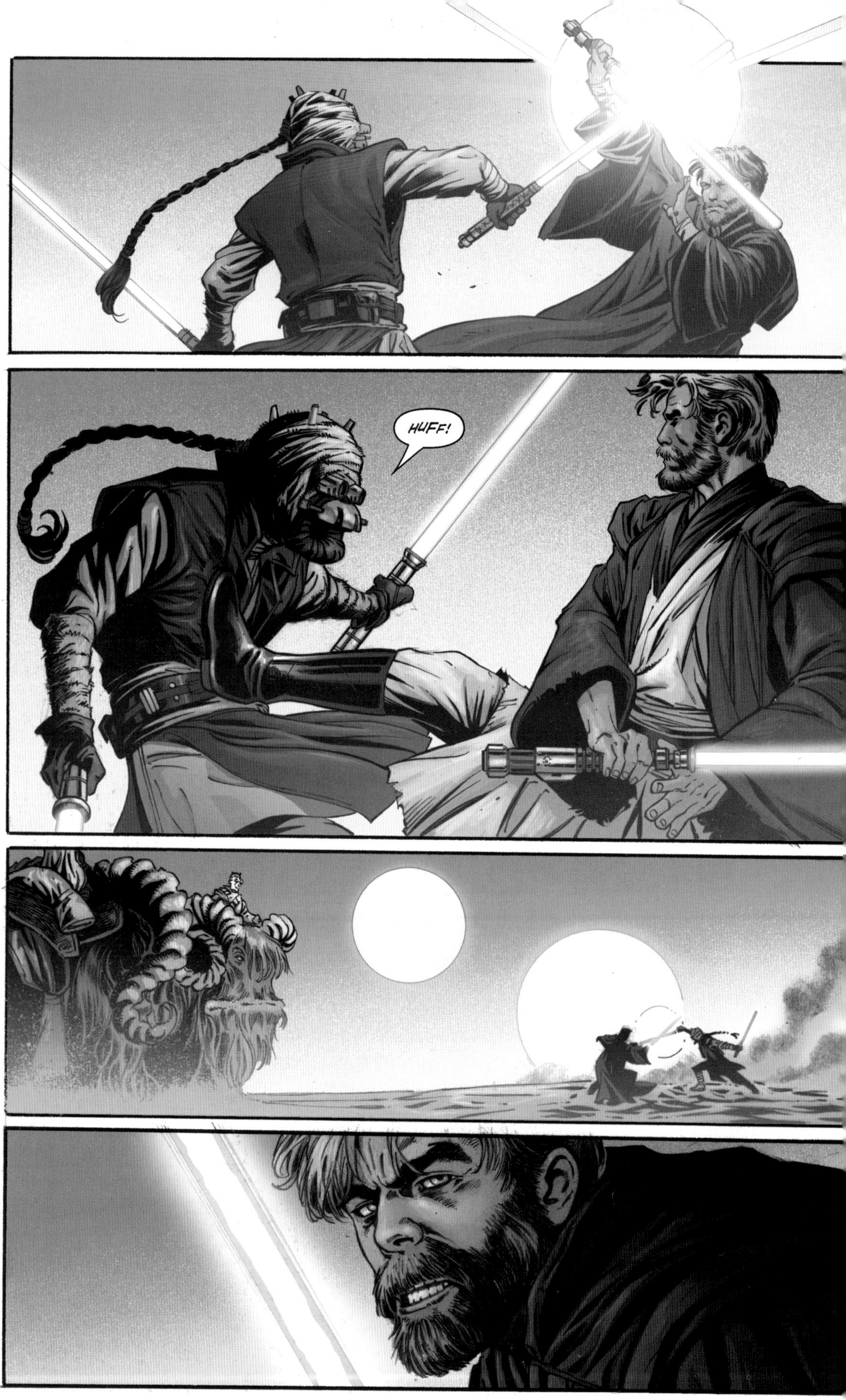
HUFF!

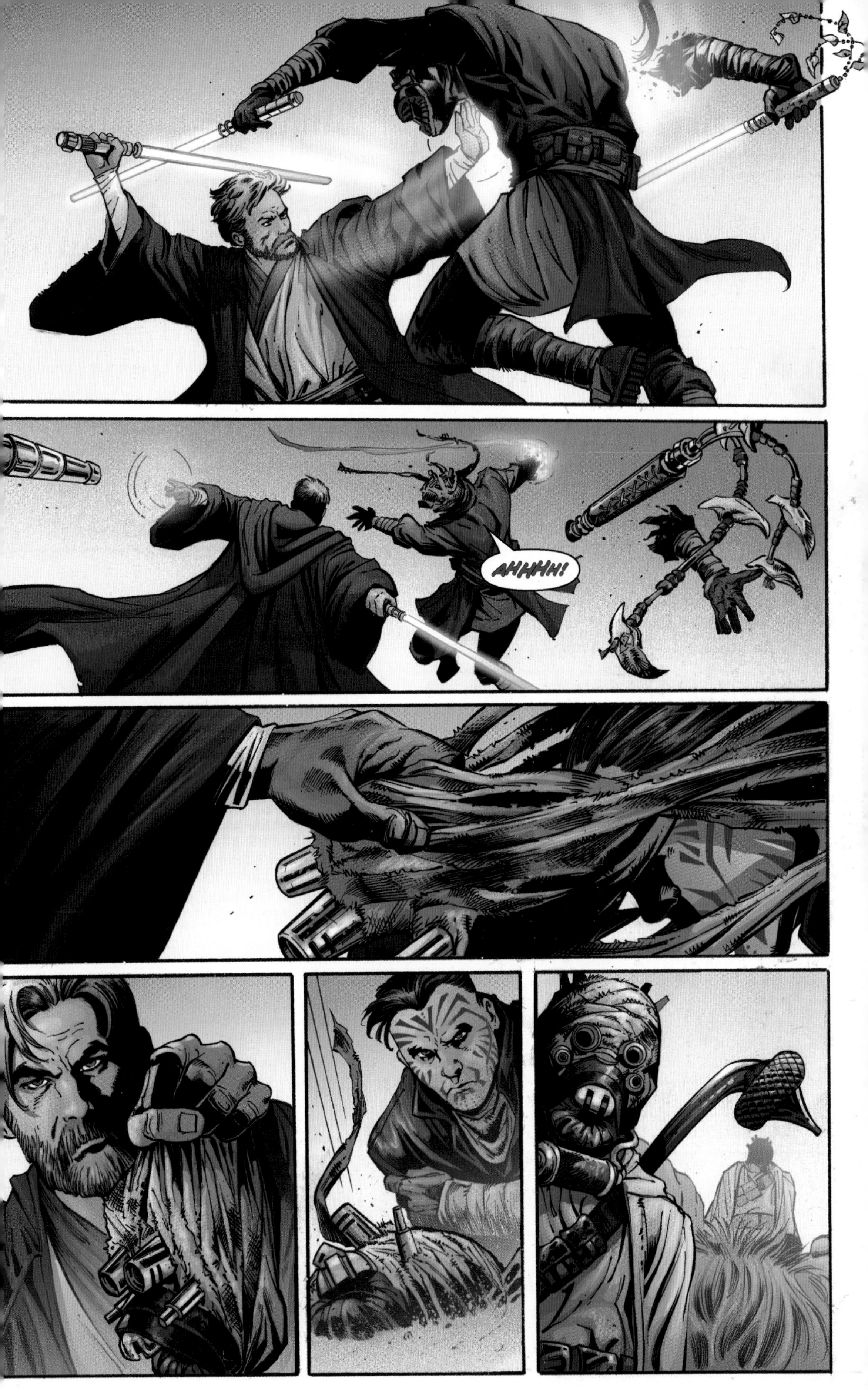
AHHHH!

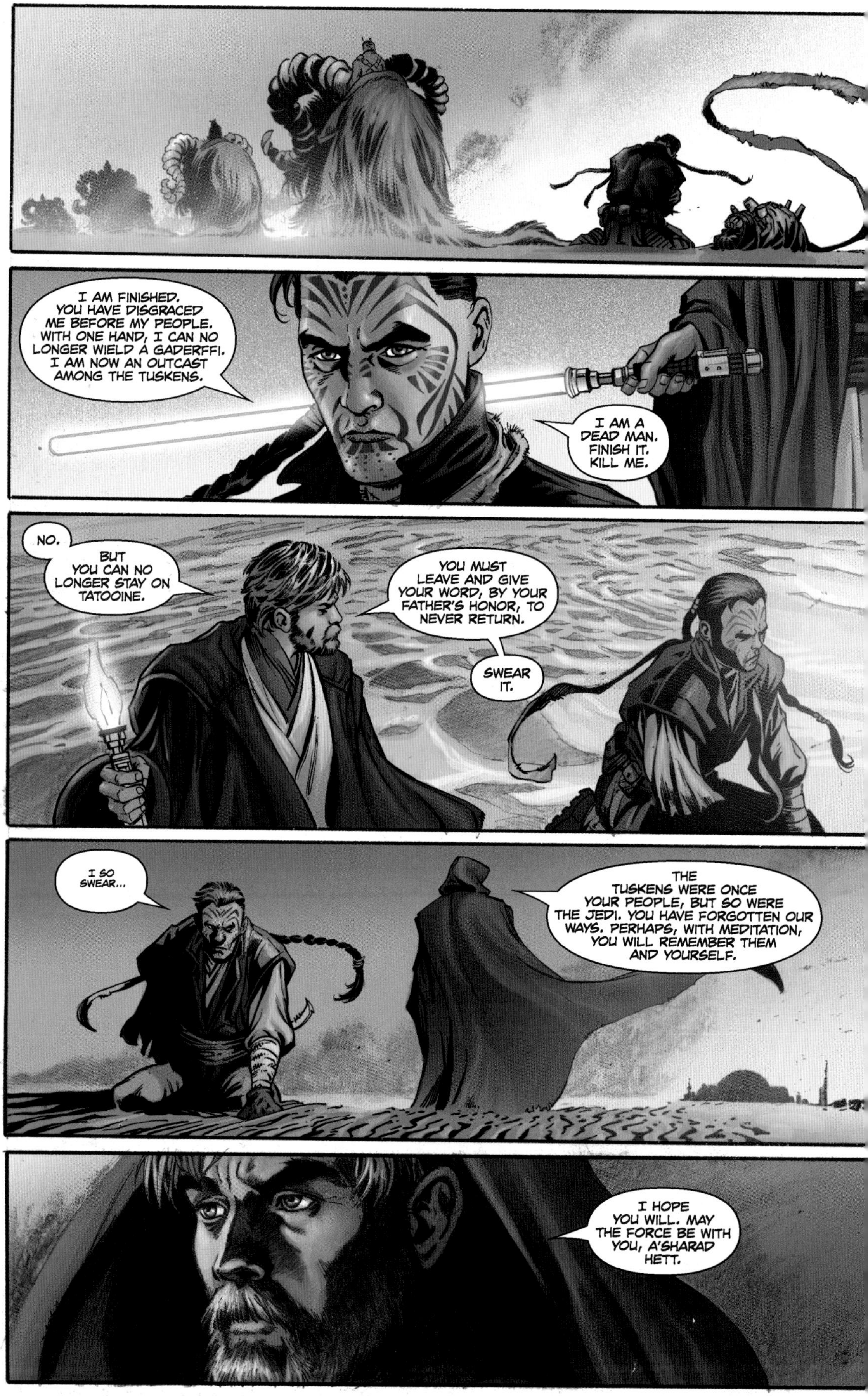
I AM FINISHED. YOU HAVE DISGRACED ME BEFORE MY PEOPLE. WITH ONE HAND, I CAN NO LONGER WIELD A GADERFFI. I AM NOW AN OUTCAST AMONG THE TUSKENS.
I AM A DEAD MAN. FINISH IT. KILL ME.
NO.
BUT YOU CAN NO LONGER STAY ON TATOOINE.
YOU MUST LEAVE AND GIVE YOUR WORD, BY YOUR FATHER'S HONOR, TO NEVER RETURN.
SWEAR IT.
I SO SWEAR...
THE TUSKENS WERE ONCE YOUR PEOPLE, BUT SO WERE THE JEDI. YOU HAVE FORGOTTEN OUR WAYS. PERHAPS, WITH MEDITATION, YOU WILL REMEMBER THEM AND YOURSELF.
I HOPE YOU WILL. MAY THE FORCE BE WITH YOU, A'SHARAD HETT.

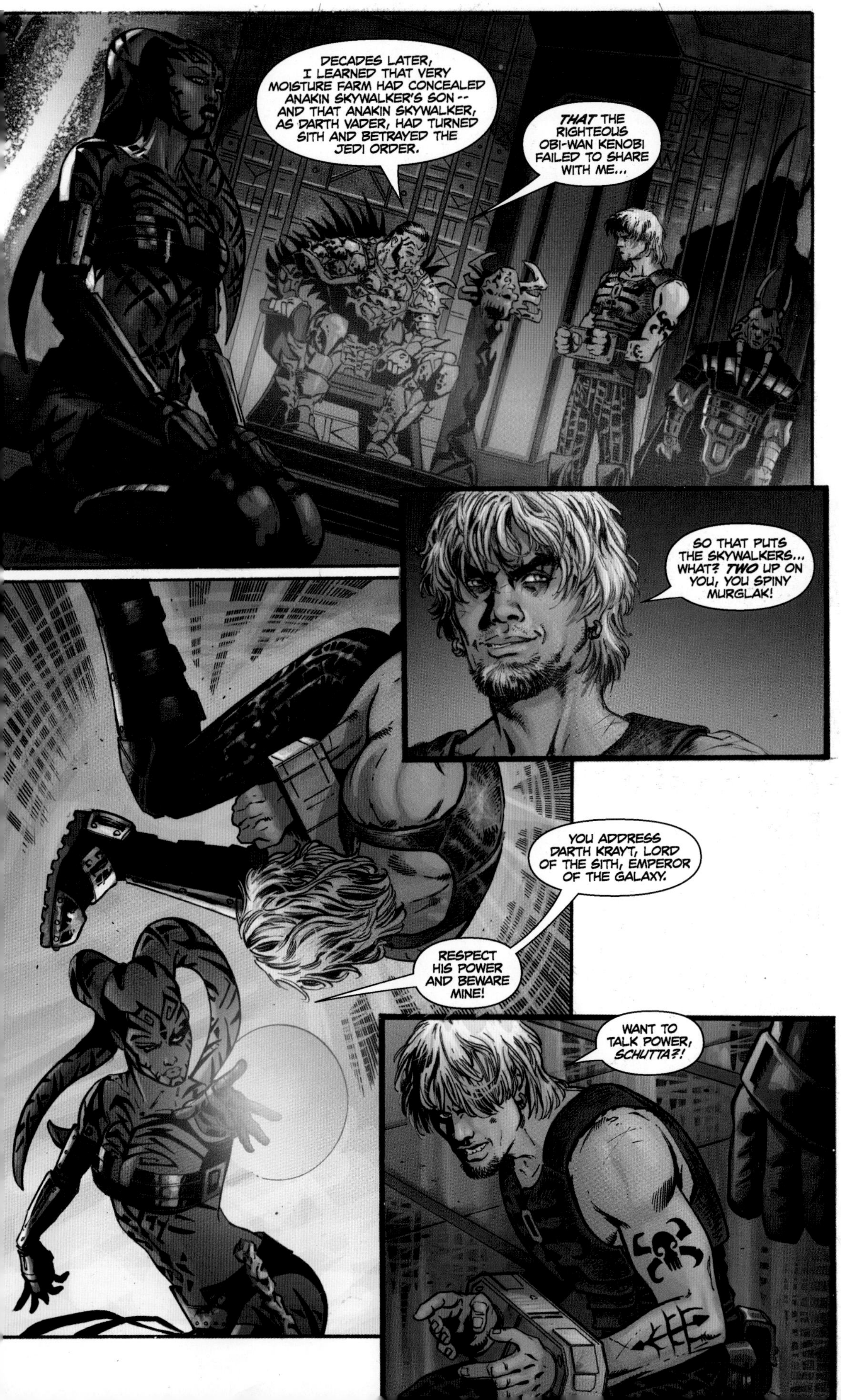
DECADES LATER, I LEARNED THAT VERY MOISTURE FARM HAD CONCEALED ANAKIN SKYWALKER'S SON -- AND THAT ANAKIN SKYWALKER, AS DARTH VADER, HAD TURNED SITH AND BETRAYED THE JEDI ORDER.
THAT THE RIGHTEOUS OBI-WAN KENOBI FAILED TO SHARE WITH ME...
SO THAT PUTS THE SKYWALKERS... WHAT? TWO UP ON YOU, YOU SPINY MURGLAK!
YOU ADDRESS DARTH KRAYT, LORD OF THE SITH, EMPEROR OF THE GALAXY.
RESPECT HIS POWER AND BEWARE MINE!
WANT TO TALK POWER, SCHUTTA?!

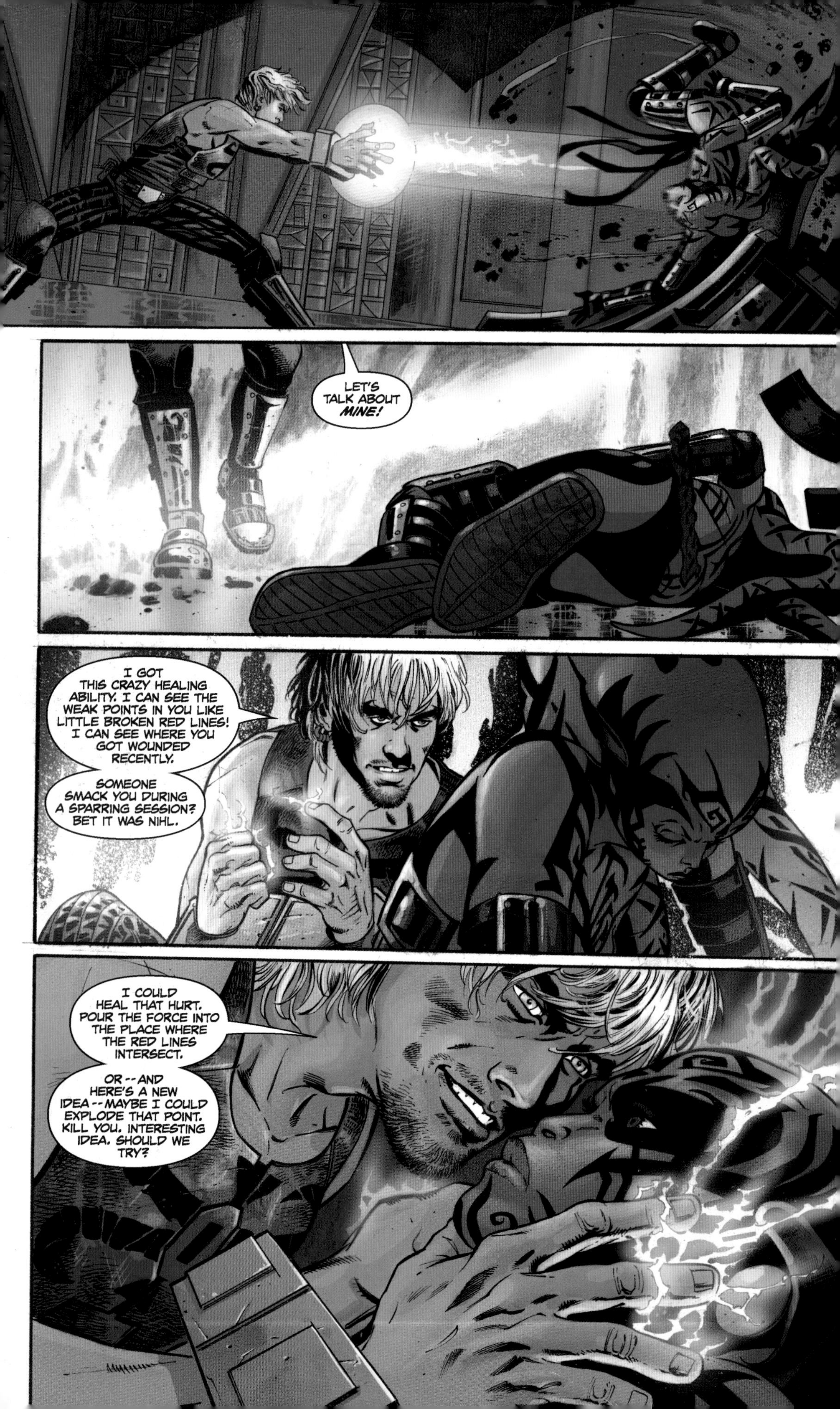
LET'S TALK ABOUT MINE!
I GOT THIS CRAZY HEALING ABILITY. I CAN SEE THE WEAK POINTS IN YOU LIKE LITTLE BROKEN RED LINES! I CAN SEE WHERE YOU GOT WOUNDED RECENTLY.
SOMEONE SMACK YOU DURING A SPARRING SESSION? BET IT WAS NIHL.
I COULD HEAL THAT HURT. POUR THE FORCE INTO THE PLACE WHERE THE RED LINES INTERSECT.
OR--AND HERE'S A NEW IDEA--MAYBE I COULD EXPLODE THAT POINT. KILL YOU. INTERESTING IDEA. SHOULD WE TRY?

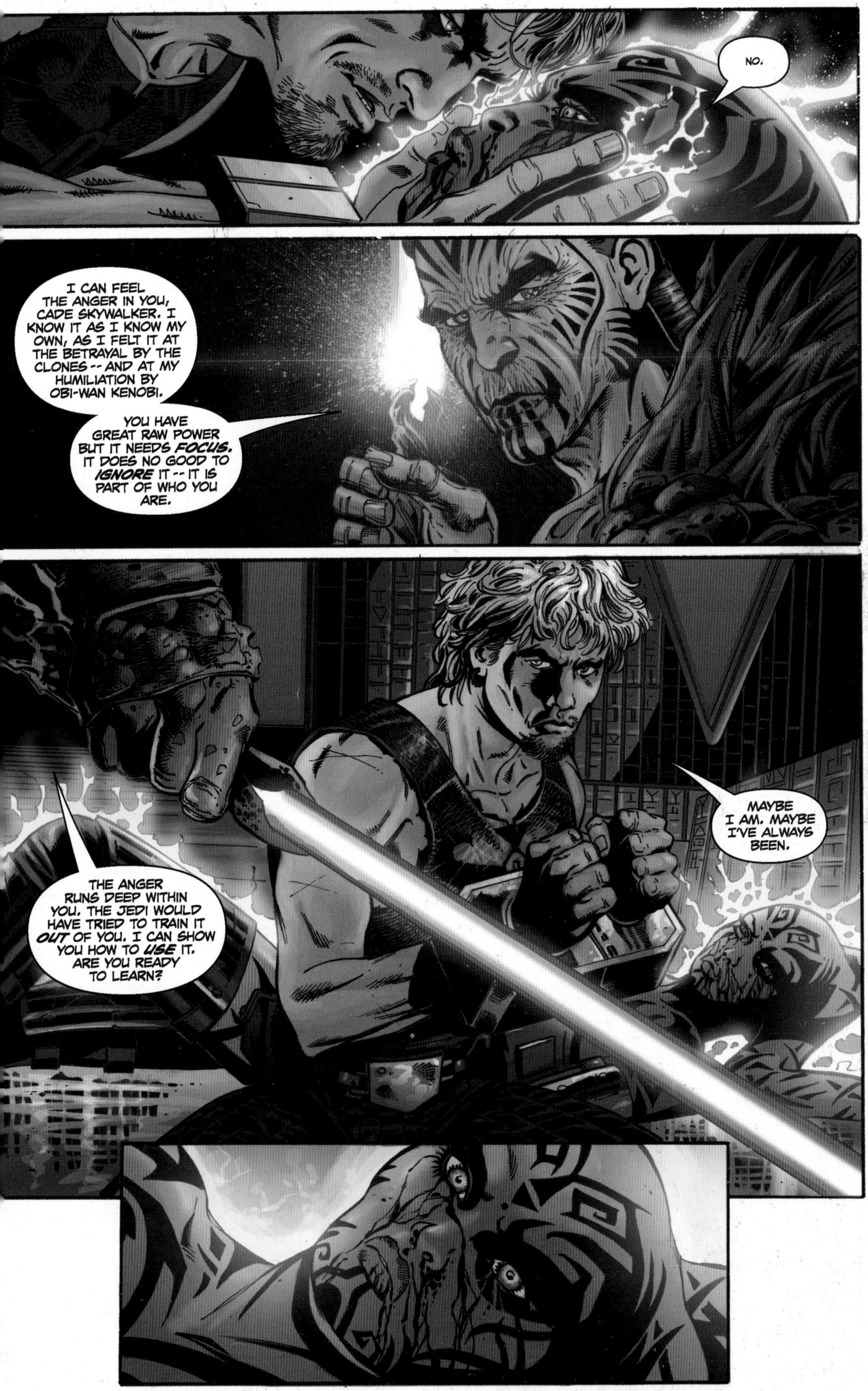
NO.
I CAN FEEL THE ANGER IN YOU, CADE SKYWALKER. I KNOW IT AS I KNOW MY OWN, AS I FELT IT AT THE BETRAYAL BY THE CLONES -- AND AT MY HUMILIATION BY OBI-WAN KENOBI.
YOU HAVE GREAT RAW POWER BUT IT NEEDS FOCUS. IT DOES NO GOOD TO IGNORE IT -- IT IS PART OF WHO YOU ARE.
THE ANGER RUNS DEEP WITHIN YOU. THE JEDI WOULD HAVE TRIED TO TRAIN IT OUT OF YOU. I CAN SHOW YOU HOW TO USE IT. ARE YOU READY TO LEARN?
MAYBE I AM. MAYBE I'VE ALWAYS BEEN.

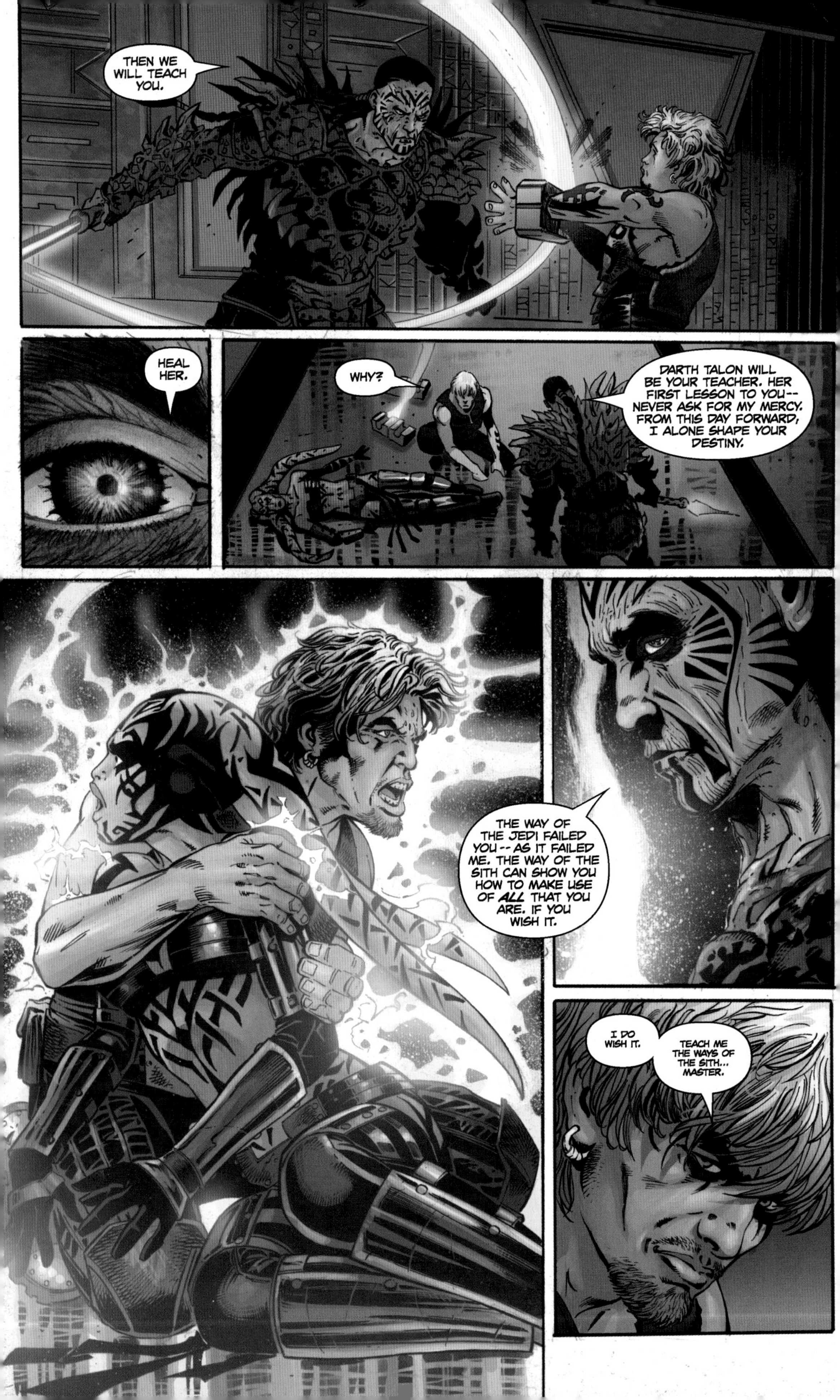
THEN WE WILL TEACH YOU.
HEAL HER.
WHY?
DARTH TALON WILL BE YOUR TEACHER. HER FIRST LESSON TO YOU-- NEVER ASK FOR MY MERCY. FROM THIS DAY FORWARD, I ALONE SHAPE YOUR DESTINY.
THE WAY OF THE JEDI FAILED YOU -- AS IT FAILED ME. THE WAY OF THE SITH CAN SHOW YOU HOW TO MAKE USE OF ALL THAT YOU ARE. IF YOU WISH IT.
I DO WISH IT.
TEACH ME THE WAYS OF THE SITH... MASTER.

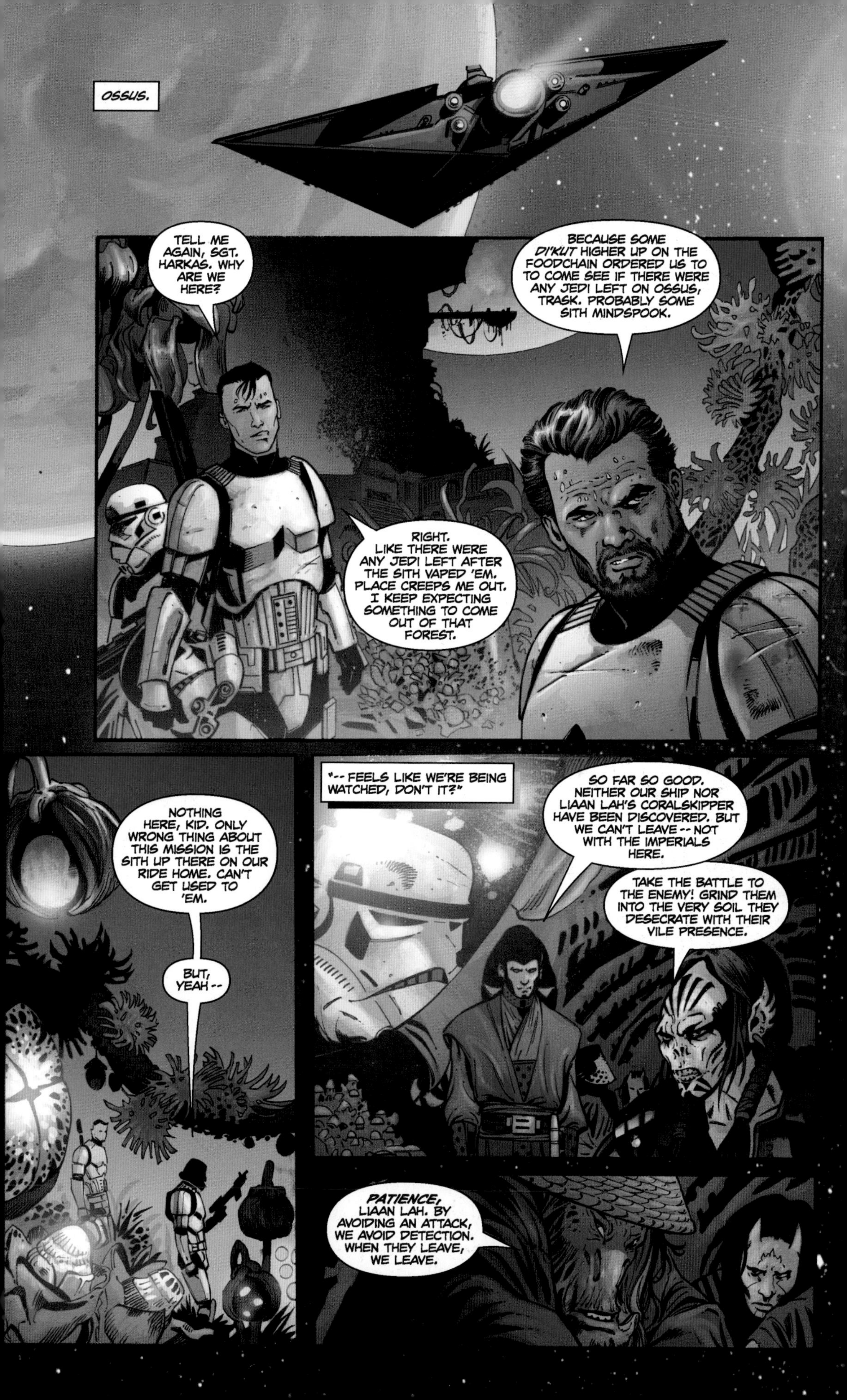
OSSUS.
TELL ME AGAIN, SGT. HARKAS. WHY ARE WE HERE?
BECAUSE SOME *DI'KUT* HIGHER UP ON THE FOODCHAIN ORDERED US TO TO COME SEE IF THERE WERE ANY JEDI LEFT ON OSSUS, TRASK. PROBABLY SOME SITH MINDSPOOK.
RIGHT. LIKE THERE WERE ANY JEDI LEFT AFTER THE SITH VAPED 'EM. PLACE CREEPS ME OUT. I KEEP EXPECTING SOMETHING TO COME OUT OF THAT FOREST.
NOTHING HERE, KID. ONLY WRONG THING ABOUT THIS MISSION IS THE SITH UP THERE ON OUR RIDE HOME. CAN'T GET USED TO 'EM.
BUT, YEAH --
"-- FEELS LIKE WE'RE BEING WATCHED, DON'T IT?"
SO FAR SO GOOD. NEITHER OUR SHIP NOR LIAAN LAH'S CORALSKIPPER HAVE BEEN DISCOVERED. BUT WE CAN'T LEAVE -- NOT WITH THE IMPERIALS HERE.
TAKE THE BATTLE TO THE ENEMY! GRIND THEM INTO THE VERY SOIL THEY DESECRATE WITH THEIR VILE PRESENCE.
PATIENCE, LIAAN LAH. BY AVOIDING AN ATTACK, WE AVOID DETECTION. WHEN THEY LEAVE, WE LEAVE.

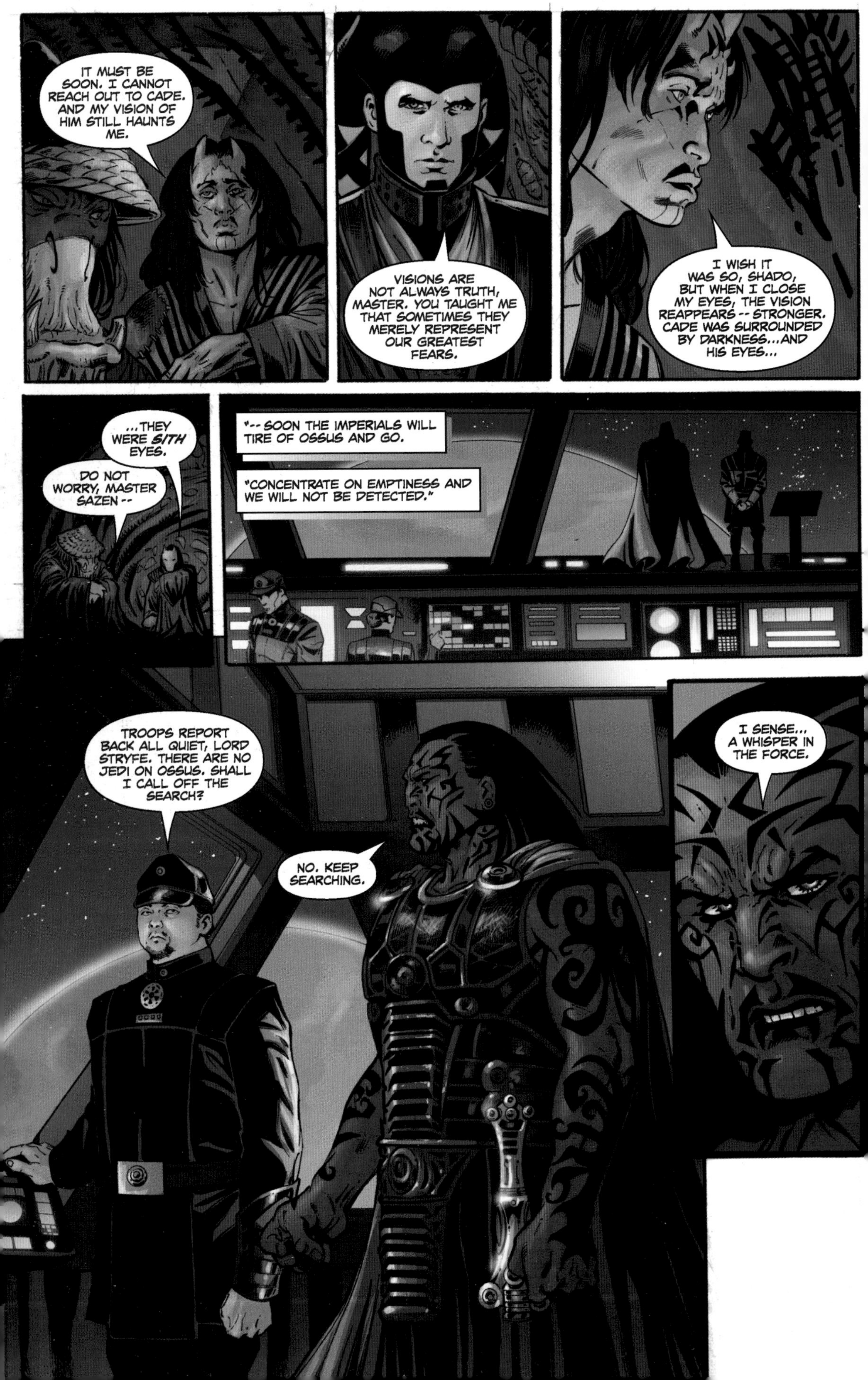
IT MUST BE SOON. I CANNOT REACH OUT TO CADE. AND MY VISION OF HIM STILL HAUNTS ME.
VISIONS ARE NOT ALWAYS TRUTH, MASTER. YOU TAUGHT ME THAT SOMETIMES THEY MERELY REPRESENT OUR GREATEST FEARS.
I WISH IT WAS SO, SHADO, BUT WHEN I CLOSE MY EYES, THE VISION REAPPEARS -- STRONGER. CADE WAS SURROUNDED BY DARKNESS...AND HIS EYES...
...THEY WERE SITH EYES.
DO NOT WORRY, MASTER SAZEN --
"-- SOON THE IMPERIALS WILL TIRE OF OSSUS AND GO.
"CONCENTRATE ON EMPTINESS AND WE WILL NOT BE DETECTED."
TROOPS REPORT BACK ALL QUIET, LORD STRYFE. THERE ARE NO JEDI ON OSSUS. SHALL I CALL OFF THE SEARCH?
NO. KEEP SEARCHING.
I SENSE... A WHISPER IN THE FORCE.

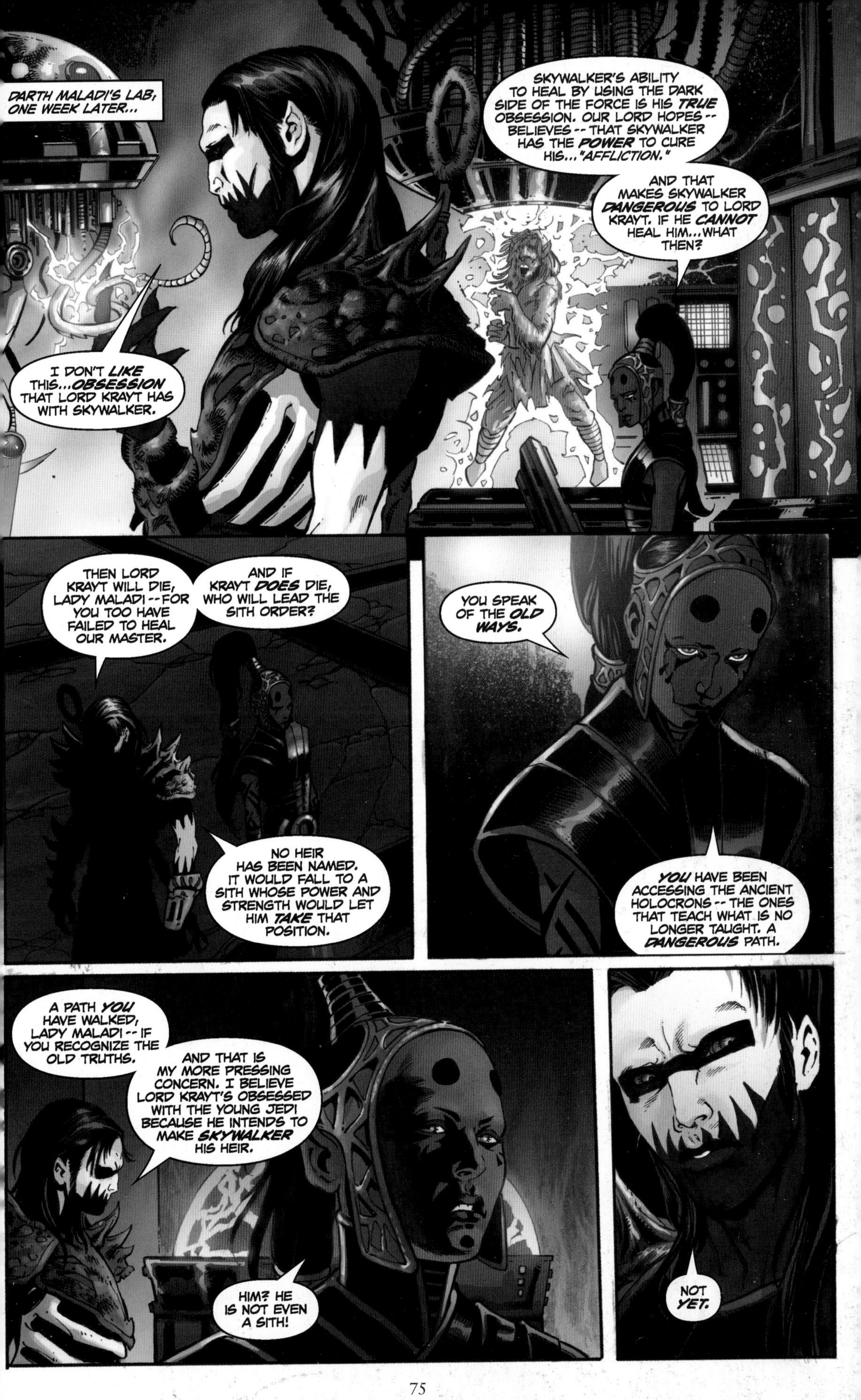
DARTH MALADI'S LAB, ONE WEEK LATER...
I DON'T LIKE THIS...OBSESSION THAT LORD KRAYT HAS WITH SKYWALKER.
SKYWALKER'S ABILITY TO HEAL BY USING THE DARK SIDE OF THE FORCE IS HIS TRUE OBSESSION. OUR LORD HOPES -- BELIEVES -- THAT SKYWALKER HAS THE POWER TO CURE HIS..."AFFLICTION."
AND THAT MAKES SKYWALKER DANGEROUS TO LORD KRAYT. IF HE CANNOT HEAL HIM...WHAT THEN?
THEN LORD KRAYT WILL DIE, LADY MALADI -- FOR YOU TOO HAVE FAILED TO HEAL OUR MASTER.
AND IF KRAYT DOES DIE, WHO WILL LEAD THE SITH ORDER?
NO HEIR HAS BEEN NAMED. IT WOULD FALL TO A SITH WHOSE POWER AND STRENGTH WOULD LET HIM TAKE THAT POSITION.
YOU SPEAK OF THE OLD WAYS.
YOU HAVE BEEN ACCESSING THE ANCIENT HOLOCRONS -- THE ONES THAT TEACH WHAT IS NO LONGER TAUGHT. A DANGEROUS PATH.
A PATH YOU HAVE WALKED, LADY MALADI -- IF YOU RECOGNIZE THE OLD TRUTHS.
AND THAT IS MY MORE PRESSING CONCERN. I BELIEVE LORD KRAYT'S OBSESSED WITH THE YOUNG JEDI BECAUSE HE INTENDS TO MAKE SKYWALKER HIS HEIR.
HIM? HE IS NOT EVEN A SITH!
NOT YET.

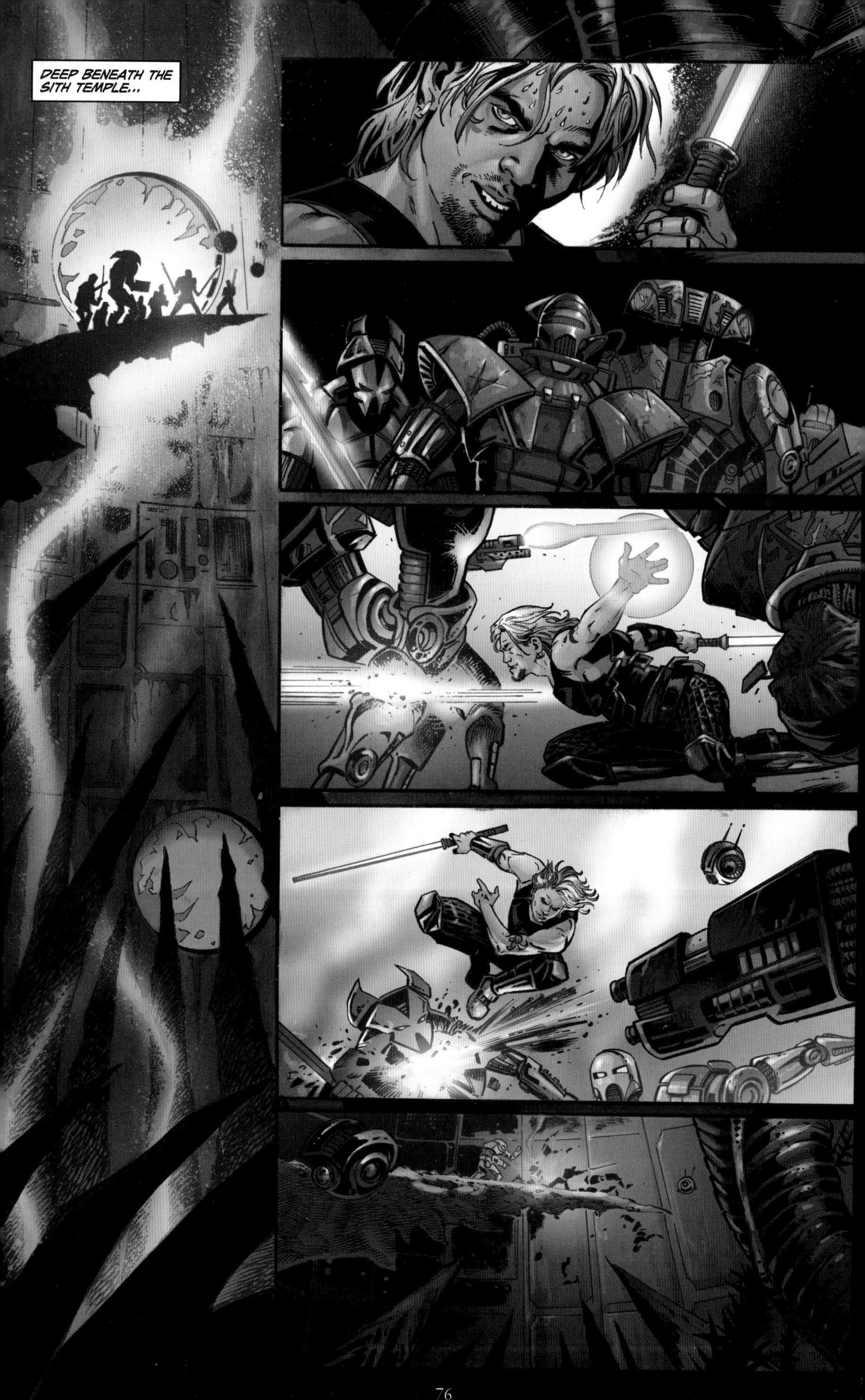
DEEP BENEATH THE SITH TEMPLE...

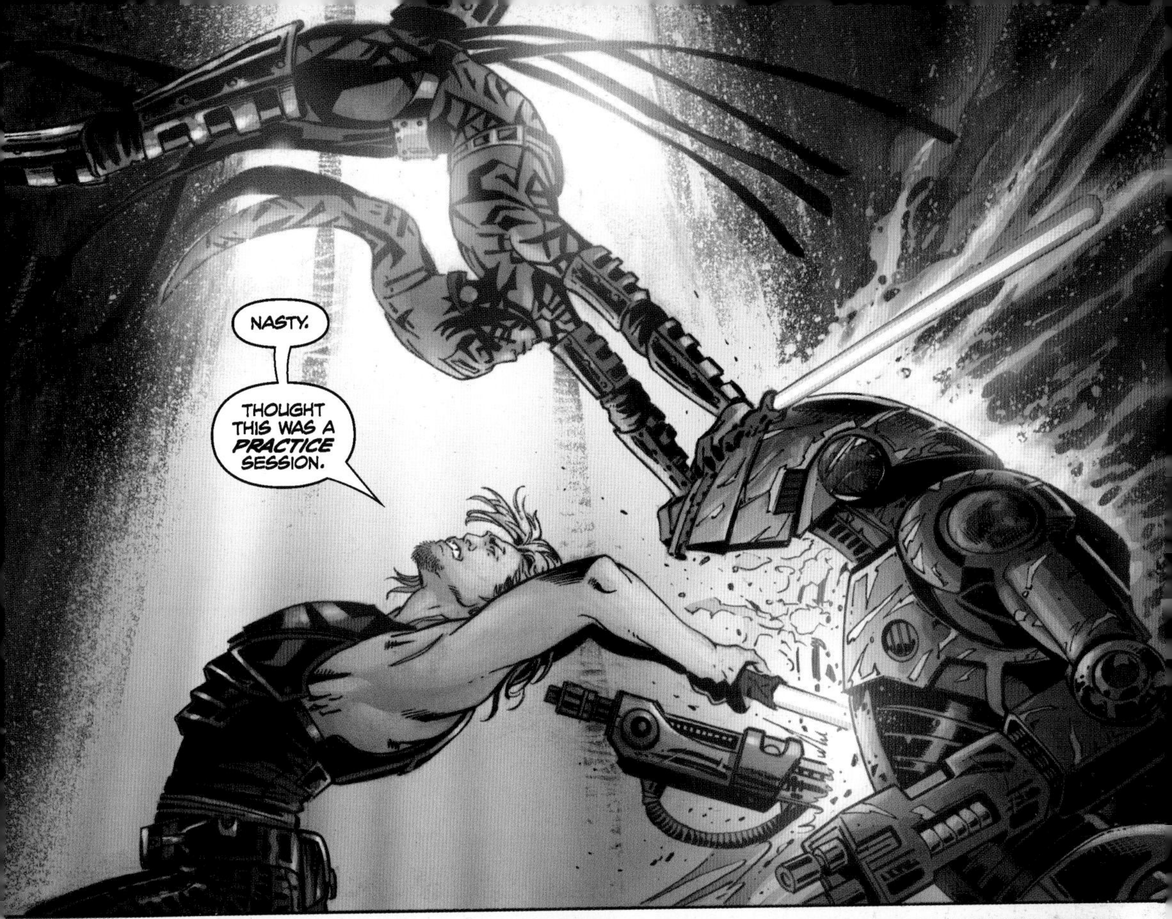
NASTY.
THOUGHT THIS WAS A *PRACTICE* SESSION.

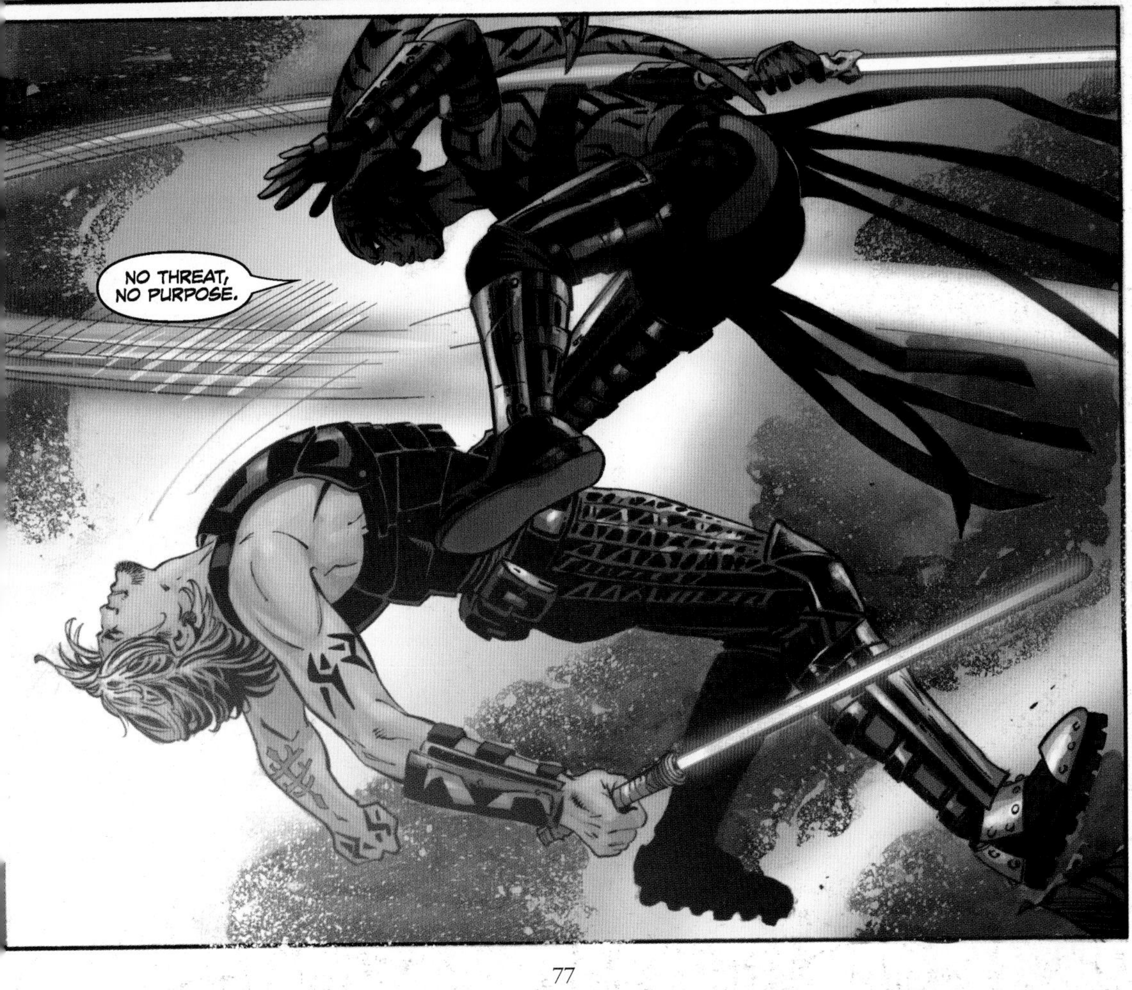
NO THREAT, NO PURPOSE.

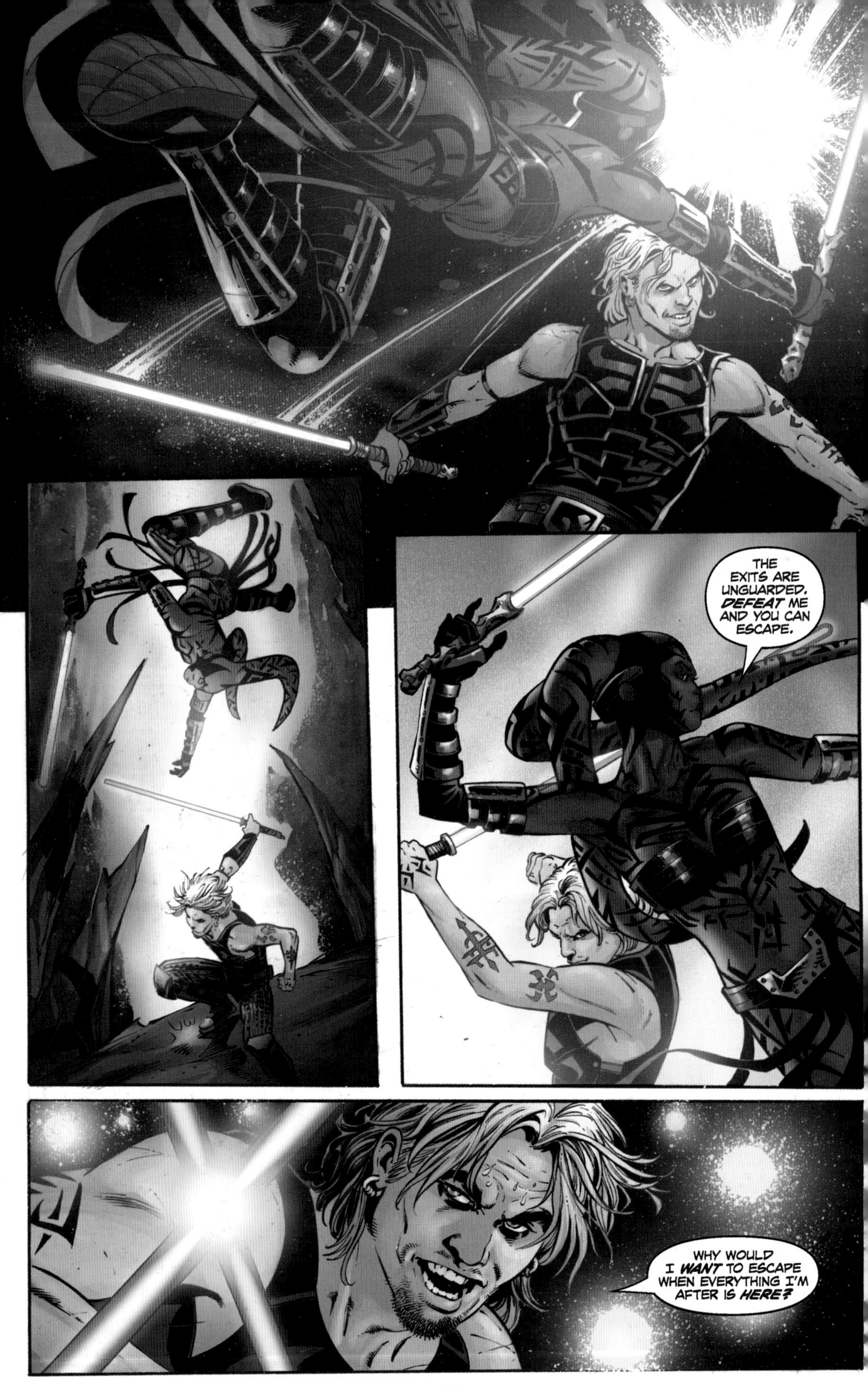
THE EXITS ARE UNGUARDED. DEFEAT ME AND YOU CAN ESCAPE.
WHY WOULD I WANT TO ESCAPE WHEN EVERYTHING I'M AFTER IS HERE?

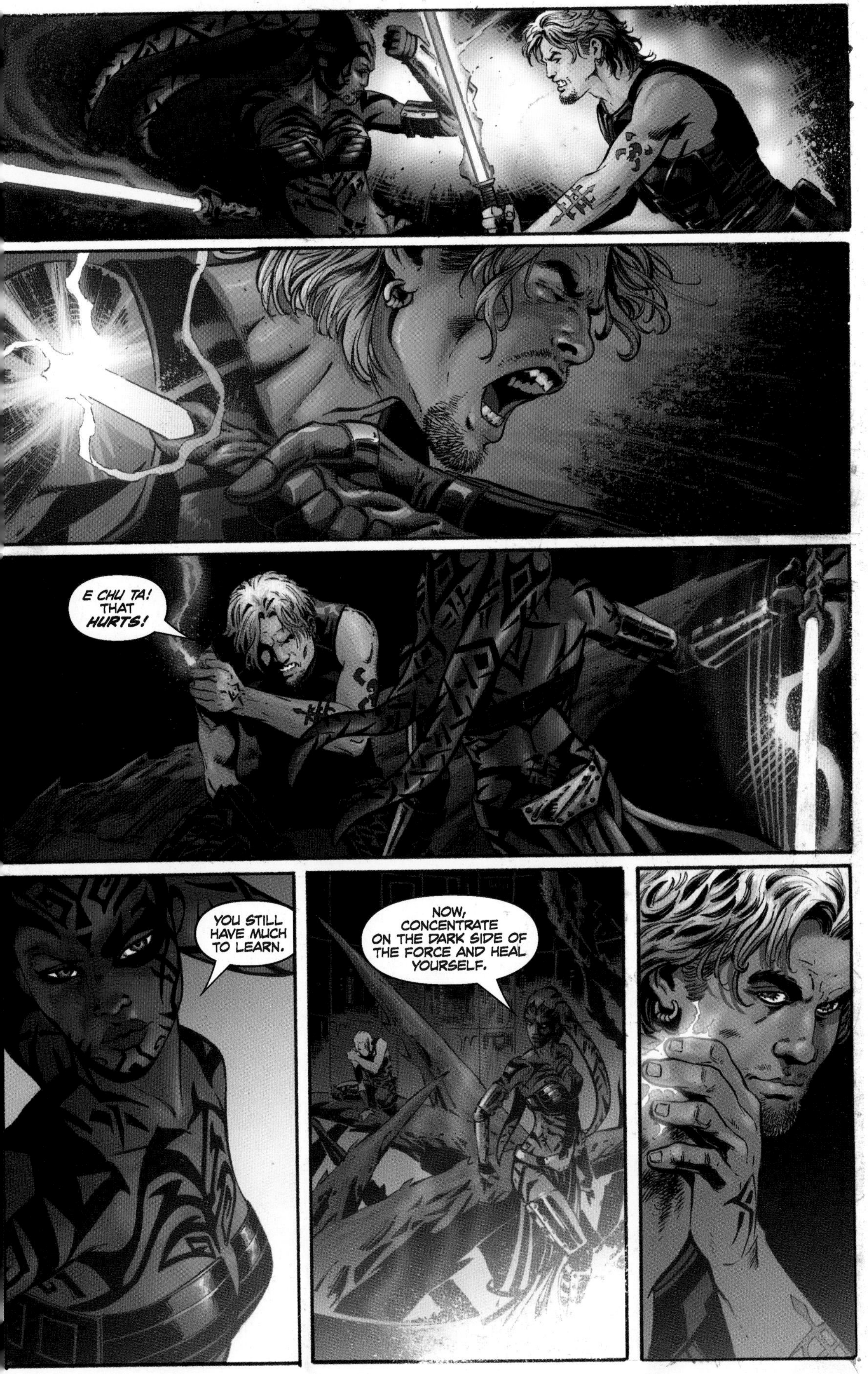
E CHU TA! THAT HURTS!
YOU STILL HAVE MUCH TO LEARN.
NOW, CONCENTRATE ON THE DARK SIDE OF THE FORCE AND HEAL YOURSELF.

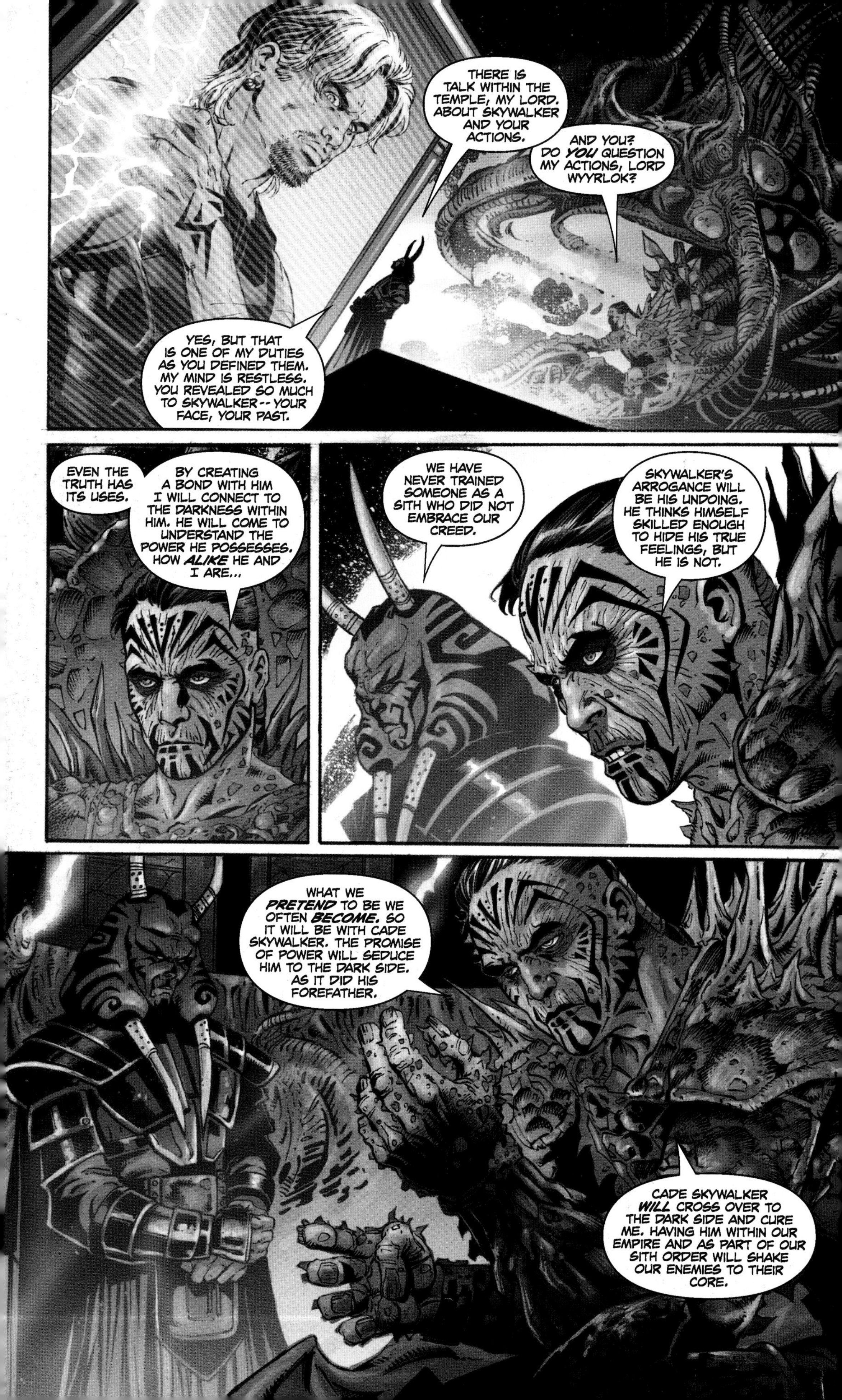
THERE IS TALK WITHIN THE TEMPLE, MY LORD. ABOUT SKYWALKER AND YOUR ACTIONS.
AND YOU? DO YOU QUESTION MY ACTIONS, LORD WYYRLOK?
YES, BUT THAT IS ONE OF MY DUTIES AS YOU DEFINED THEM. MY MIND IS RESTLESS. YOU REVEALED SO MUCH TO SKYWALKER-- YOUR FACE, YOUR PAST.
EVEN THE TRUTH HAS ITS USES.
BY CREATING A BOND WITH HIM I WILL CONNECT TO THE DARKNESS WITHIN HIM. HE WILL COME TO UNDERSTAND THE POWER HE POSSESSES. HOW ALIKE HE AND I ARE...
WE HAVE NEVER TRAINED SOMEONE AS A SITH WHO DID NOT EMBRACE OUR CREED.
SKYWALKER'S ARROGANCE WILL BE HIS UNDOING. HE THINKS HIMSELF SKILLED ENOUGH TO HIDE HIS TRUE FEELINGS, BUT HE IS NOT.
WHAT WE PRETEND TO BE WE OFTEN BECOME. SO IT WILL BE WITH CADE SKYWALKER. THE PROMISE OF POWER WILL SEDUCE HIM TO THE DARK SIDE. AS IT DID HIS FOREFATHER.
CADE SKYWALKER WILL CROSS OVER TO THE DARK SIDE AND CURE ME. HAVING HIM WITHIN OUR EMPIRE AND AS PART OF OUR SITH ORDER WILL SHAKE OUR ENEMIES TO THEIR CORE.

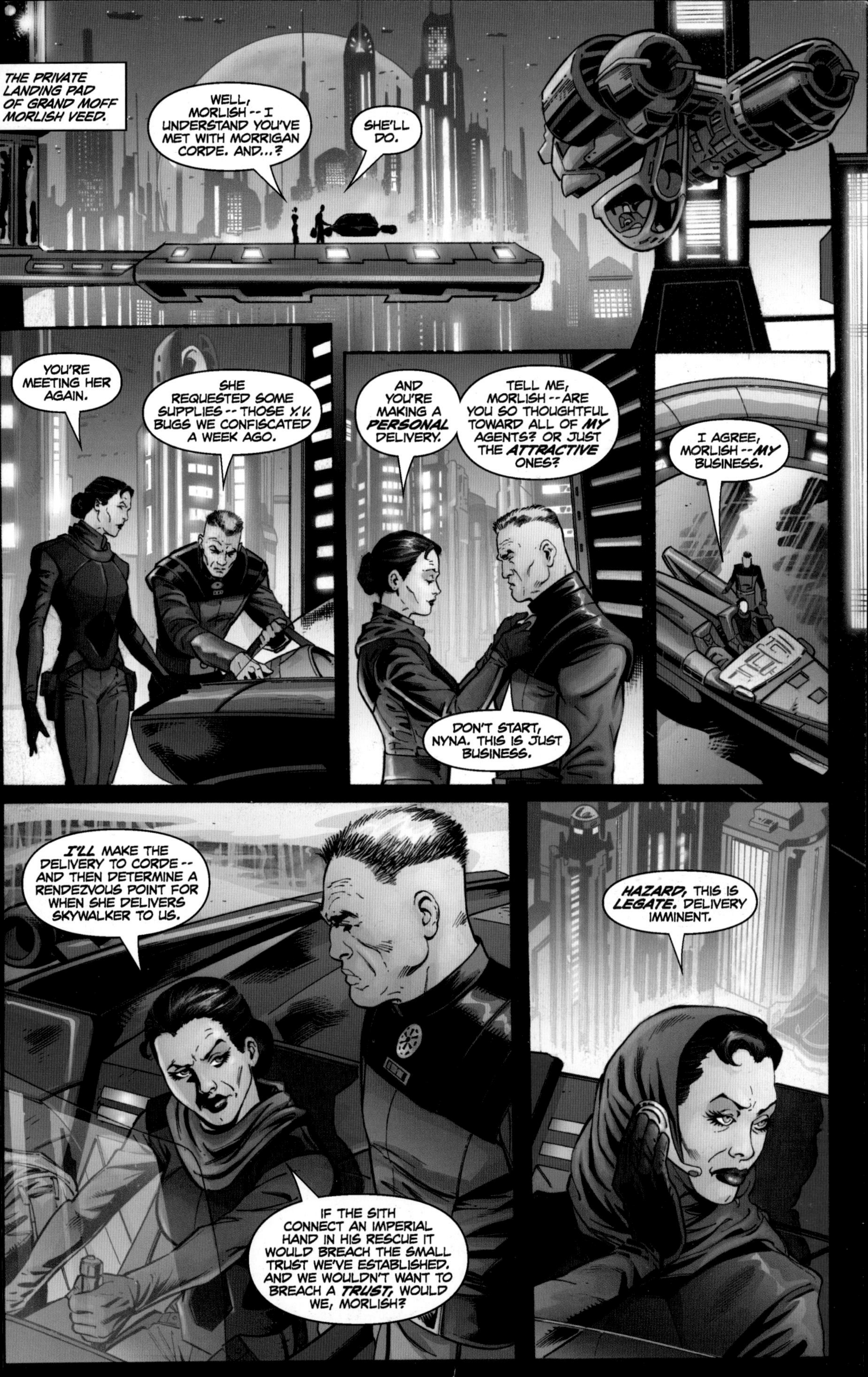
THE PRIVATE LANDING PAD OF GRAND MOFF MORLISH VEED.
WELL, MORLISH -- I UNDERSTAND YOU'VE MET WITH MORRIGAN CORDE. AND...?
SHE'LL DO.
YOU'RE MEETING HER AGAIN.
SHE REQUESTED SOME SUPPLIES -- THOSE Y.V. BUGS WE CONFISCATED A WEEK AGO.
AND YOU'RE MAKING A PERSONAL DELIVERY.
TELL ME, MORLISH -- ARE YOU SO THOUGHTFUL TOWARD ALL OF MY AGENTS? OR JUST THE ATTRACTIVE ONES?
DON'T START, NYNA. THIS IS JUST BUSINESS.
I AGREE, MORLISH -- MY BUSINESS.
I'LL MAKE THE DELIVERY TO CORDE -- AND THEN DETERMINE A RENDEZVOUS POINT FOR WHEN SHE DELIVERS SKYWALKER TO US.
IF THE SITH CONNECT AN IMPERIAL HAND IN HIS RESCUE IT WOULD BREACH THE SMALL TRUST WE'VE ESTABLISHED. AND WE WOULDN'T WANT TO BREACH A TRUST, WOULD WE, MORLISH?
HAZARD, THIS IS LEGATE. DELIVERY IMMINENT.

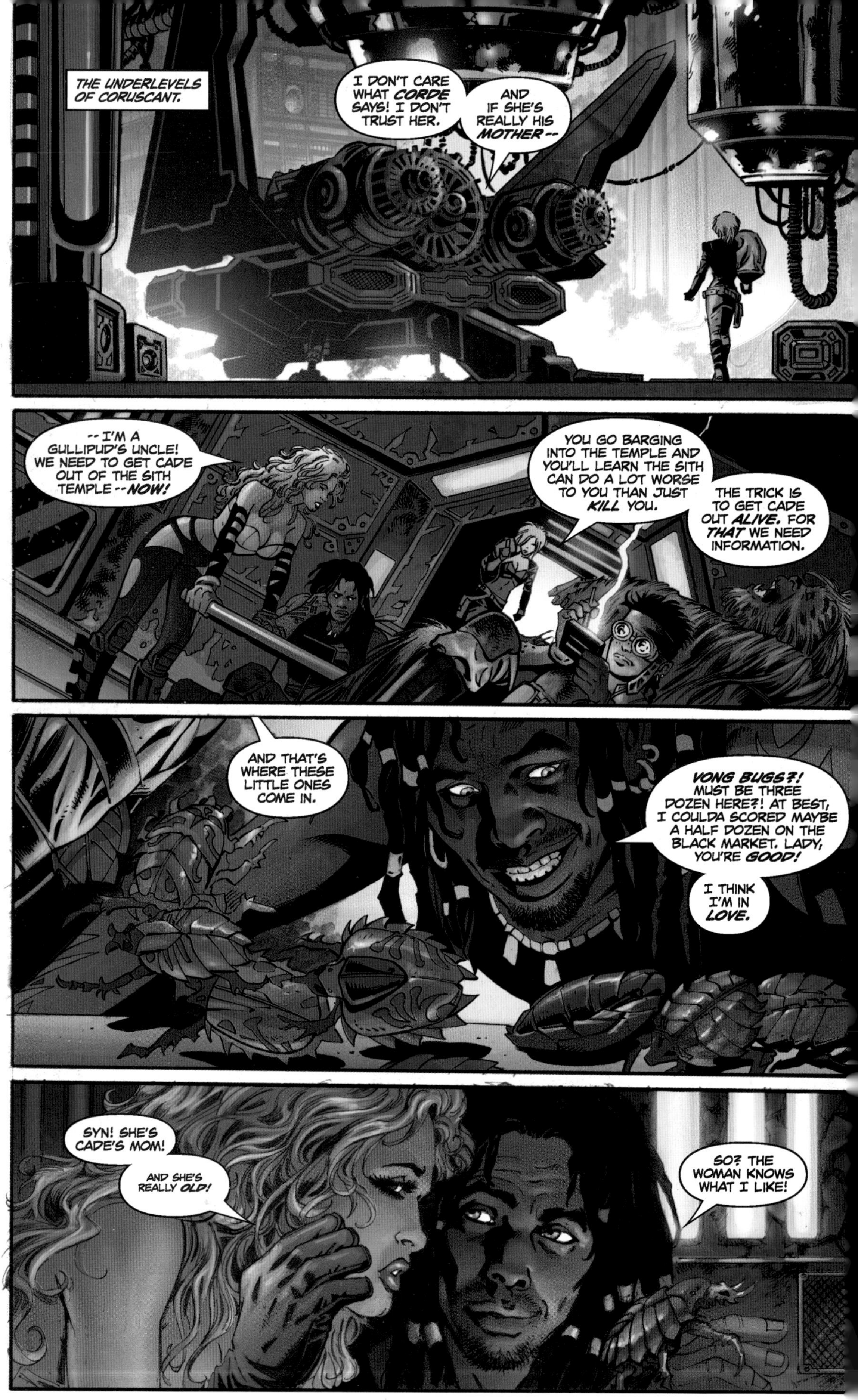
THE UNDERLEVELS OF CORUSCANT.
I DON'T CARE WHAT CORDE SAYS! I DON'T TRUST HER.
AND IF SHE'S REALLY HIS MOTHER --
-- I'M A GULLIPUD'S UNCLE! WE NEED TO GET CADE OUT OF THE SITH TEMPLE -- NOW!
YOU GO BARGING INTO THE TEMPLE AND YOU'LL LEARN THE SITH CAN DO A LOT WORSE TO YOU THAN JUST KILL YOU.
THE TRICK IS TO GET CADE OUT ALIVE. FOR THAT WE NEED INFORMATION.
AND THAT'S WHERE THESE LITTLE ONES COME IN.
VONG BUGS?! MUST BE THREE DOZEN HERE?! AT BEST, I COULDA SCORED MAYBE A HALF DOZEN ON THE BLACK MARKET. LADY, YOU'RE GOOD!
I THINK I'M IN LOVE.
SYN! SHE'S CADE'S MOM!
AND SHE'S REALLY OLD!
SO? THE WOMAN KNOWS WHAT I LIKE!

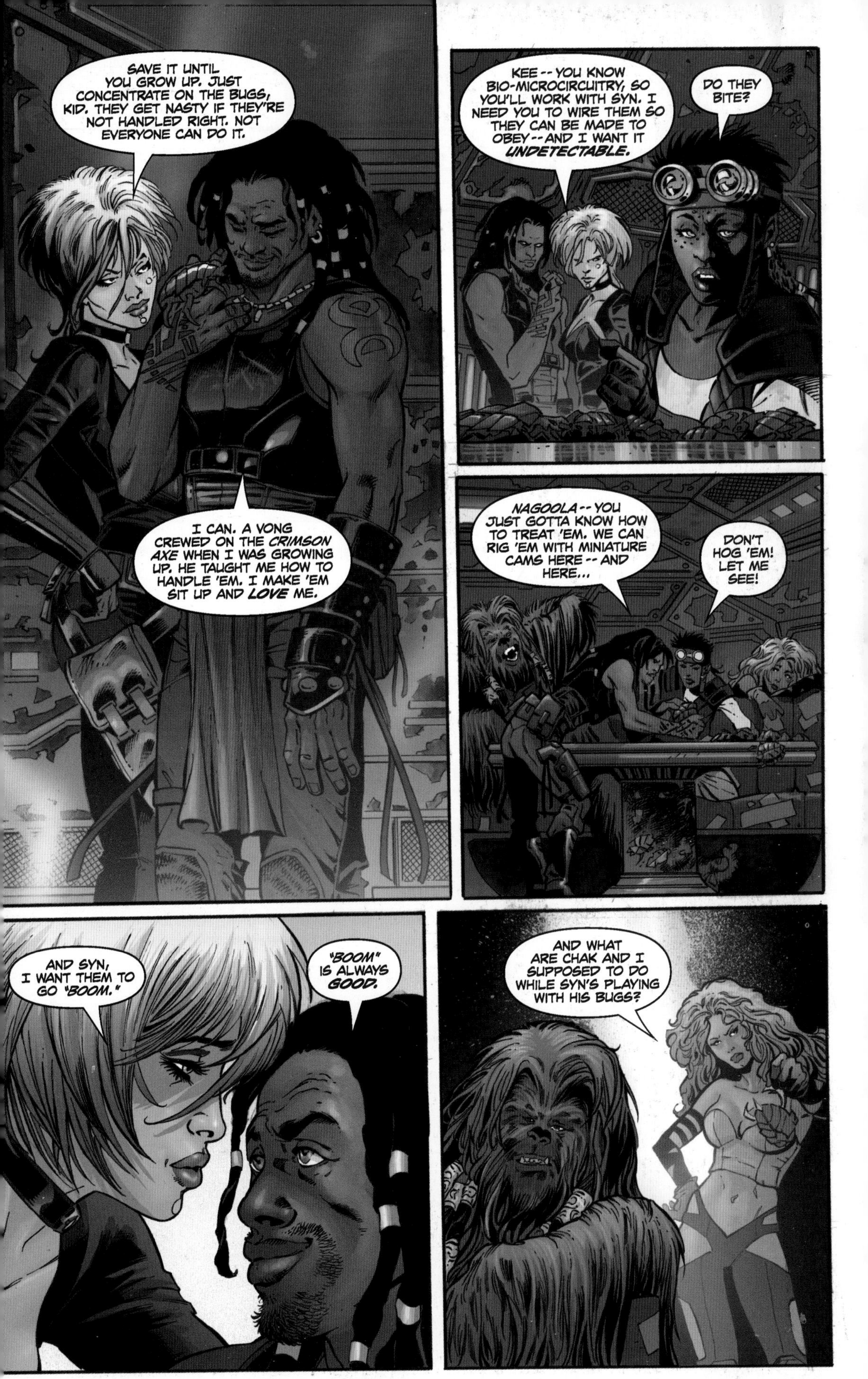
SAVE IT UNTIL YOU GROW UP. JUST CONCENTRATE ON THE BUGS, KID. THEY GET NASTY IF THEY'RE NOT HANDLED RIGHT. NOT EVERYONE CAN DO IT.
I CAN. A VONG CREWED ON THE CRIMSON AXE WHEN I WAS GROWING UP. HE TAUGHT ME HOW TO HANDLE 'EM. I MAKE 'EM SIT UP AND LOVE ME.
KEE -- YOU KNOW BIO-MICROCIRCUITRY, SO YOU'LL WORK WITH SYN. I NEED YOU TO WIRE THEM SO THEY CAN BE MADE TO OBEY -- AND I WANT IT UNDETECTABLE.
DO THEY BITE?
NAGOOLA -- YOU JUST GOTTA KNOW HOW TO TREAT 'EM. WE CAN RIG 'EM WITH MINIATURE CAMS HERE -- AND HERE...
DON'T HOG 'EM! LET ME SEE!
AND SYN, I WANT THEM TO GO "BOOM."
"BOOM" IS ALWAYS GOOD.
AND WHAT ARE CHAK AND I SUPPOSED TO DO WHILE SYN'S PLAYING WITH HIS BUGS?

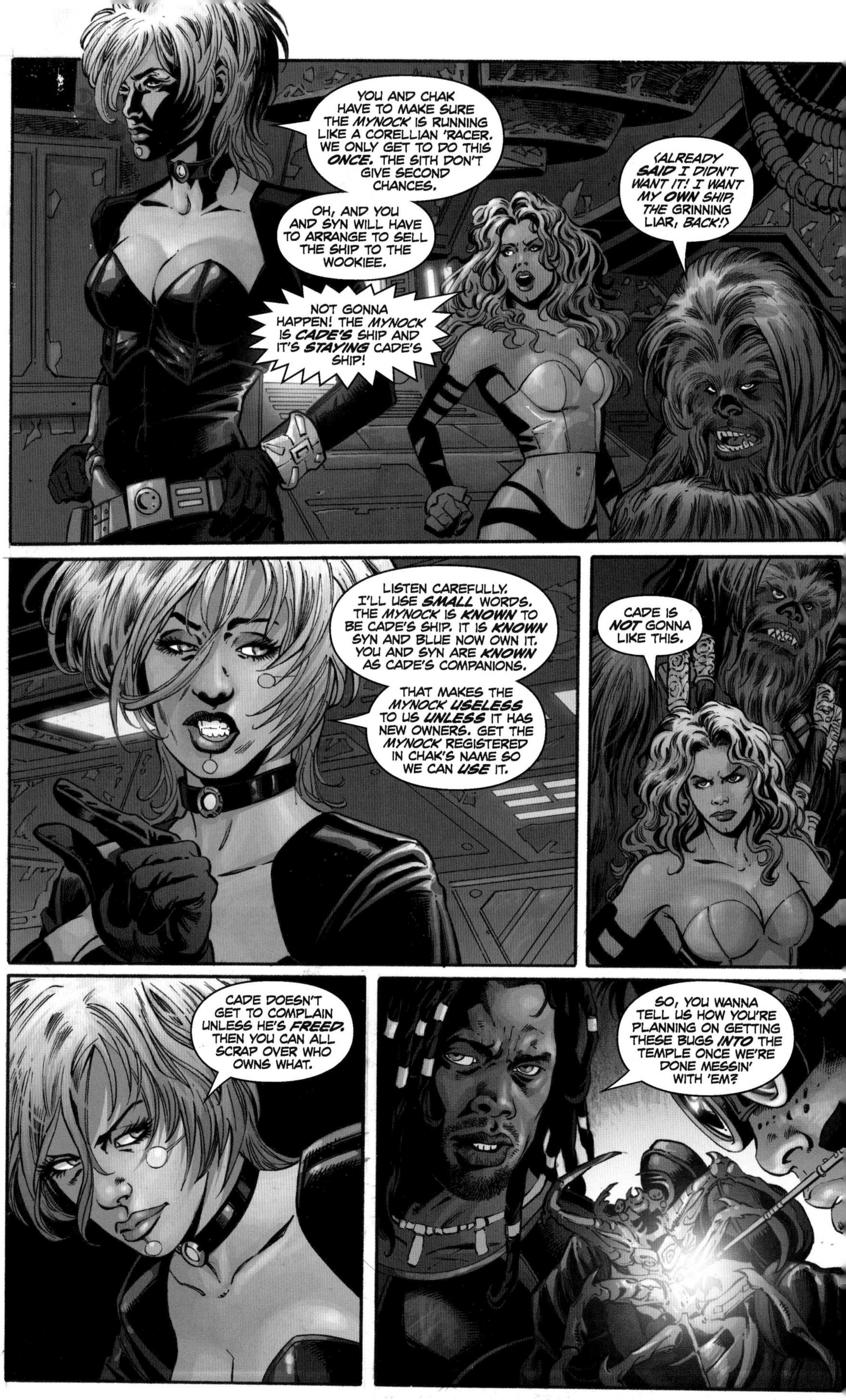
YOU AND CHAK HAVE TO MAKE SURE THE MYNOCK IS RUNNING LIKE A CORELLIAN 'RACER. WE ONLY GET TO DO THIS ONCE. THE SITH DON'T GIVE SECOND CHANCES.
OH, AND YOU AND SYN WILL HAVE TO ARRANGE TO SELL THE SHIP TO THE WOOKIEE.
<ALREADY SAID I DIDN'T WANT IT! I WANT MY OWN SHIP, THE GRINNING LIAR, BACK!>
NOT GONNA HAPPEN! THE MYNOCK IS CADE'S SHIP AND IT'S STAYING CADE'S SHIP!
LISTEN CAREFULLY. I'LL USE SMALL WORDS. THE MYNOCK IS KNOWN TO BE CADE'S SHIP. IT IS KNOWN SYN AND BLUE NOW OWN IT. YOU AND SYN ARE KNOWN AS CADE'S COMPANIONS.
THAT MAKES THE MYNOCK USELESS TO US UNLESS IT HAS NEW OWNERS. GET THE MYNOCK REGISTERED IN CHAK'S NAME SO WE CAN USE IT.
CADE IS NOT GONNA LIKE THIS.
CADE DOESN'T GET TO COMPLAIN UNLESS HE'S FREED. THEN YOU CAN ALL SCRAP OVER WHO OWNS WHAT.
SO, YOU WANNA TELL US HOW YOU'RE PLANNING ON GETTING THESE BUGS INTO THE TEMPLE ONCE WE'RE DONE MESSIN' WITH 'EM?

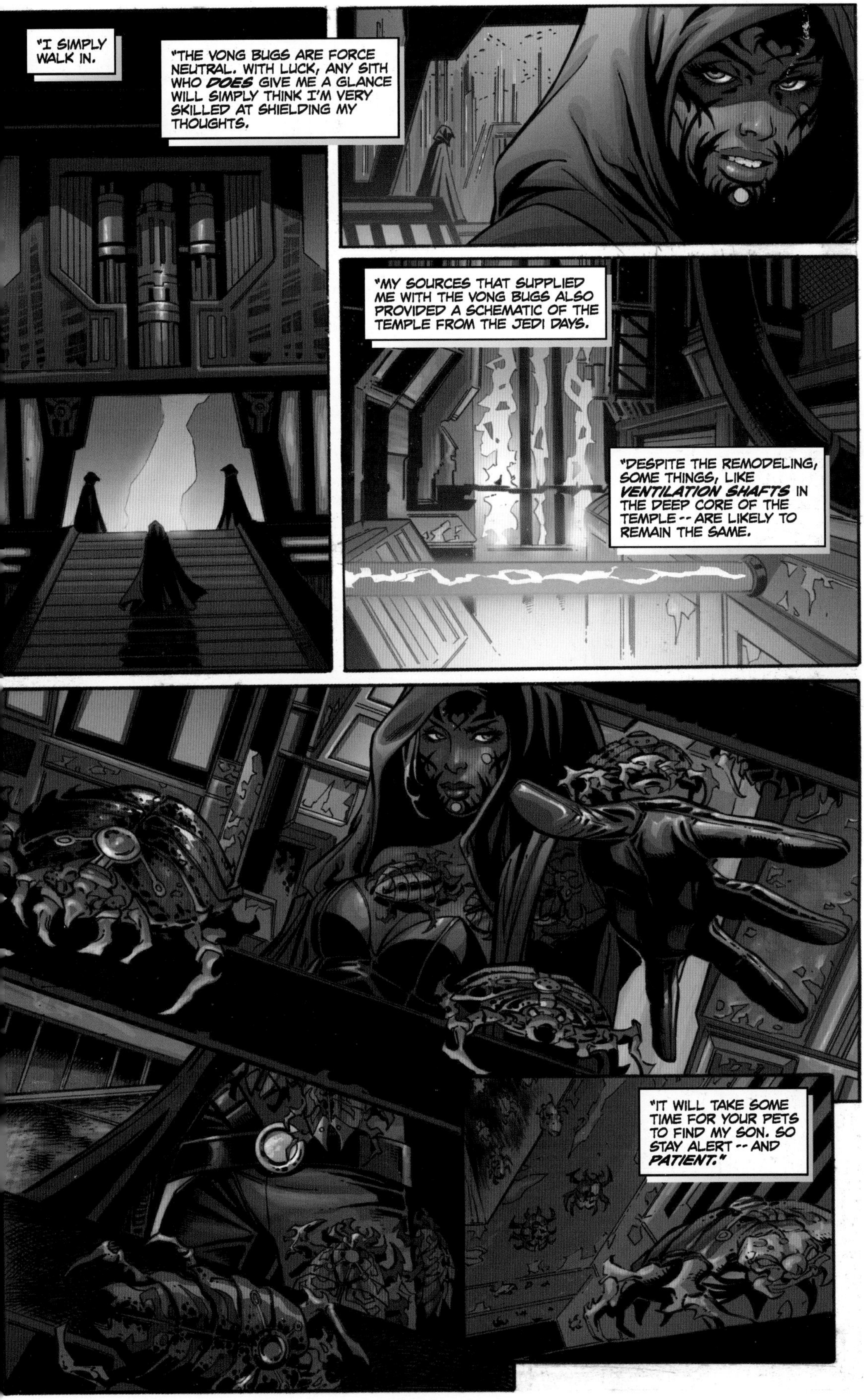
"I SIMPLY WALK IN.
"THE VONG BUGS ARE FORCE NEUTRAL. WITH LUCK, ANY SITH WHO DOES GIVE ME A GLANCE WILL SIMPLY THINK I'M VERY SKILLED AT SHIELDING MY THOUGHTS.
"MY SOURCES THAT SUPPLIED ME WITH THE VONG BUGS ALSO PROVIDED A SCHEMATIC OF THE TEMPLE FROM THE JEDI DAYS.
"DESPITE THE REMODELING, SOME THINGS, LIKE VENTILATION SHAFTS IN THE DEEP CORE OF THE TEMPLE -- ARE LIKELY TO REMAIN THE SAME.
"IT WILL TAKE SOME TIME FOR YOUR PETS TO FIND MY SON. SO STAY ALERT -- AND PATIENT."

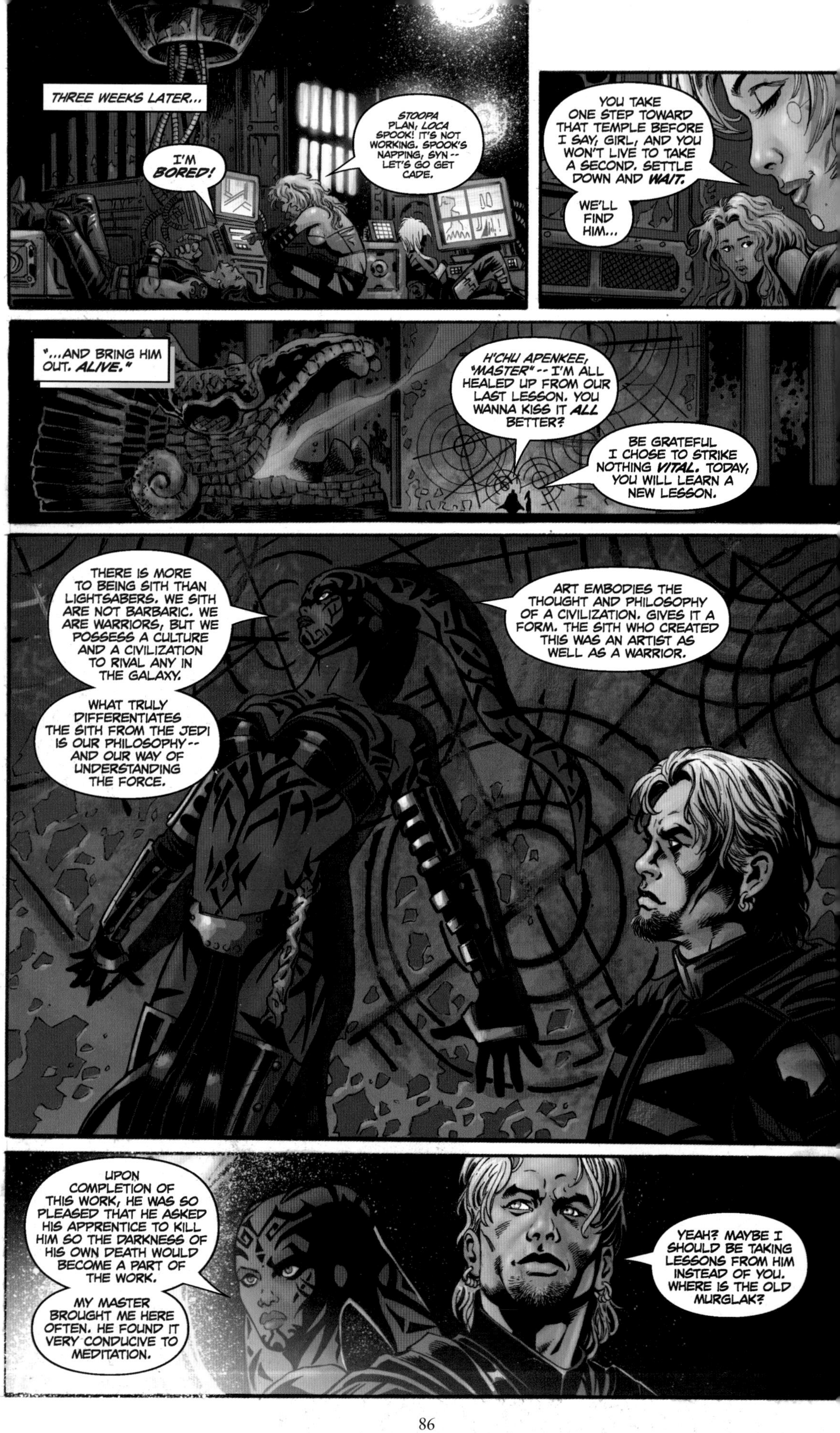
THREE WEEKS LATER...
I'M BORED!
STOOPA PLAN, LOCA SPOOK! IT'S NOT WORKING. SPOOK'S NAPPING, SYN -- LET'S GO GET CADE.
YOU TAKE ONE STEP TOWARD THAT TEMPLE BEFORE I SAY, GIRL, AND YOU WON'T LIVE TO TAKE A SECOND. SETTLE DOWN AND WAIT.
WE'LL FIND HIM...
"...AND BRING HIM OUT. ALIVE."
H'CHU APENKEE, "MASTER" -- I'M ALL HEALED UP FROM OUR LAST LESSON. YOU WANNA KISS IT ALL BETTER?
BE GRATEFUL I CHOSE TO STRIKE NOTHING VITAL. TODAY, YOU WILL LEARN A NEW LESSON.
THERE IS MORE TO BEING SITH THAN LIGHTSABERS. WE SITH ARE NOT BARBARIC. WE ARE WARRIORS, BUT WE POSSESS A CULTURE AND A CIVILIZATION TO RIVAL ANY IN THE GALAXY.
WHAT TRULY DIFFERENTIATES THE SITH FROM THE JEDI IS OUR PHILOSOPHY -- AND OUR WAY OF UNDERSTANDING THE FORCE.
ART EMBODIES THE THOUGHT AND PHILOSOPHY OF A CIVILIZATION. GIVES IT A FORM. THE SITH WHO CREATED THIS WAS AN ARTIST AS WELL AS A WARRIOR.
UPON COMPLETION OF THIS WORK, HE WAS SO PLEASED THAT HE ASKED HIS APPRENTICE TO KILL HIM SO THE DARKNESS OF HIS OWN DEATH WOULD BECOME A PART OF THE WORK.
MY MASTER BROUGHT ME HERE OFTEN. HE FOUND IT VERY CONDUCIVE TO MEDITATION.
YEAH? MAYBE I SHOULD BE TAKING LESSONS FROM HIM INSTEAD OF YOU. WHERE IS THE OLD MURGLAK?

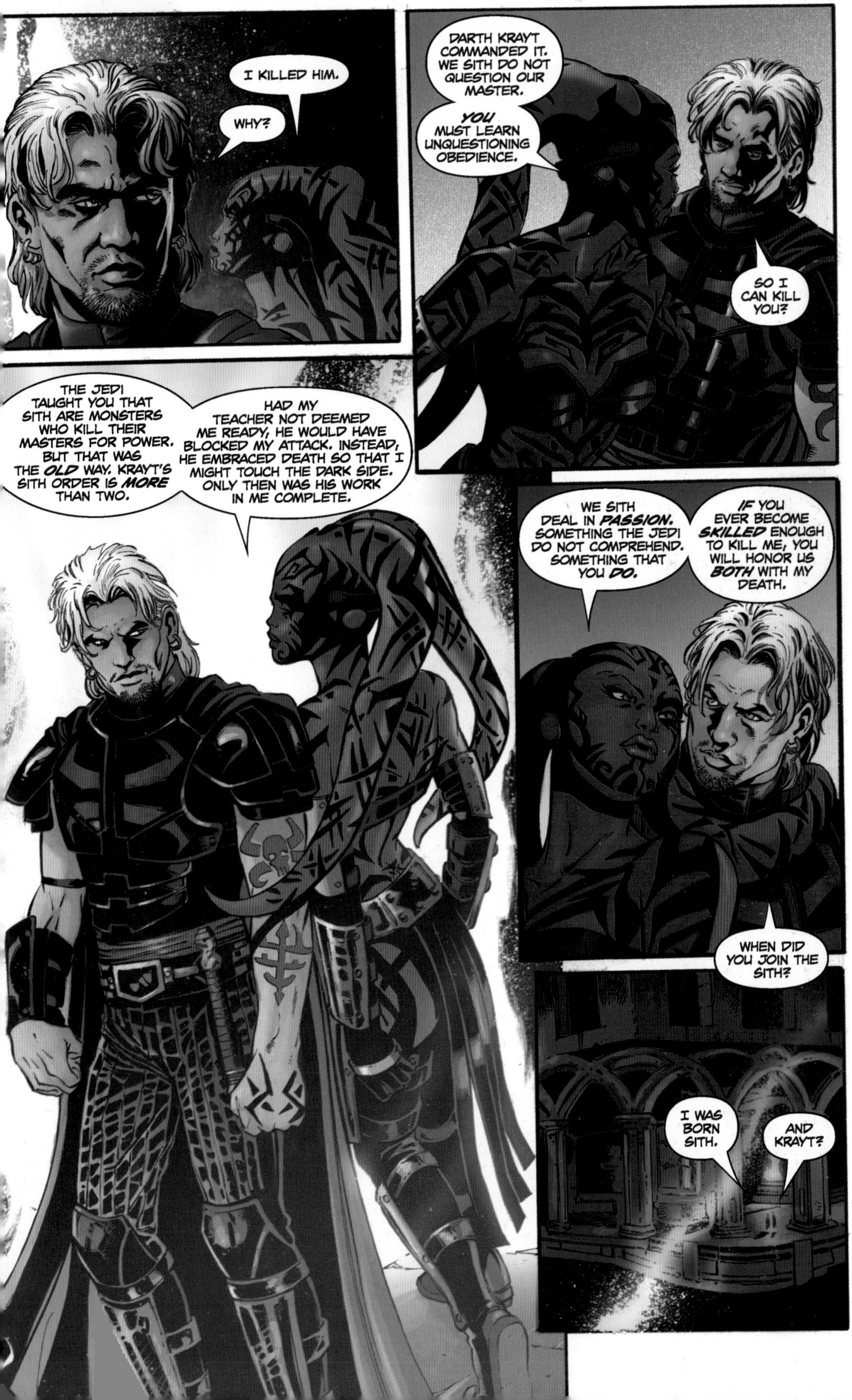
I KILLED HIM.
WHY?
DARTH KRAYT COMMANDED IT. WE SITH DO NOT QUESTION OUR MASTER.
YOU MUST LEARN UNQUESTIONING OBEDIENCE.
SO I CAN KILL YOU?
THE JEDI TAUGHT YOU THAT SITH ARE MONSTERS WHO KILL THEIR MASTERS FOR POWER. BUT THAT WAS THE OLD WAY. KRAYT'S SITH ORDER IS MORE THAN TWO.
HAD MY TEACHER NOT DEEMED ME READY, HE WOULD HAVE BLOCKED MY ATTACK. INSTEAD, HE EMBRACED DEATH SO THAT I MIGHT TOUCH THE DARK SIDE. ONLY THEN WAS HIS WORK IN ME COMPLETE.
WE SITH DEAL IN PASSION. SOMETHING THE JEDI DO NOT COMPREHEND. SOMETHING THAT YOU DO.
IF YOU EVER BECOME SKILLED ENOUGH TO KILL ME, YOU WILL HONOR US BOTH WITH MY DEATH.
WHEN DID YOU JOIN THE SITH?
I WAS BORN SITH.
AND KRAYT?

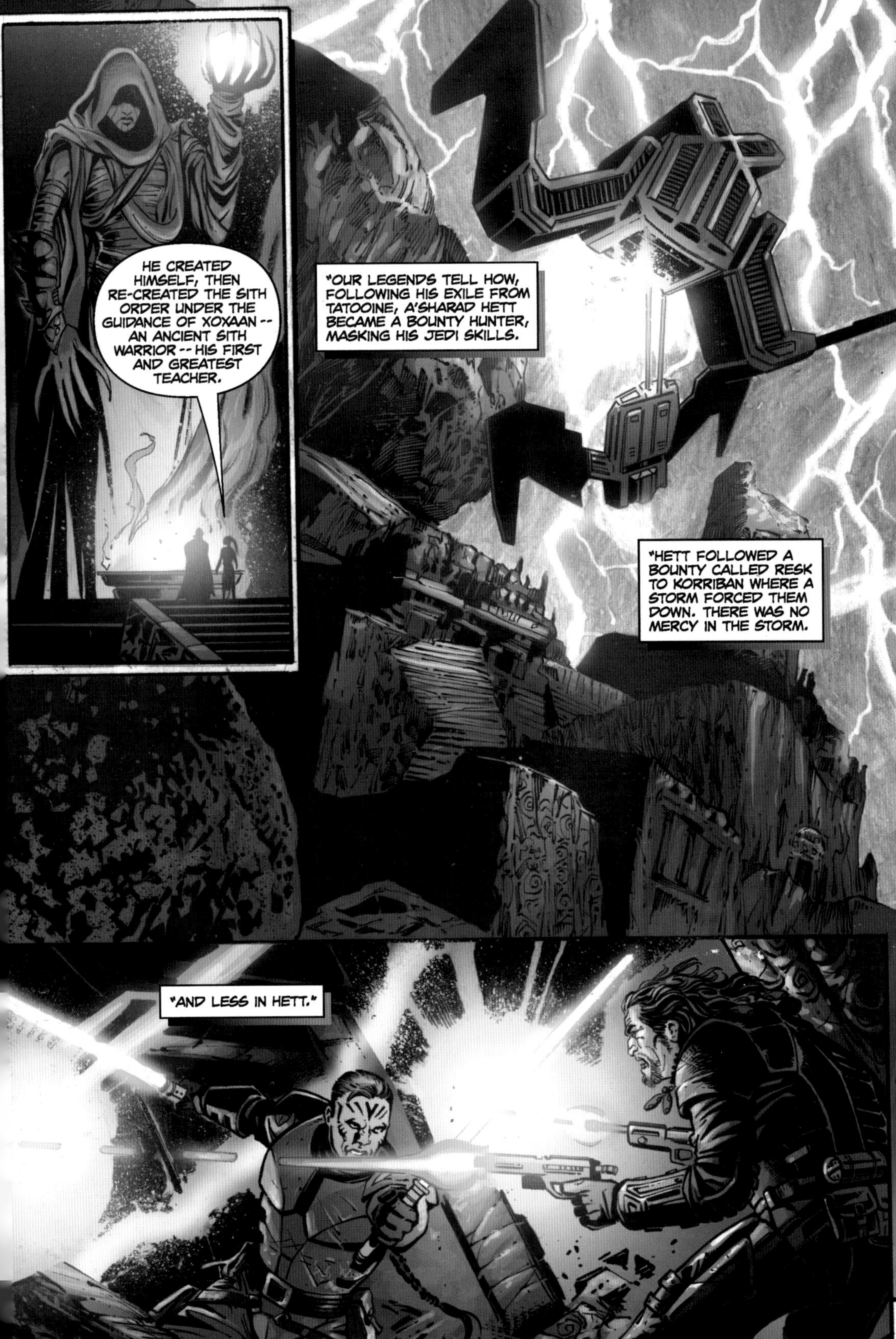
HE CREATED HIMSELF, THEN RE-CREATED THE SITH ORDER UNDER THE GUIDANCE OF XOXAAN -- AN ANCIENT SITH WARRIOR -- HIS FIRST AND GREATEST TEACHER.
"OUR LEGENDS TELL HOW, FOLLOWING HIS EXILE FROM TATOOINE, A'SHARAD HETT BECAME A BOUNTY HUNTER, MASKING HIS JEDI SKILLS.
"HETT FOLLOWED A BOUNTY CALLED RESK TO KORRIBAN WHERE A STORM FORCED THEM DOWN. THERE WAS NO MERCY IN THE STORM.
"AND LESS IN HETT."

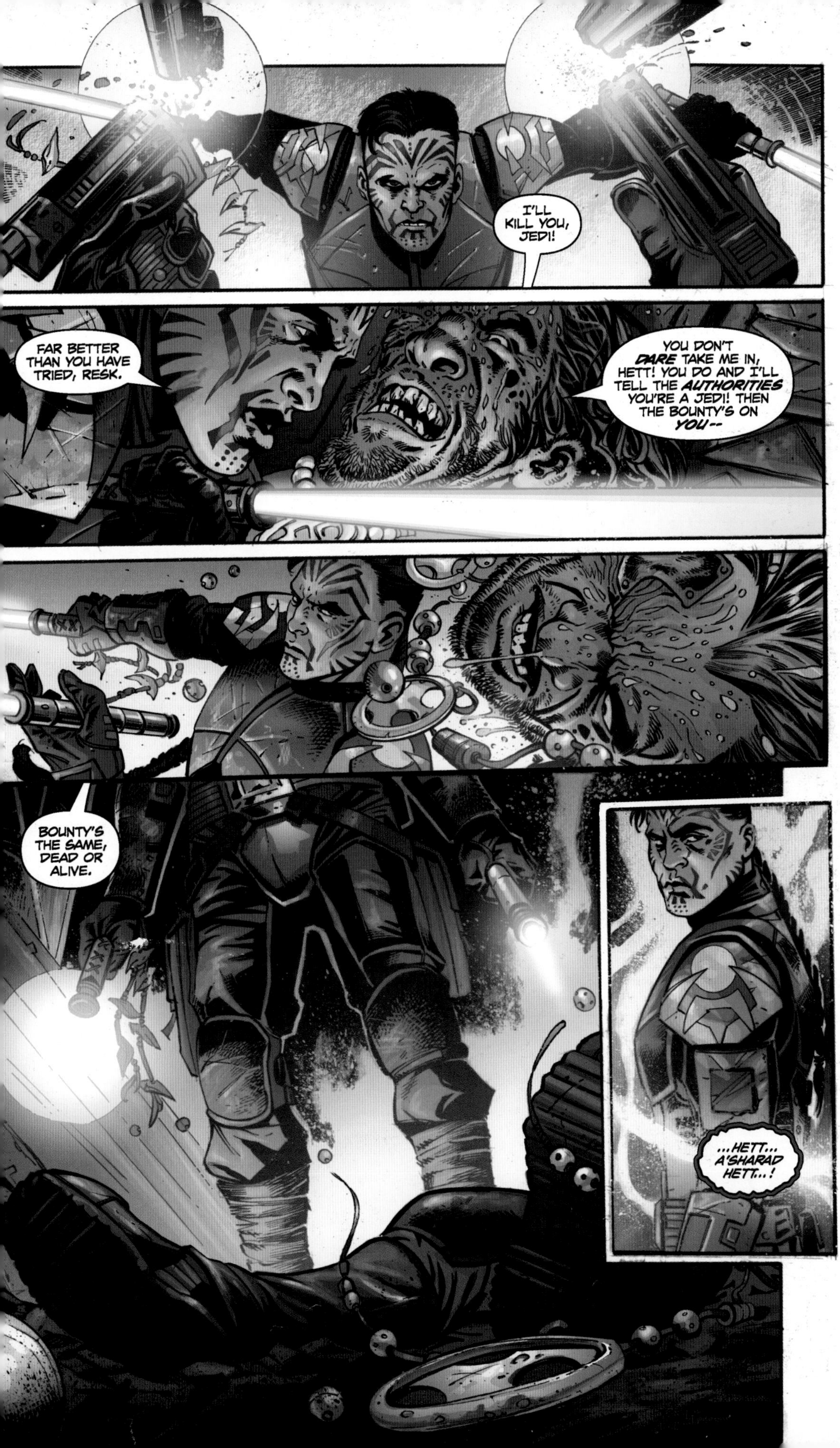
I'LL KILL YOU, JEDI!
FAR BETTER THAN YOU HAVE TRIED, RESK.
YOU DON'T DARE TAKE ME IN, HETT! YOU DO AND I'LL TELL THE AUTHORITIES YOU'RE A JEDI! THEN THE BOUNTY'S ON YOU--
BOUNTY'S THE SAME, DEAD OR ALIVE.
...HETT... A'SHARAD HETT...!

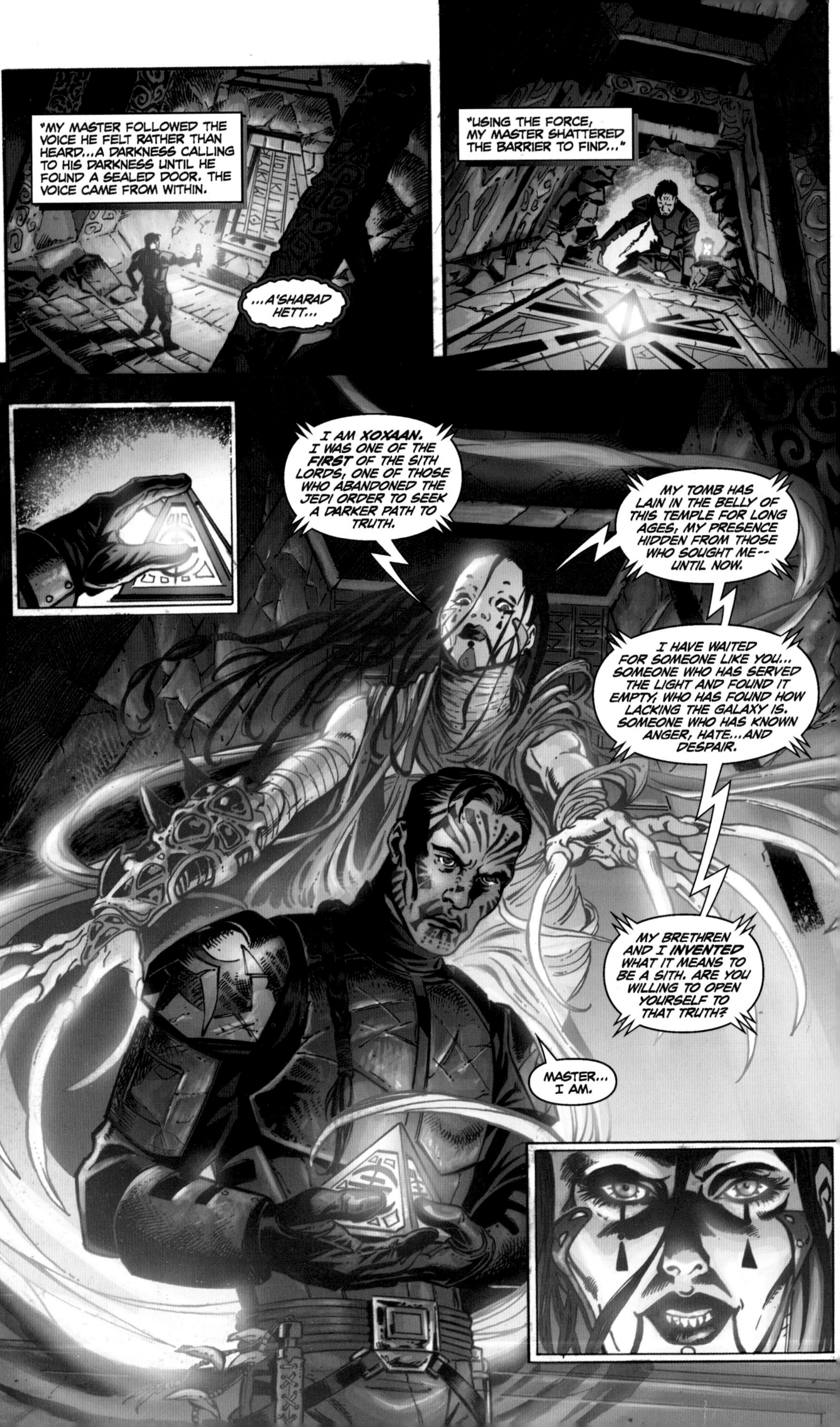
"MY MASTER FOLLOWED THE VOICE HE FELT RATHER THAN HEARD...A DARKNESS CALLING TO HIS DARKNESS UNTIL HE FOUND A SEALED DOOR. THE VOICE CAME FROM WITHIN.
...A'SHARAD HETT...
"USING THE FORCE, MY MASTER SHATTERED THE BARRIER TO FIND..."
I AM XOXAAN. I WAS ONE OF THE FIRST OF THE SITH LORDS; ONE OF THOSE WHO ABANDONED THE JEDI ORDER TO SEEK A DARKER PATH TO TRUTH.
MY TOMB HAS LAIN IN THE BELLY OF THIS TEMPLE FOR LONG AGES, MY PRESENCE HIDDEN FROM THOSE WHO SOUGHT ME--UNTIL NOW.
I HAVE WAITED FOR SOMEONE LIKE YOU... SOMEONE WHO HAS SERVED THE LIGHT AND FOUND IT EMPTY; WHO HAS FOUND HOW LACKING THE GALAXY IS. SOMEONE WHO HAS KNOWN ANGER, HATE...AND DESPAIR.
MY BRETHREN AND I INVENTED WHAT IT MEANS TO BE A SITH. ARE YOU WILLING TO OPEN YOURSELF TO THAT TRUTH?
MASTER... I AM.

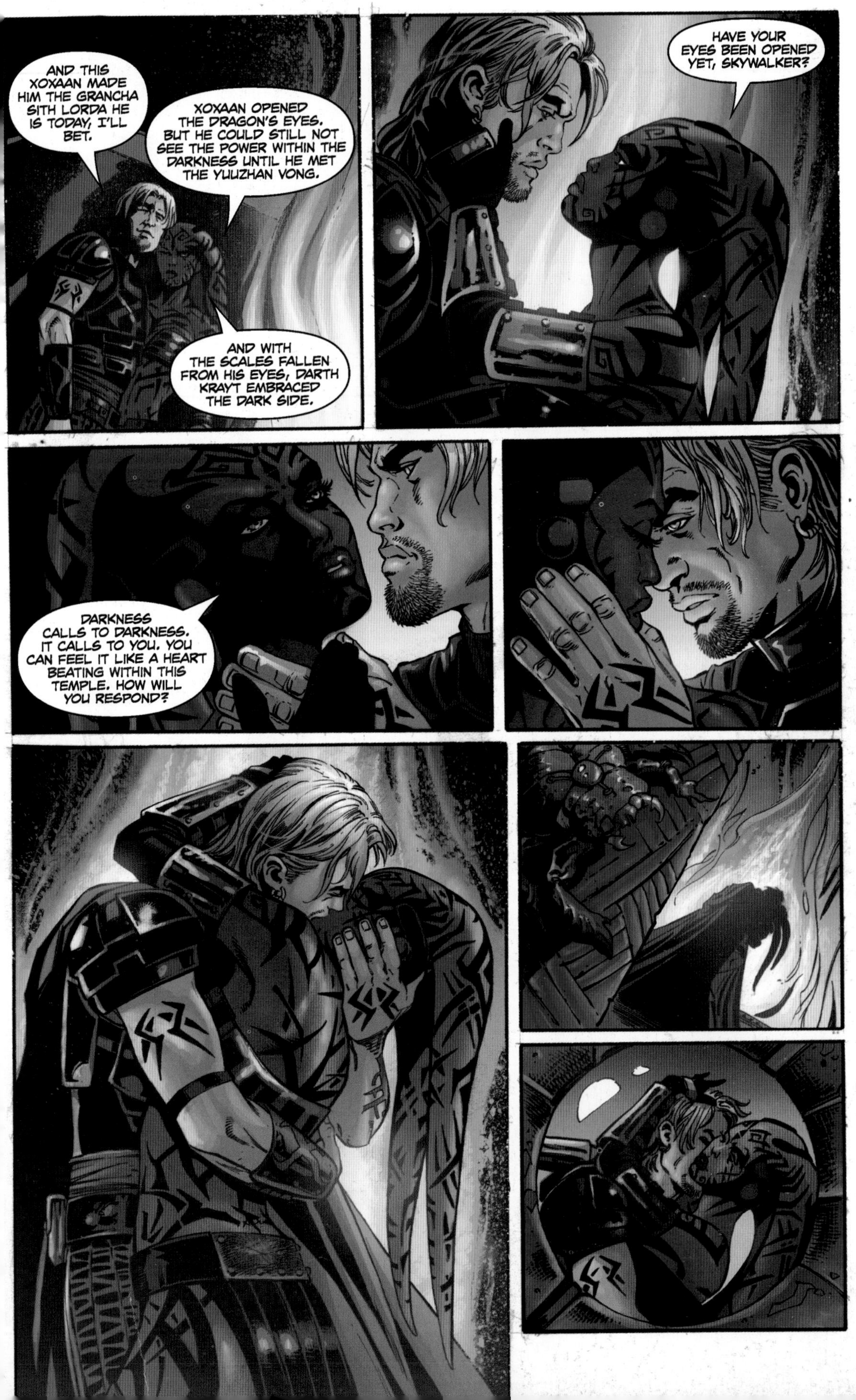
AND THIS XOXAAN MADE HIM THE GRANCHA SITH LORDA HE IS TODAY, I'LL BET.
XOXAAN OPENED THE DRAGON'S EYES. BUT HE COULD STILL NOT SEE THE POWER WITHIN THE DARKNESS UNTIL HE MET THE YUUZHAN VONG.
AND WITH THE SCALES FALLEN FROM HIS EYES, DARTH KRAYT EMBRACED THE DARK SIDE.
HAVE YOUR EYES BEEN OPENED YET, SKYWALKER?
DARKNESS CALLS TO DARKNESS. IT CALLS TO YOU. YOU CAN FEEL IT LIKE A HEART BEATING WITHIN THIS TEMPLE. HOW WILL YOU RESPOND?

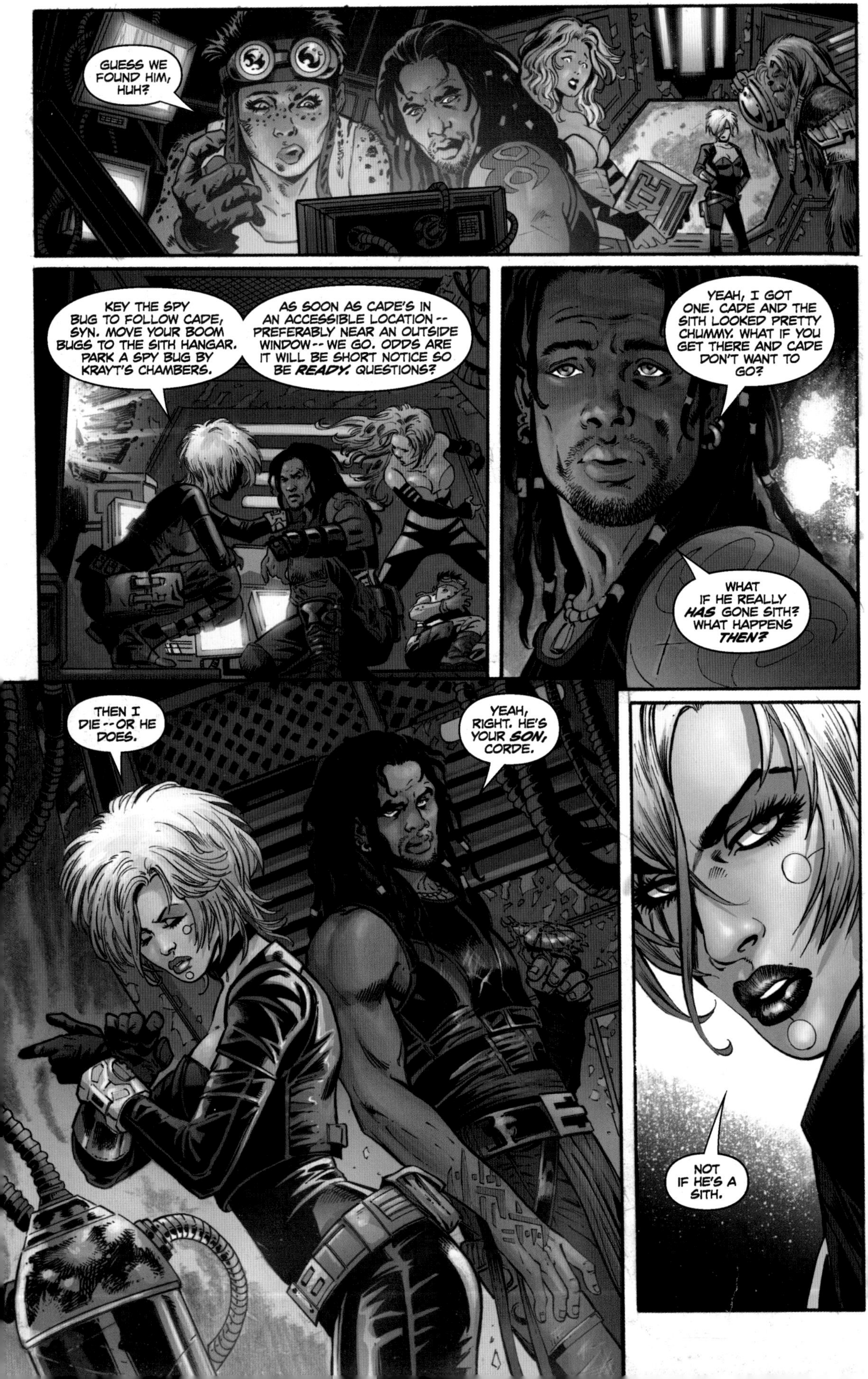
GUESS WE FOUND HIM, HUH?
KEY THE SPY BUG TO FOLLOW CADE, SYN. MOVE YOUR BOOM BUGS TO THE SITH HANGAR. PARK A SPY BUG BY KRAYT'S CHAMBERS.
AS SOON AS CADE'S IN AN ACCESSIBLE LOCATION -- PREFERABLY NEAR AN OUTSIDE WINDOW -- WE GO. ODDS ARE IT WILL BE SHORT NOTICE SO BE *READY.* QUESTIONS?
YEAH, I GOT ONE. CADE AND THE SITH LOOKED PRETTY CHUMMY. WHAT IF YOU GET THERE AND CADE DON'T WANT TO GO?
WHAT IF HE REALLY *HAS* GONE SITH? WHAT HAPPENS *THEN?*
THEN I DIE -- OR HE DOES.
YEAH, RIGHT. HE'S YOUR *SON,* CORDE.
NOT IF HE'S A SITH.

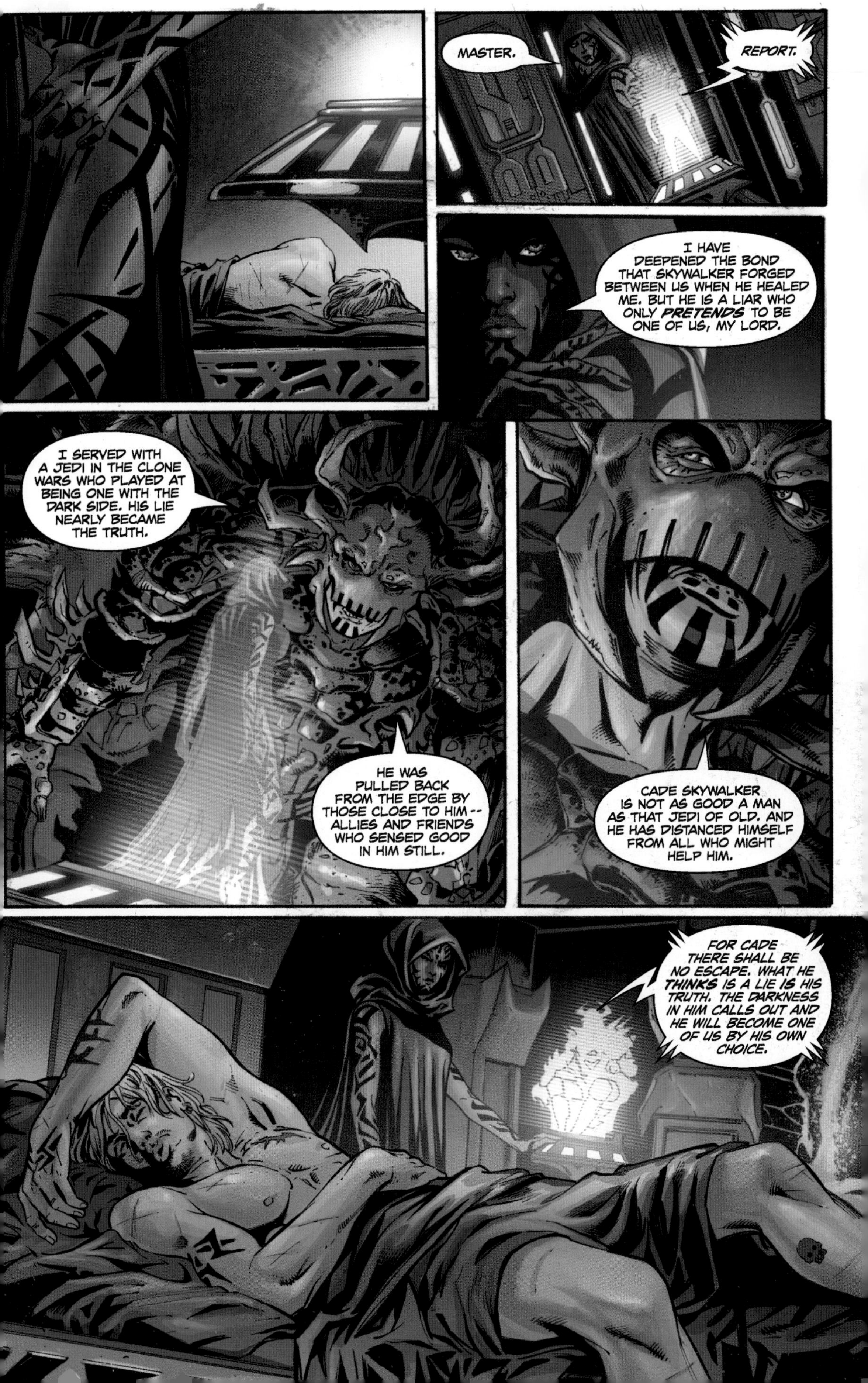
MASTER.
REPORT.
I HAVE DEEPENED THE BOND THAT SKYWALKER FORGED BETWEEN US WHEN HE HEALED ME. BUT HE IS A LIAR WHO ONLY *PRETENDS* TO BE ONE OF US, MY LORD.
I SERVED WITH A JEDI IN THE CLONE WARS WHO PLAYED AT BEING ONE WITH THE DARK SIDE. HIS LIE NEARLY BECAME THE TRUTH.
HE WAS PULLED BACK FROM THE EDGE BY THOSE CLOSE TO HIM -- ALLIES AND FRIENDS WHO SENSED GOOD IN HIM STILL.
CADE SKYWALKER IS NOT AS GOOD A MAN AS THAT JEDI OF OLD. AND HE HAS DISTANCED HIMSELF FROM ALL WHO MIGHT HELP HIM.
FOR CADE THERE SHALL BE NO ESCAPE. WHAT HE **THINKS** IS A LIE **IS** HIS TRUTH. THE DARKNESS IN HIM CALLS OUT AND HE WILL BECOME ONE OF US BY HIS OWN CHOICE.

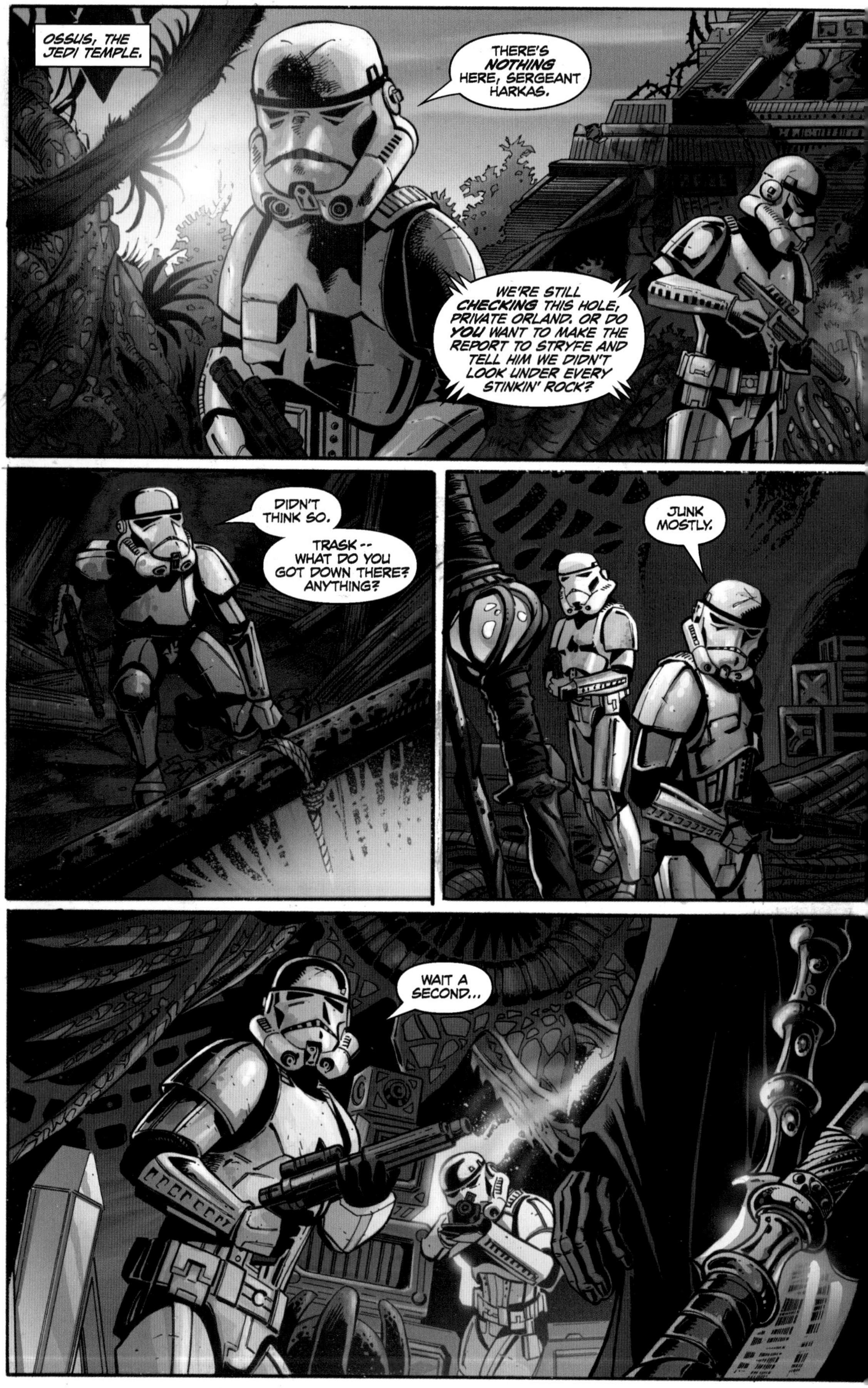
OSSUS, THE JEDI TEMPLE.
THERE'S NOTHING HERE, SERGEANT HARKAS.
WE'RE STILL CHECKING THIS HOLE, PRIVATE ORLAND. OR DO YOU WANT TO MAKE THE REPORT TO STRYFE AND TELL HIM WE DIDN'T LOOK UNDER EVERY STINKIN' ROCK?
DIDN'T THINK SO.
TRASK -- WHAT DO YOU GOT DOWN THERE? ANYTHING?
JUNK MOSTLY.
WAIT A SECOND...

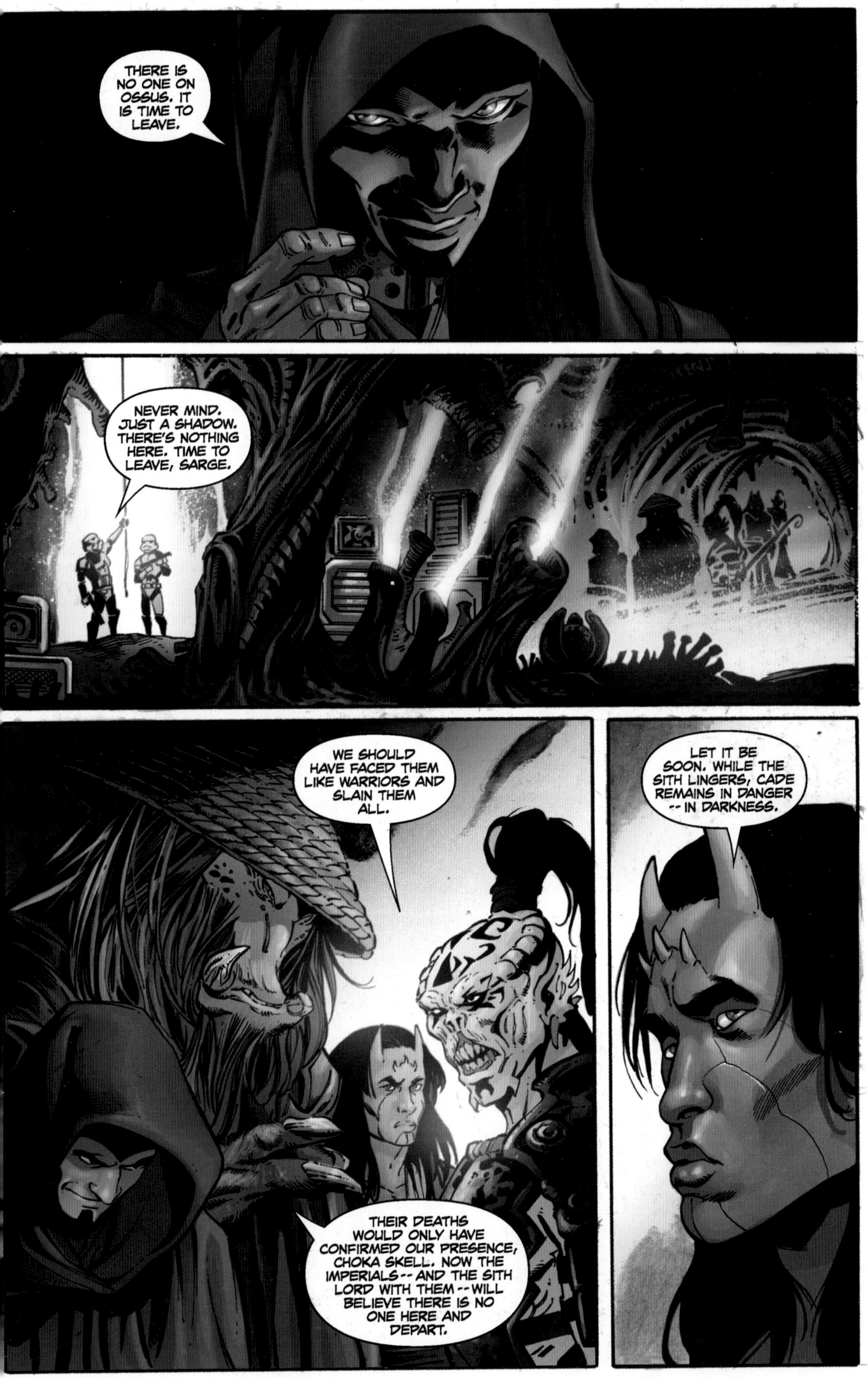
THERE IS NO ONE ON OSSUS. IT IS TIME TO LEAVE.
NEVER MIND. JUST A SHADOW. THERE'S NOTHING HERE. TIME TO LEAVE, SARGE.
WE SHOULD HAVE FACED THEM LIKE WARRIORS AND SLAIN THEM ALL.
THEIR DEATHS WOULD ONLY HAVE CONFIRMED OUR PRESENCE, CHOKA SKELL. NOW THE IMPERIALS-- AND THE SITH LORD WITH THEM --WILL BELIEVE THERE IS NO ONE HERE AND DEPART.
LET IT BE SOON. WHILE THE SITH LINGERS, CADE REMAINS IN DANGER -- IN DARKNESS.

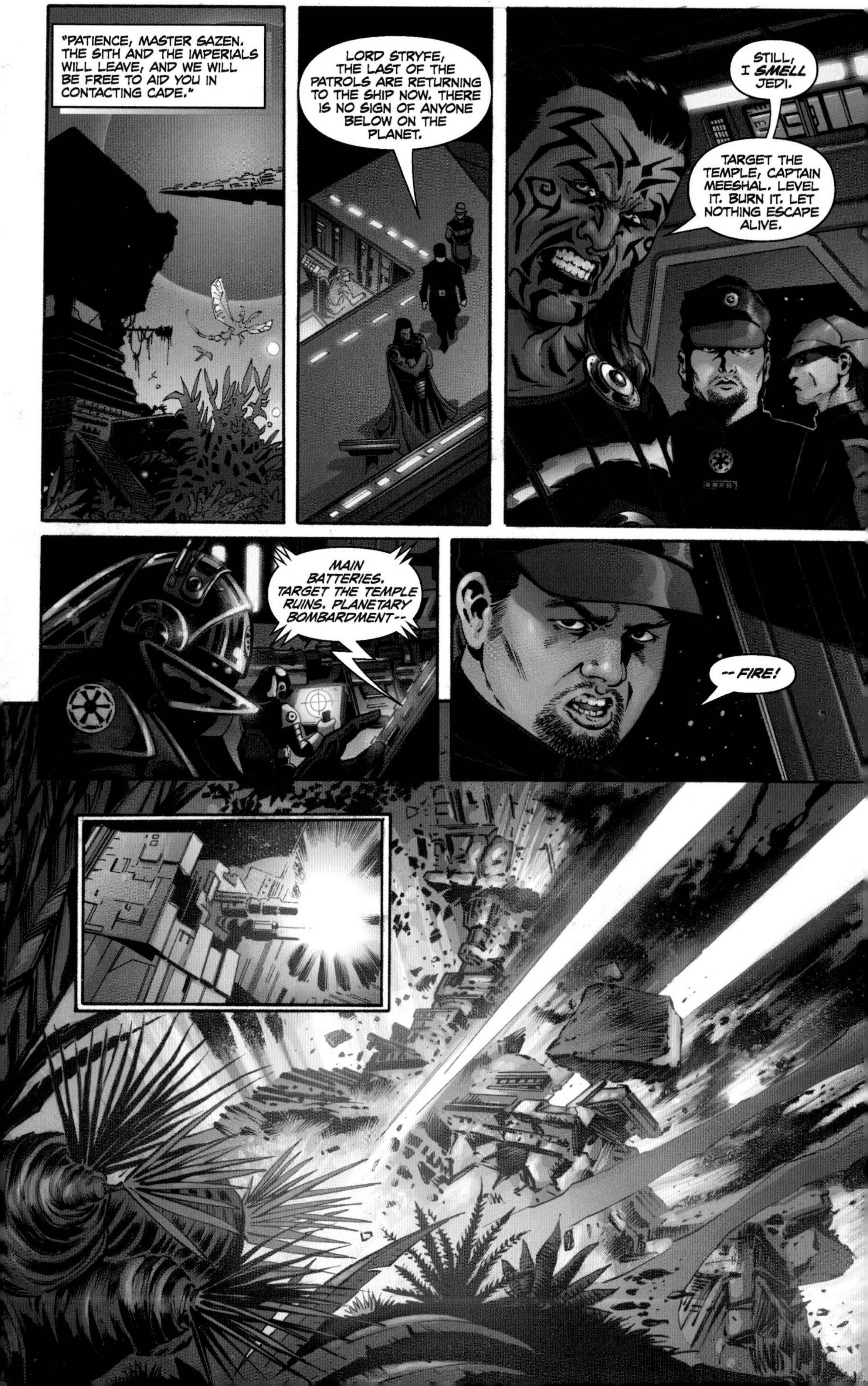
"PATIENCE, MASTER SAZEN. THE SITH AND THE IMPERIALS WILL LEAVE, AND WE WILL BE FREE TO AID YOU IN CONTACTING CADE."
LORD STRYFE, THE LAST OF THE PATROLS ARE RETURNING TO THE SHIP NOW. THERE IS NO SIGN OF ANYONE BELOW ON THE PLANET.
STILL, I SMELL JEDI.
TARGET THE TEMPLE, CAPTAIN MEESHAL. LEVEL IT. BURN IT. LET NOTHING ESCAPE ALIVE.
MAIN BATTERIES. TARGET THE TEMPLE RUINS. PLANETARY BOMBARDMENT--
--FIRE!

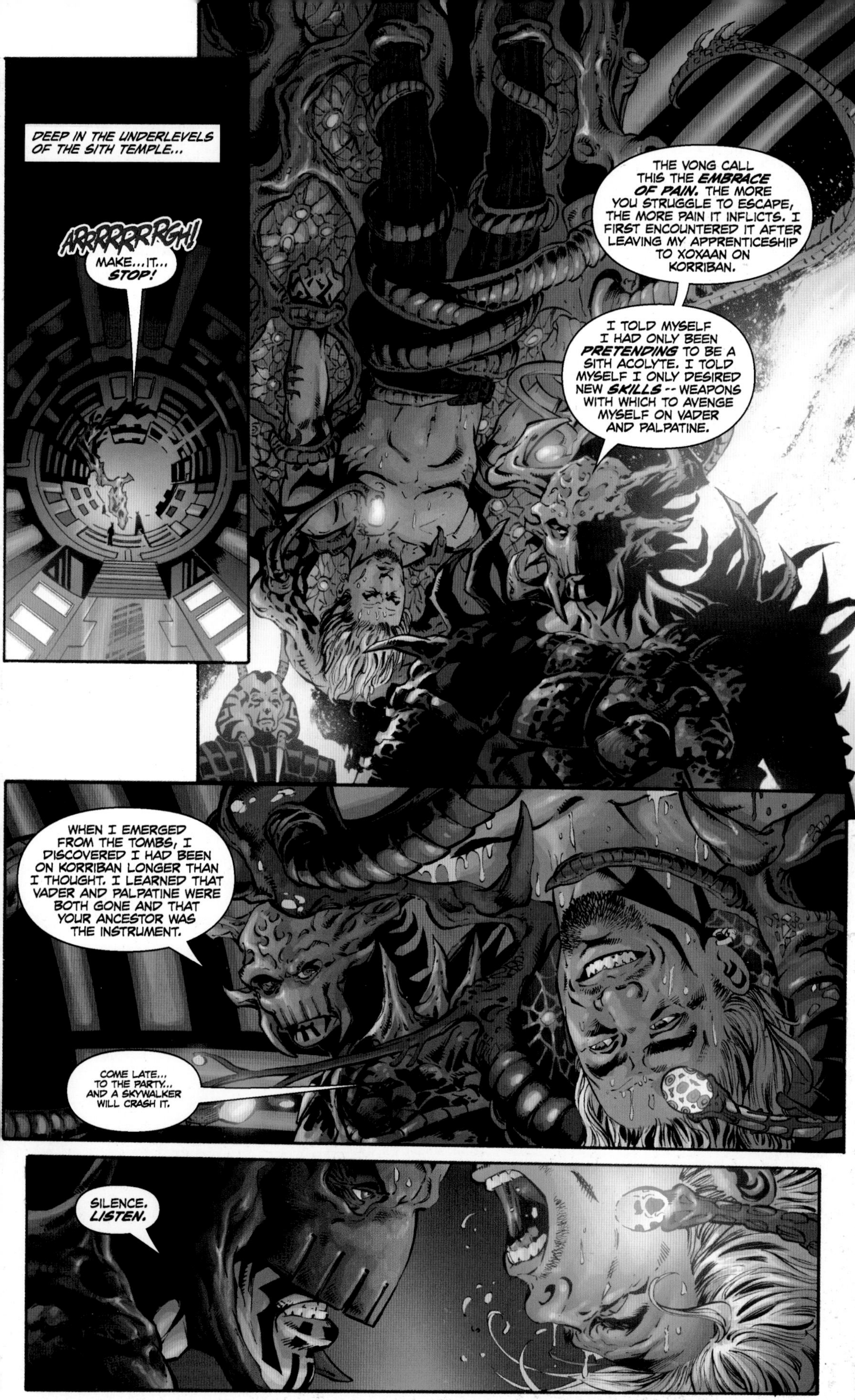
DEEP IN THE UNDERLEVELS OF THE SITH TEMPLE...
ARRRRRRRGH! MAKE...IT... STOP!
THE VONG CALL THIS THE EMBRACE OF PAIN. THE MORE YOU STRUGGLE TO ESCAPE, THE MORE PAIN IT INFLICTS. I FIRST ENCOUNTERED IT AFTER LEAVING MY APPRENTICESHIP TO XOXAAN ON KORRIBAN.
I TOLD MYSELF I HAD ONLY BEEN PRETENDING TO BE A SITH ACOLYTE. I TOLD MYSELF I ONLY DESIRED NEW SKILLS -- WEAPONS WITH WHICH TO AVENGE MYSELF ON VADER AND PALPATINE.
WHEN I EMERGED FROM THE TOMBS, I DISCOVERED I HAD BEEN ON KORRIBAN LONGER THAN I THOUGHT. I LEARNED THAT VADER AND PALPATINE WERE BOTH GONE AND THAT YOUR ANCESTOR WAS THE INSTRUMENT.
COME LATE... TO THE PARTY... AND A SKYWALKER WILL CRASH IT.
SILENCE. LISTEN.

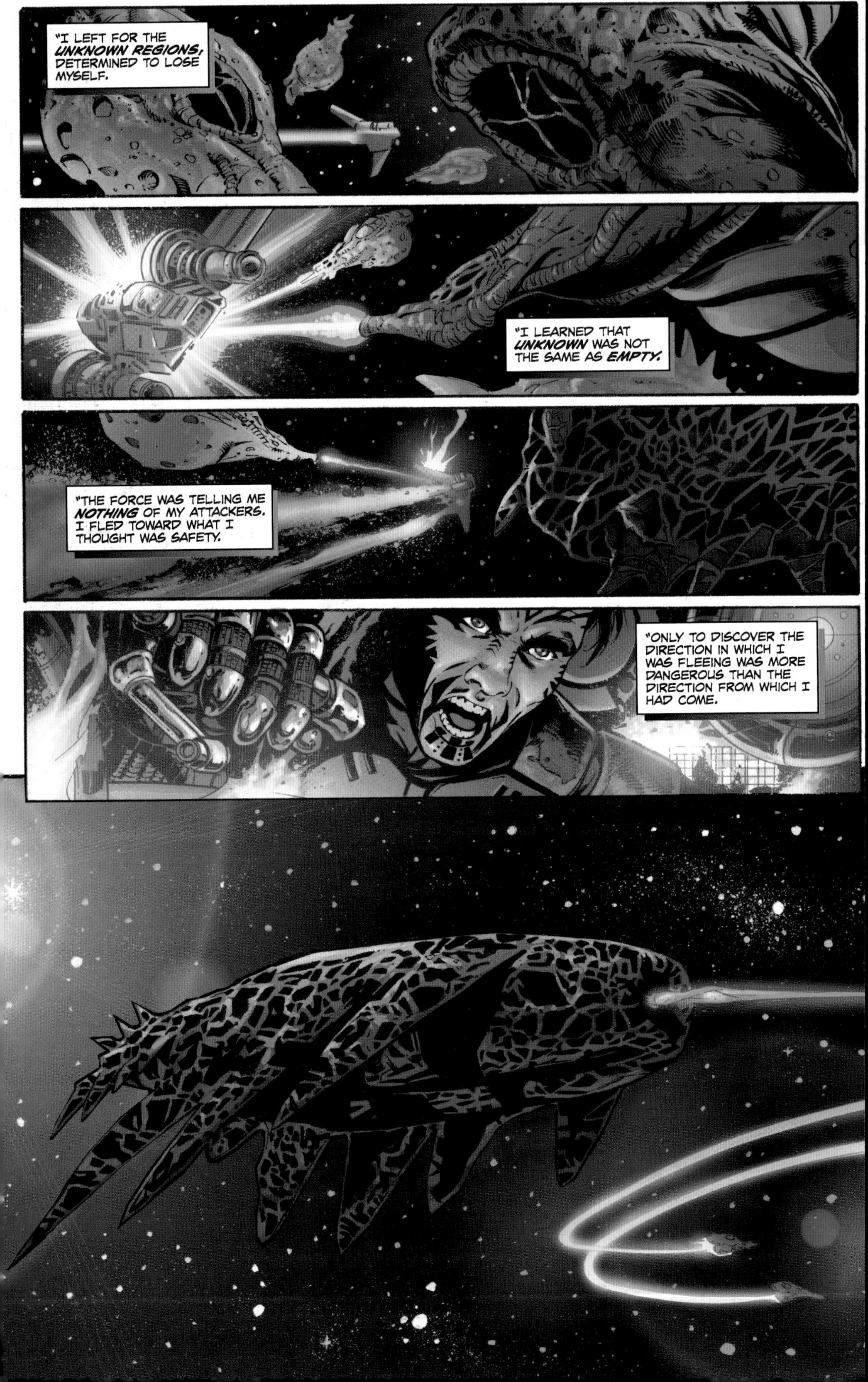
"I LEFT FOR THE *UNKNOWN REGIONS;* DETERMINED TO LOSE MYSELF.
"I LEARNED THAT *UNKNOWN* WAS NOT THE SAME AS *EMPTY.*
"THE FORCE WAS TELLING ME *NOTHING* OF MY ATTACKERS. I FLED TOWARD WHAT I THOUGHT WAS SAFETY.
"ONLY TO DISCOVER THE DIRECTION IN WHICH I WAS FLEEING WAS MORE DANGEROUS THAN THE DIRECTION FROM WHICH I HAD COME.

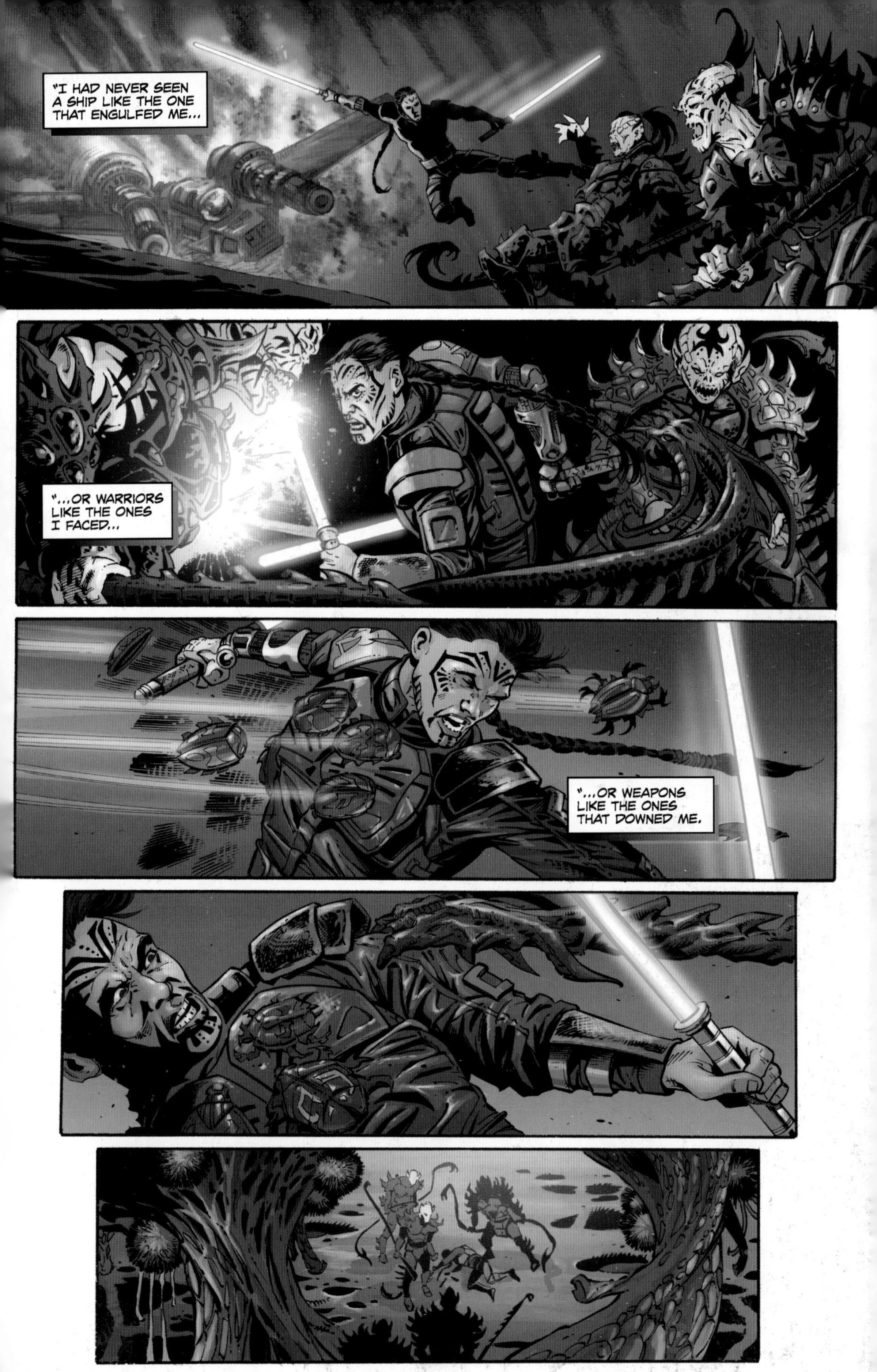
"I HAD NEVER SEEN A SHIP LIKE THE ONE THAT ENGULFED ME...
"...OR WARRIORS LIKE THE ONES I FACED...
"...OR WEAPONS LIKE THE ONES THAT DOWNED ME.

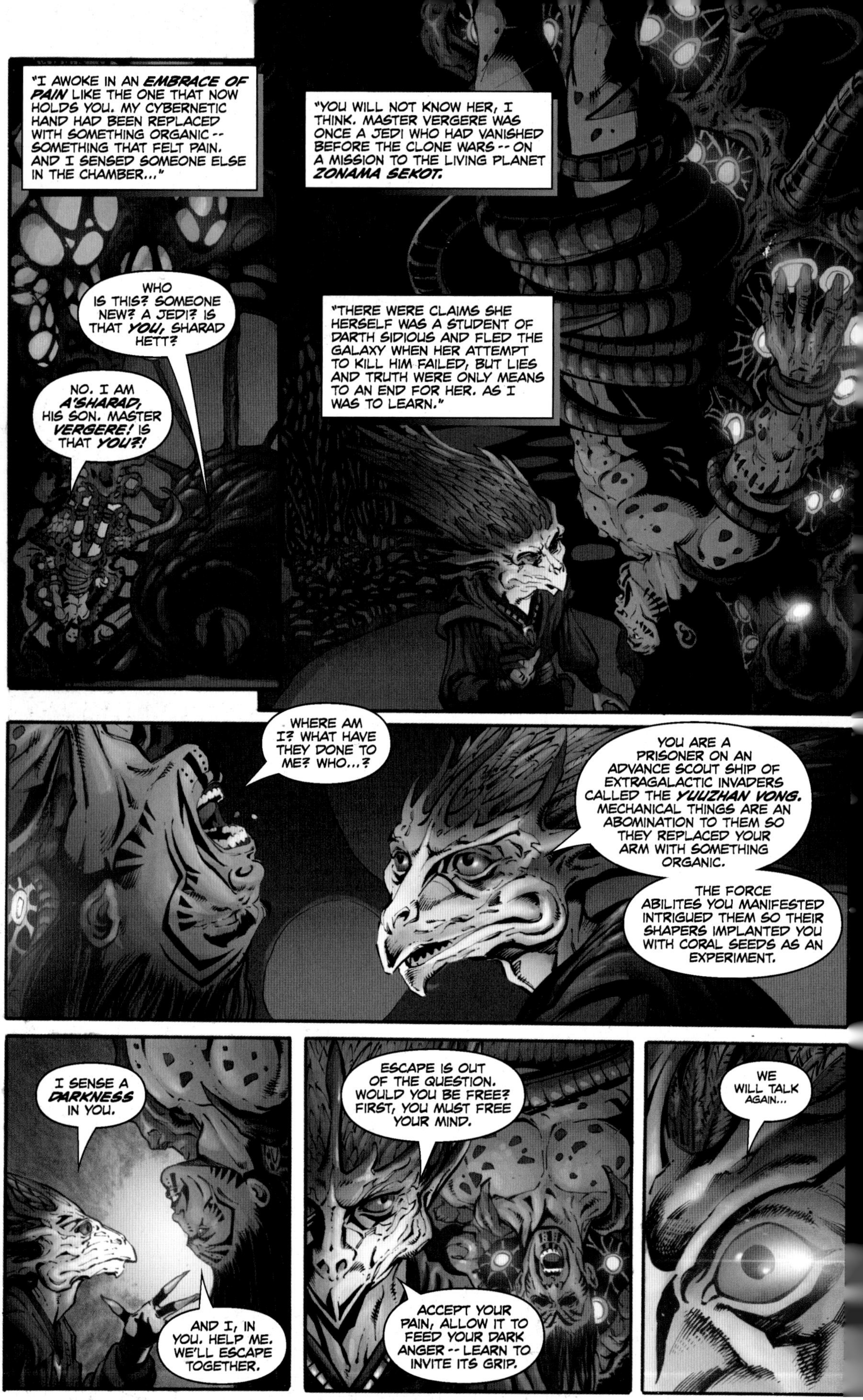
"I AWOKE IN AN EMBRACE OF PAIN LIKE THE ONE THAT NOW HOLDS YOU. MY CYBERNETIC HAND HAD BEEN REPLACED WITH SOMETHING ORGANIC -- SOMETHING THAT FELT PAIN. AND I SENSED SOMEONE ELSE IN THE CHAMBER..."
WHO IS THIS? SOMEONE NEW? A JEDI? IS THAT YOU, SHARAD HETT?
NO. I AM A'SHARAD, HIS SON. MASTER VERGERE! IS THAT YOU?!
"YOU WILL NOT KNOW HER, I THINK. MASTER VERGERE WAS ONCE A JEDI WHO HAD VANISHED BEFORE THE CLONE WARS -- ON A MISSION TO THE LIVING PLANET ZONAMA SEKOT.
"THERE WERE CLAIMS SHE HERSELF WAS A STUDENT OF DARTH SIDIOUS AND FLED THE GALAXY WHEN HER ATTEMPT TO KILL HIM FAILED, BUT LIES AND TRUTH WERE ONLY MEANS TO AN END FOR HER. AS I WAS TO LEARN."
WHERE AM I? WHAT HAVE THEY DONE TO ME? WHO...?
YOU ARE A PRISONER ON AN ADVANCE SCOUT SHIP OF EXTRAGALACTIC INVADERS CALLED THE YUUZHAN VONG. MECHANICAL THINGS ARE AN ABOMINATION TO THEM SO THEY REPLACED YOUR ARM WITH SOMETHING ORGANIC.
THE FORCE ABILITES YOU MANIFESTED INTRIGUED THEM SO THEIR SHAPERS IMPLANTED YOU WITH CORAL SEEDS AS AN EXPERIMENT.
I SENSE A DARKNESS IN YOU.
AND I, IN YOU. HELP ME. WE'LL ESCAPE TOGETHER.
ESCAPE IS OUT OF THE QUESTION. WOULD YOU BE FREE? FIRST, YOU MUST FREE YOUR MIND.
ACCEPT YOUR PAIN, ALLOW IT TO FEED YOUR DARK ANGER -- LEARN TO INVITE ITS GRIP.
WE WILL TALK AGAIN...

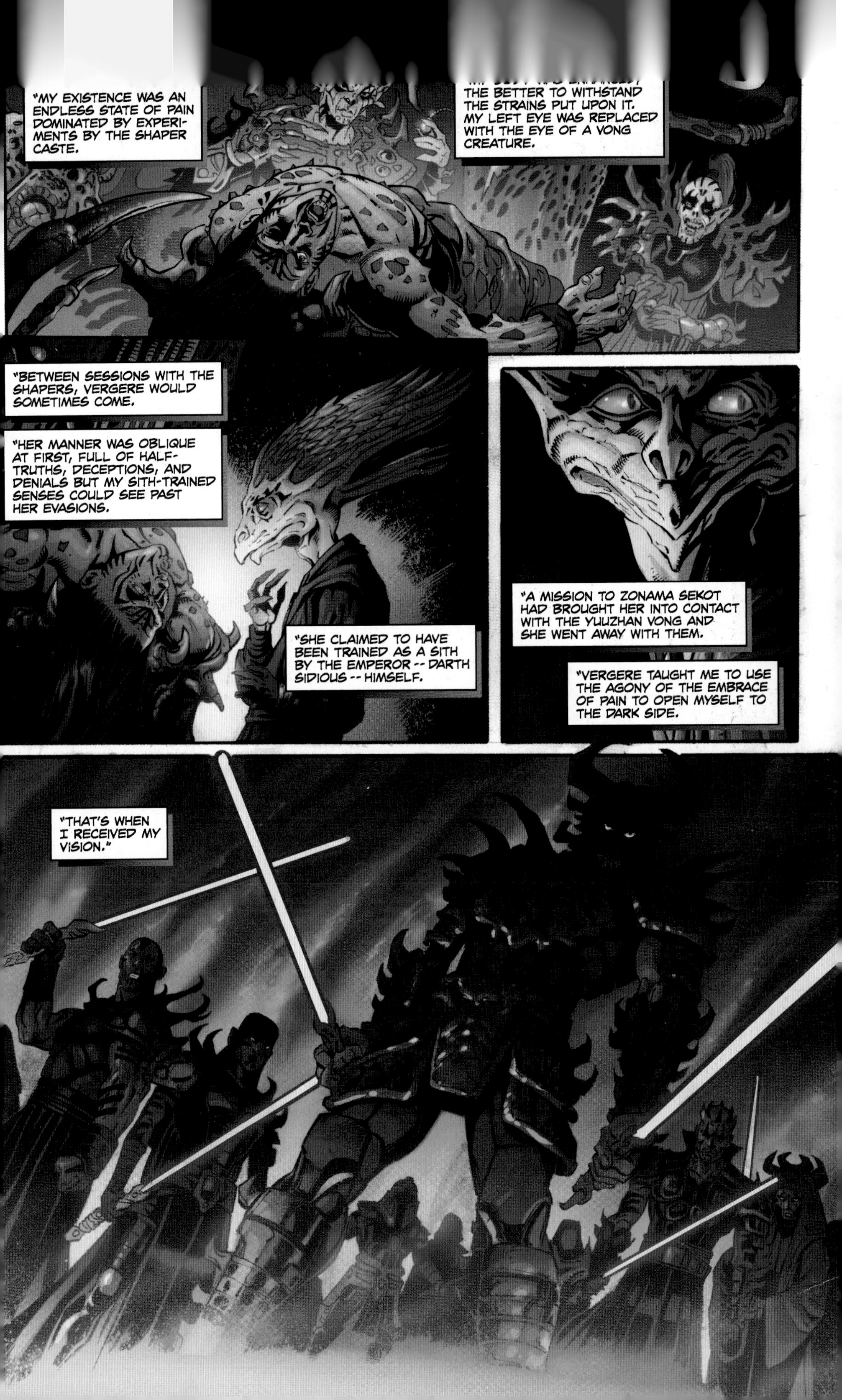
"MY EXISTENCE WAS AN ENDLESS STATE OF PAIN DOMINATED BY EXPERIMENTS BY THE SHAPER CASTE.
THE BETTER TO WITHSTAND THE STRAINS PUT UPON IT. MY LEFT EYE WAS REPLACED WITH THE EYE OF A VONG CREATURE.
"BETWEEN SESSIONS WITH THE SHAPERS, VERGERE WOULD SOMETIMES COME.
"HER MANNER WAS OBLIQUE AT FIRST, FULL OF HALF-TRUTHS, DECEPTIONS, AND DENIALS BUT MY SITH-TRAINED SENSES COULD SEE PAST HER EVASIONS.
"SHE CLAIMED TO HAVE BEEN TRAINED AS A SITH BY THE EMPEROR -- DARTH SIDIOUS -- HIMSELF.
"A MISSION TO ZONAMA SEKOT HAD BROUGHT HER INTO CONTACT WITH THE YUUZHAN VONG AND SHE WENT AWAY WITH THEM.
"VERGERE TAUGHT ME TO USE THE AGONY OF THE EMBRACE OF PAIN TO OPEN MYSELF TO THE DARK SIDE.
"THAT'S WHEN I RECEIVED MY VISION."

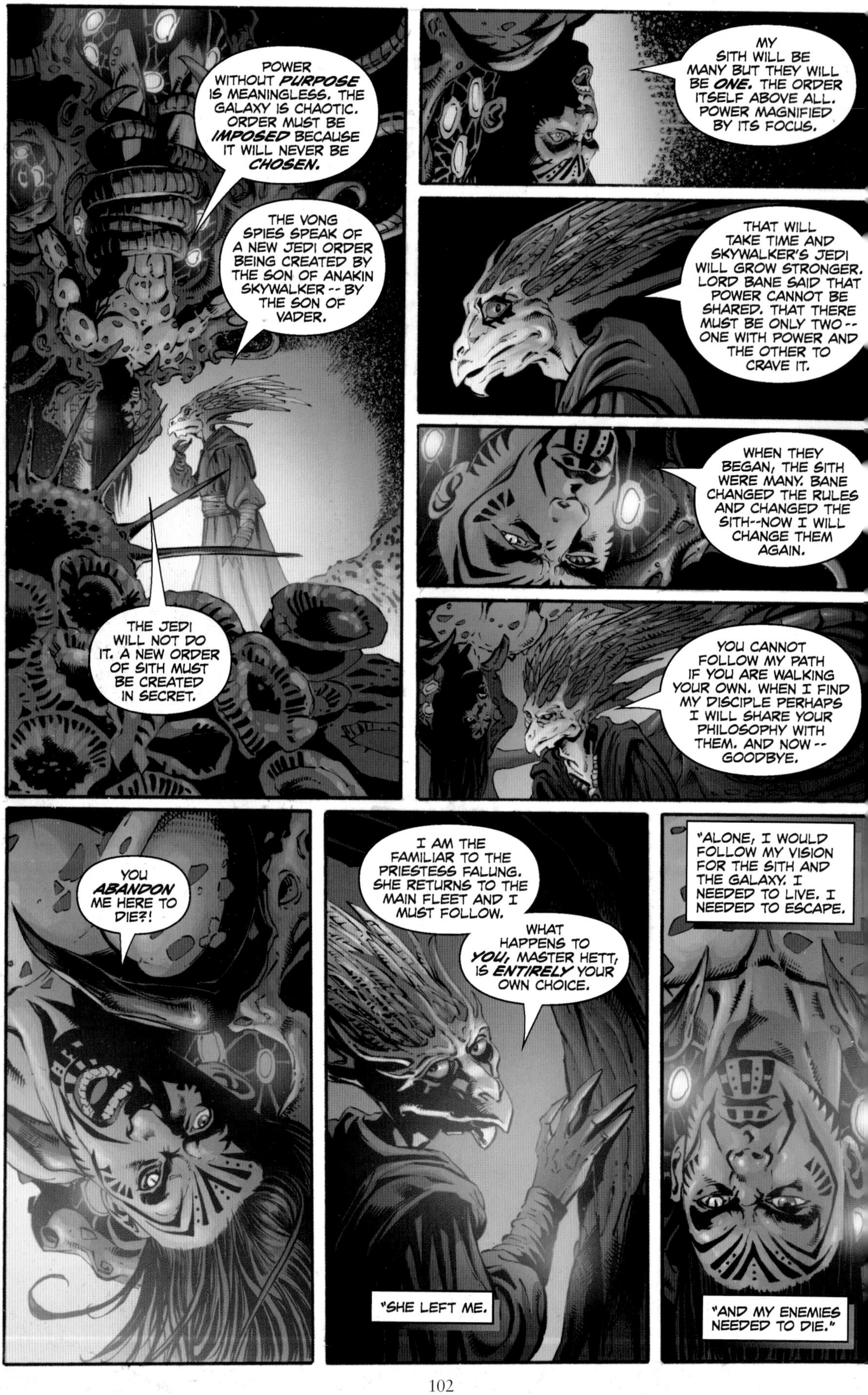
POWER WITHOUT PURPOSE IS MEANINGLESS. THE GALAXY IS CHAOTIC. ORDER MUST BE IMPOSED BECAUSE IT WILL NEVER BE CHOSEN.
THE VONG SPIES SPEAK OF A NEW JEDI ORDER BEING CREATED BY THE SON OF ANAKIN SKYWALKER -- BY THE SON OF VADER.
THE JEDI WILL NOT DO IT. A NEW ORDER OF SITH MUST BE CREATED IN SECRET.
MY SITH WILL BE MANY BUT THEY WILL BE ONE. THE ORDER ITSELF ABOVE ALL. POWER MAGNIFIED BY ITS FOCUS.
THAT WILL TAKE TIME AND SKYWALKER'S JEDI WILL GROW STRONGER. LORD BANE SAID THAT POWER CANNOT BE SHARED. THAT THERE MUST BE ONLY TWO -- ONE WITH POWER AND THE OTHER TO CRAVE IT.
WHEN THEY BEGAN, THE SITH WERE MANY. BANE CHANGED THE RULES AND CHANGED THE SITH--NOW I WILL CHANGE THEM AGAIN.
YOU CANNOT FOLLOW MY PATH IF YOU ARE WALKING YOUR OWN. WHEN I FIND MY DISCIPLE PERHAPS I WILL SHARE YOUR PHILOSOPHY WITH THEM. AND NOW -- GOODBYE.
YOU ABANDON ME HERE TO DIE?!
I AM THE FAMILIAR TO THE PRIESTESS FALUNG. SHE RETURNS TO THE MAIN FLEET AND I MUST FOLLOW.
WHAT HAPPENS TO YOU, MASTER HETT, IS ENTIRELY YOUR OWN CHOICE.
"SHE LEFT ME.
"ALONE, I WOULD FOLLOW MY VISION FOR THE SITH AND THE GALAXY. I NEEDED TO LIVE. I NEEDED TO ESCAPE.
"AND MY ENEMIES NEEDED TO DIE."

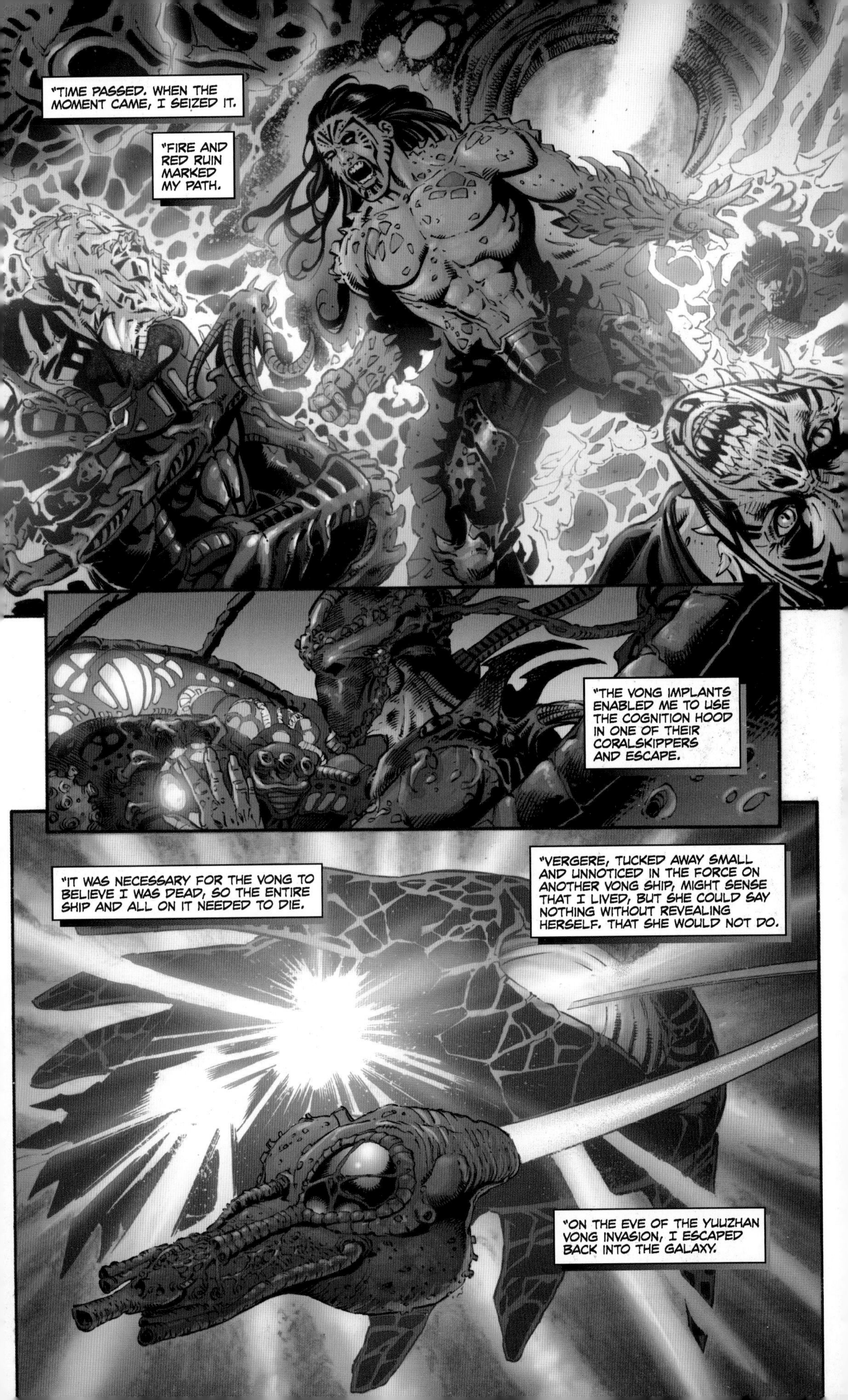
"TIME PASSED. WHEN THE MOMENT CAME, I SEIZED IT.
"FIRE AND RED RUIN MARKED MY PATH.
"THE VONG IMPLANTS ENABLED ME TO USE THE COGNITION HOOD IN ONE OF THEIR CORALSKIPPERS AND ESCAPE.
"IT WAS NECESSARY FOR THE VONG TO BELIEVE I WAS DEAD, SO THE ENTIRE SHIP AND ALL ON IT NEEDED TO DIE.
"VERGERE, TUCKED AWAY SMALL AND UNNOTICED IN THE FORCE ON ANOTHER VONG SHIP, MIGHT SENSE THAT I LIVED, BUT SHE COULD SAY NOTHING WITHOUT REVEALING HERSELF. THAT SHE WOULD NOT DO.
"ON THE EVE OF THE YUUZHAN VONG INVASION, I ESCAPED BACK INTO THE GALAXY.

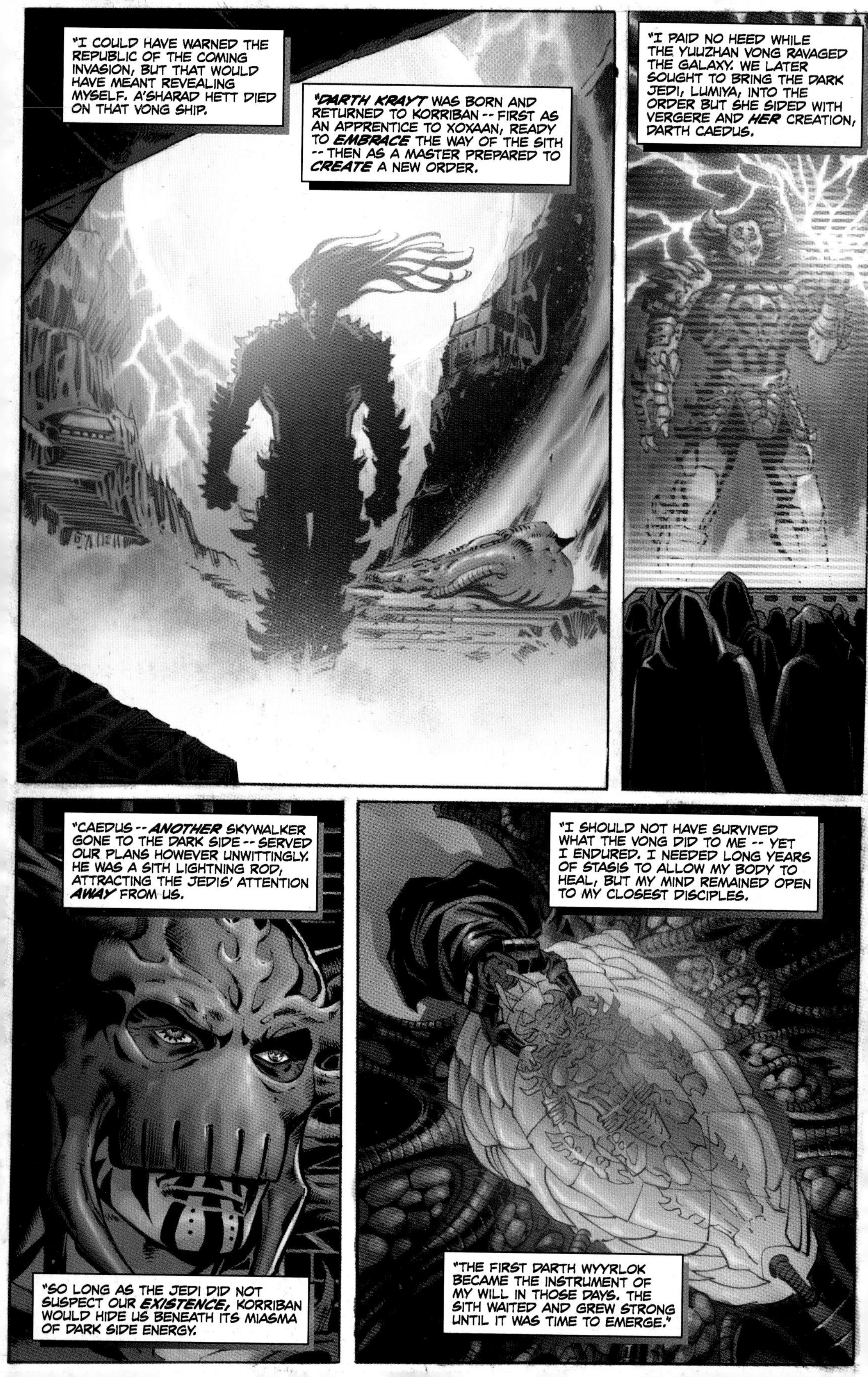
"I COULD HAVE WARNED THE REPUBLIC OF THE COMING INVASION, BUT THAT WOULD HAVE MEANT REVEALING MYSELF. A'SHARAD HETT DIED ON THAT VONG SHIP.
"DARTH KRAYT WAS BORN AND RETURNED TO KORRIBAN -- FIRST AS AN APPRENTICE TO XOXAAN, READY TO EMBRACE THE WAY OF THE SITH -- THEN AS A MASTER PREPARED TO CREATE A NEW ORDER.
"I PAID NO HEED WHILE THE YUUZHAN VONG RAVAGED THE GALAXY. WE LATER SOUGHT TO BRING THE DARK JEDI, LUMIYA, INTO THE ORDER BUT SHE SIDED WITH VERGERE AND HER CREATION, DARTH CAEDUS.
"CAEDUS -- ANOTHER SKYWALKER GONE TO THE DARK SIDE -- SERVED OUR PLANS HOWEVER UNWITTINGLY. HE WAS A SITH LIGHTNING ROD, ATTRACTING THE JEDIS' ATTENTION AWAY FROM US.
"SO LONG AS THE JEDI DID NOT SUSPECT OUR EXISTENCE, KORRIBAN WOULD HIDE US BENEATH ITS MIASMA OF DARK SIDE ENERGY.
"I SHOULD NOT HAVE SURVIVED WHAT THE VONG DID TO ME -- YET I ENDURED. I NEEDED LONG YEARS OF STASIS TO ALLOW MY BODY TO HEAL, BUT MY MIND REMAINED OPEN TO MY CLOSEST DISCIPLES.
"THE FIRST DARTH WYYRLOK BECAME THE INSTRUMENT OF MY WILL IN THOSE DAYS. THE SITH WAITED AND GREW STRONG UNTIL IT WAS TIME TO EMERGE."

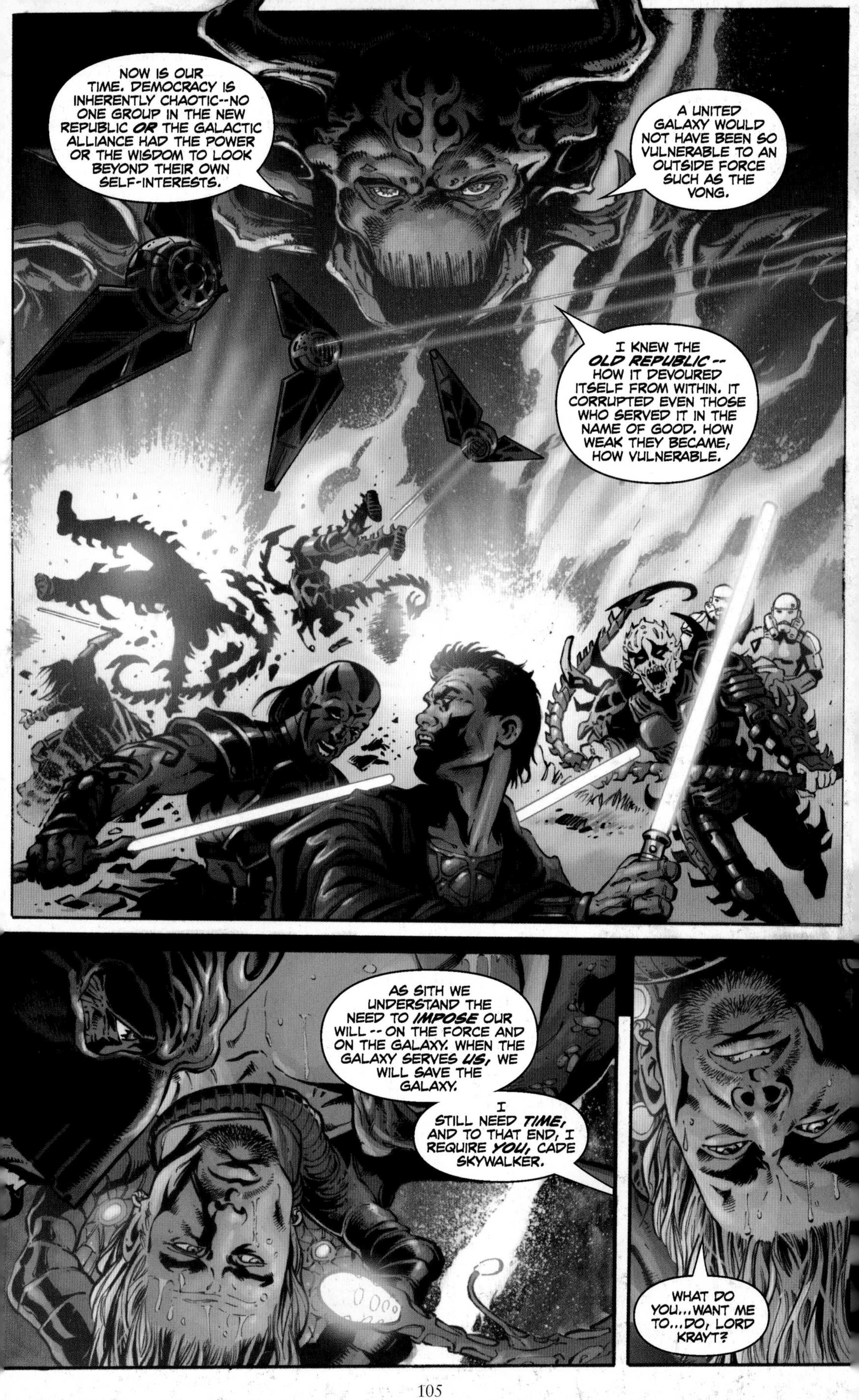
NOW IS OUR TIME. DEMOCRACY IS INHERENTLY CHAOTIC--NO ONE GROUP IN THE NEW REPUBLIC OR THE GALACTIC ALLIANCE HAD THE POWER OR THE WISDOM TO LOOK BEYOND THEIR OWN SELF-INTERESTS.
A UNITED GALAXY WOULD NOT HAVE BEEN SO VULNERABLE TO AN OUTSIDE FORCE SUCH AS THE VONG.
I KNEW THE OLD REPUBLIC -- HOW IT DEVOURED ITSELF FROM WITHIN. IT CORRUPTED EVEN THOSE WHO SERVED IT IN THE NAME OF GOOD. HOW WEAK THEY BECAME, HOW VULNERABLE.
AS SITH WE UNDERSTAND THE NEED TO IMPOSE OUR WILL -- ON THE FORCE AND ON THE GALAXY. WHEN THE GALAXY SERVES US, WE WILL SAVE THE GALAXY.
I STILL NEED TIME, AND TO THAT END, I REQUIRE YOU, CADE SKYWALKER.
WHAT DO YOU...WANT ME TO...DO, LORD KRAYT?

THE GROWTHS CAUSED BY THE CORAL SEEDS THE VONG IMPLANTED IN ME CONTINUE TO GROW. THEY THREATEN TO CONSUME ME. IN ORDER TO REALIZE MY VISION...

...I NEED *HEALING.*

I CAN'T.

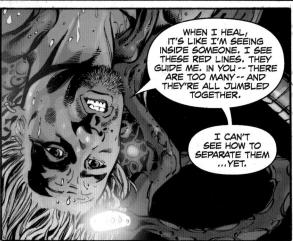

WHEN I HEAL, IT'S LIKE I'M SEEING INSIDE SOMEONE. I SEE THESE RED LINES. THEY GUIDE ME. IN YOU -- THERE ARE TOO MANY -- AND THEY'RE ALL JUMBLED TOGETHER.

I CAN'T SEE HOW TO SEPARATE THEM ...YET.

YOU NEED TO FOCUS YOUR THOUGHTS. THE EMBRACE WILL TEACH YOU THAT. IT WILL BIND THE BROKEN PLACES IN YOU WITH DARK THREADS OF PAIN.

PERHAPS THEN YOU WILL BE ABLE TO TAP INTO THE POWER OF THE DARK SIDE AND BE OF USE TO ME.

THE FIRST TIME DARTH NIHL EXPERIENCED THE EMBRACE, HIS ANGER AND PAIN WERE SO KEEN THAT HE SLEW AN ENTIRE VILLAGE.

THE EMBRACE WILL TEACH YOU PAIN AND FEAR. IT WILL TEACH YOU THE POWER THAT LIES IN HATE. THEN YOU WILL BE PREPARED TO TAKE ON YOUR OWN DARK LEGACY.

BUT FIRST, YOU WILL LEARN DESPAIR...

AAAAAAAA!

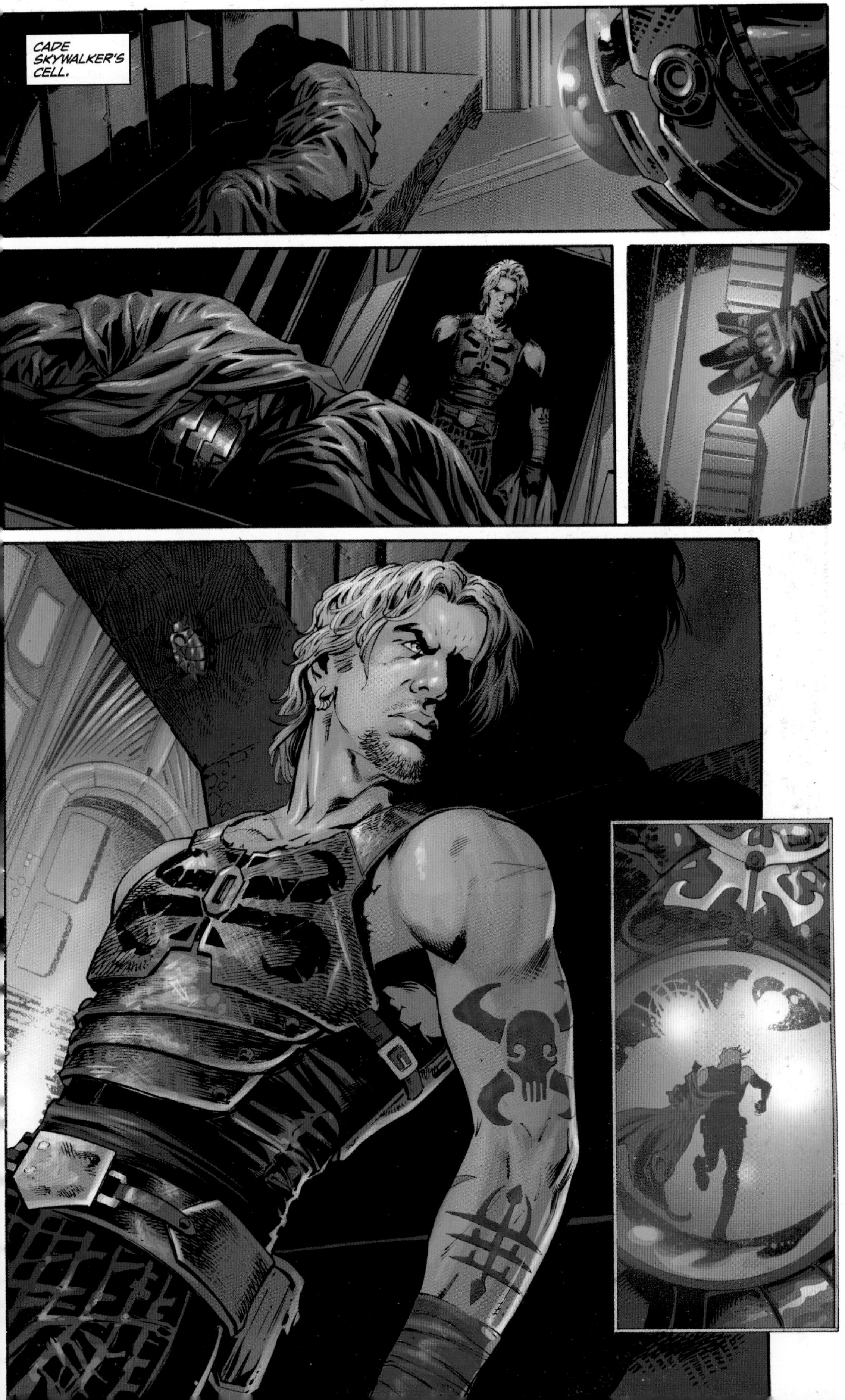
CADE SKYWALKER'S CELL.

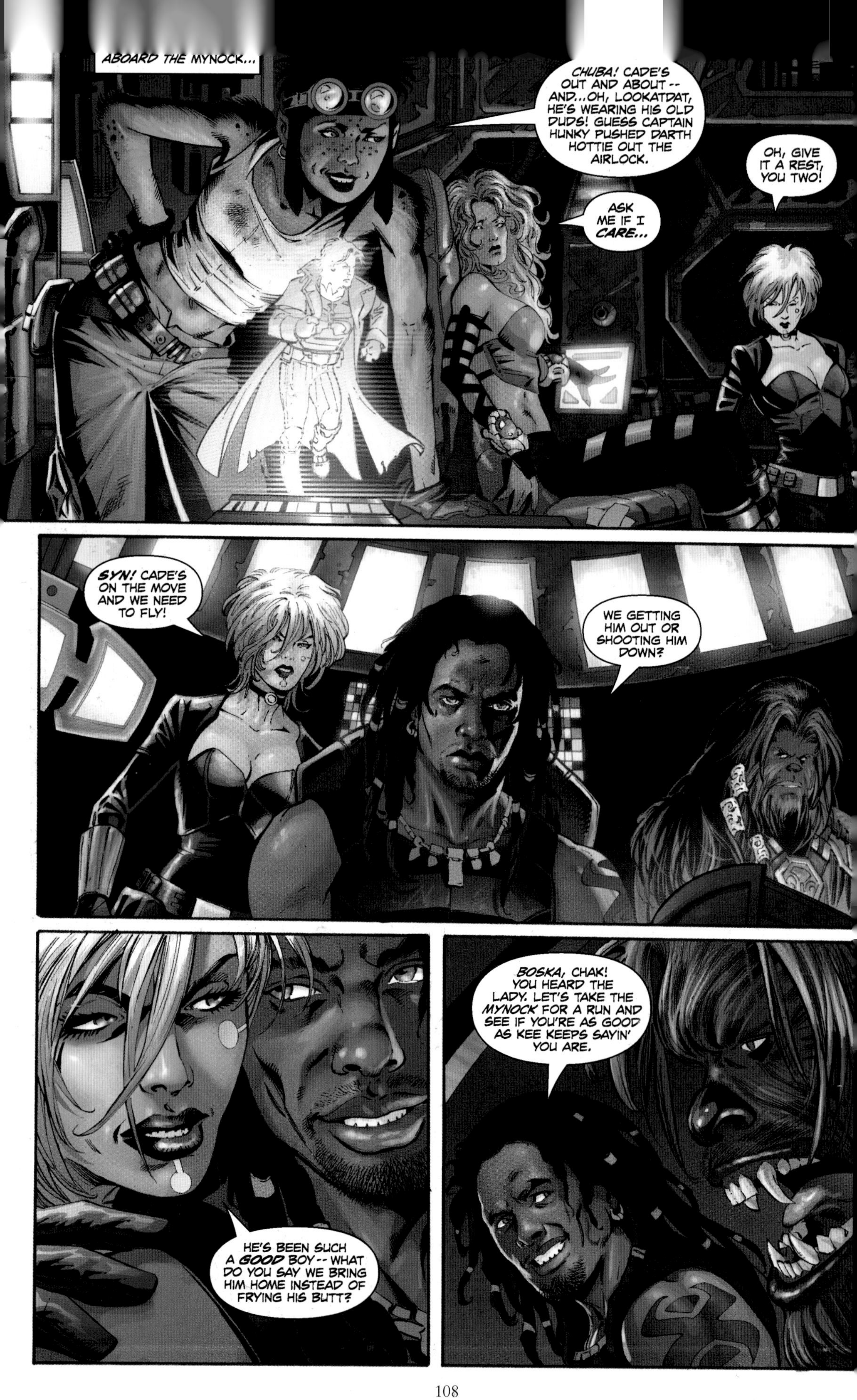
ABOARD THE MYNOCK...
CHUBA! CADE'S OUT AND ABOUT -- AND...OH, LOOKATDAT, HE'S WEARING HIS OLD DUDS! GUESS CAPTAIN HUNKY PUSHED DARTH HOTTIE OUT THE AIRLOCK.
ASK ME IF I CARE...
OH, GIVE IT A REST, YOU TWO!
SYN! CADE'S ON THE MOVE AND WE NEED TO FLY!
WE GETTING HIM OUT OR SHOOTING HIM DOWN?
HE'S BEEN SUCH A GOOD BOY -- WHAT DO YOU SAY WE BRING HIM HOME INSTEAD OF FRYING HIS BUTT?
BOSKA, CHAK! YOU HEARD THE LADY. LET'S TAKE THE MYNOCK FOR A RUN AND SEE IF YOU'RE AS GOOD AS KEE KEEPS SAYIN' YOU ARE.

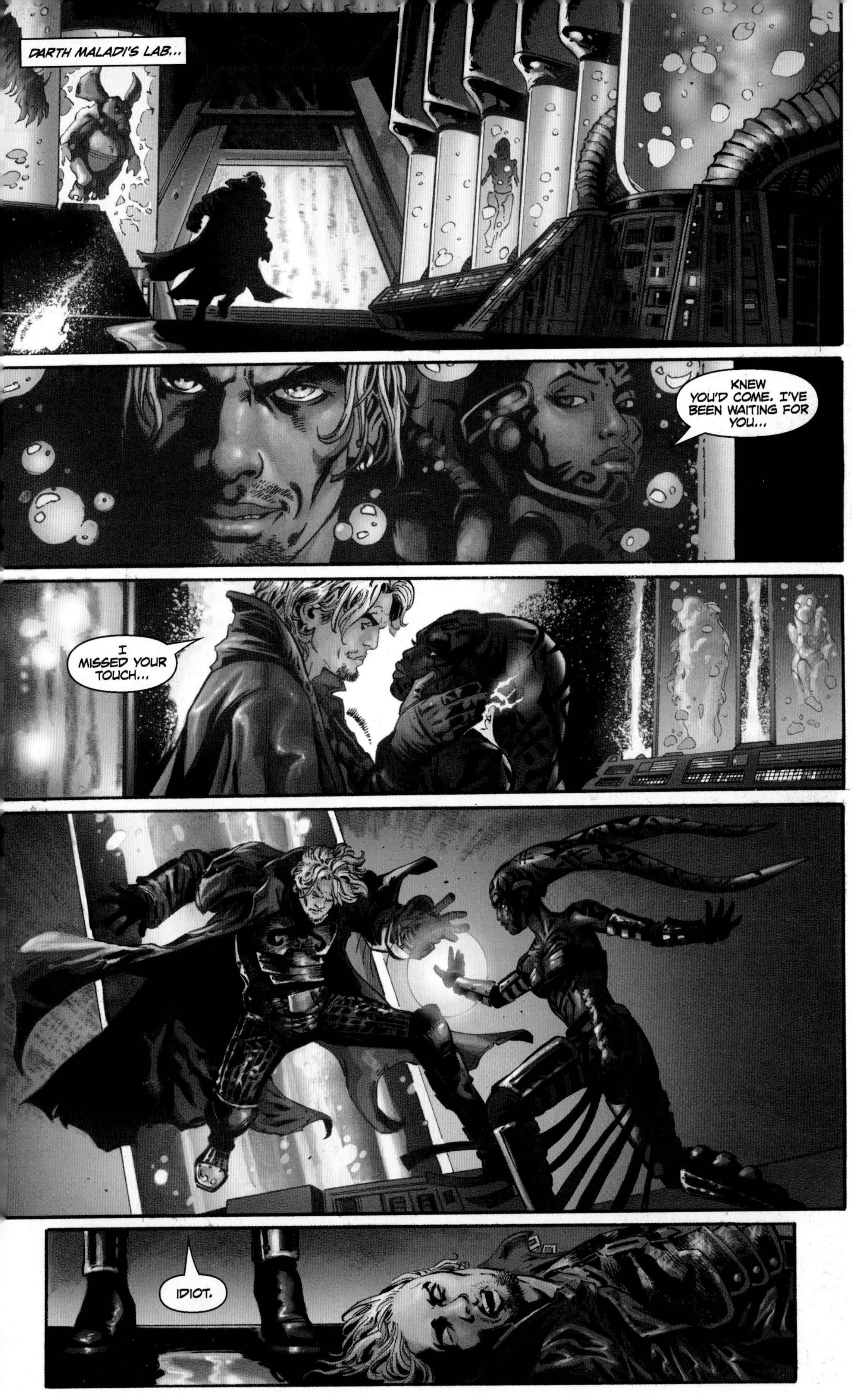
DARTH MALADI'S LAB...
KNEW YOU'D COME. I'VE BEEN WAITING FOR YOU...
I MISSED YOUR TOUCH...
IDIOT.

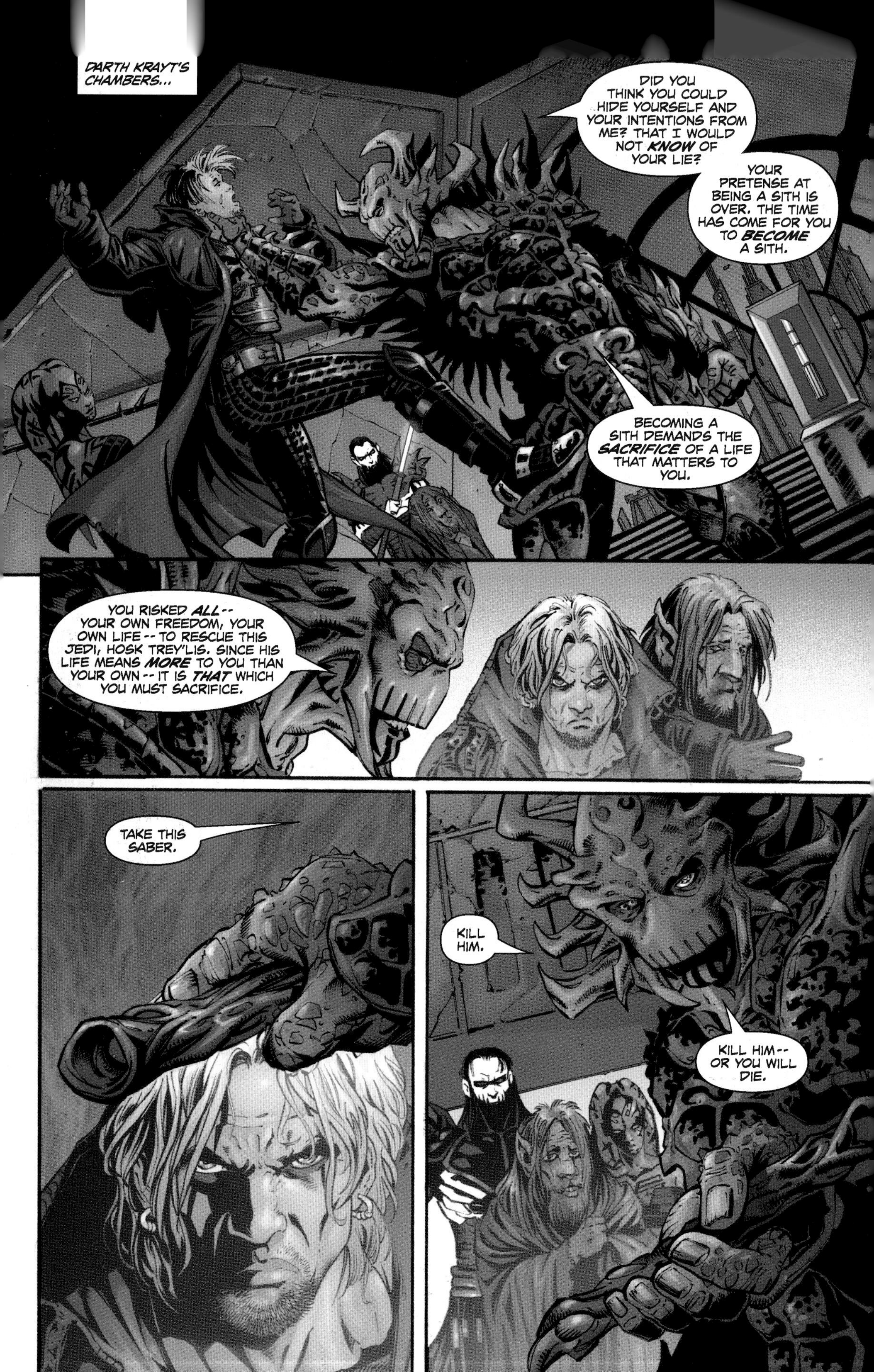
DARTH KRAYT'S CHAMBERS...
DID YOU THINK YOU COULD HIDE YOURSELF AND YOUR INTENTIONS FROM ME? THAT I WOULD NOT KNOW OF YOUR LIE?
YOUR PRETENSE AT BEING A SITH IS OVER. THE TIME HAS COME FOR YOU TO BECOME A SITH.
BECOMING A SITH DEMANDS THE SACRIFICE OF A LIFE THAT MATTERS TO YOU.
YOU RISKED ALL -- YOUR OWN FREEDOM, YOUR OWN LIFE -- TO RESCUE THIS JEDI, HOSK TREY'LIS. SINCE HIS LIFE MEANS MORE TO YOU THAN YOUR OWN -- IT IS THAT WHICH YOU MUST SACRIFICE.
TAKE THIS SABER.
KILL HIM.
KILL HIM -- OR YOU WILL DIE.

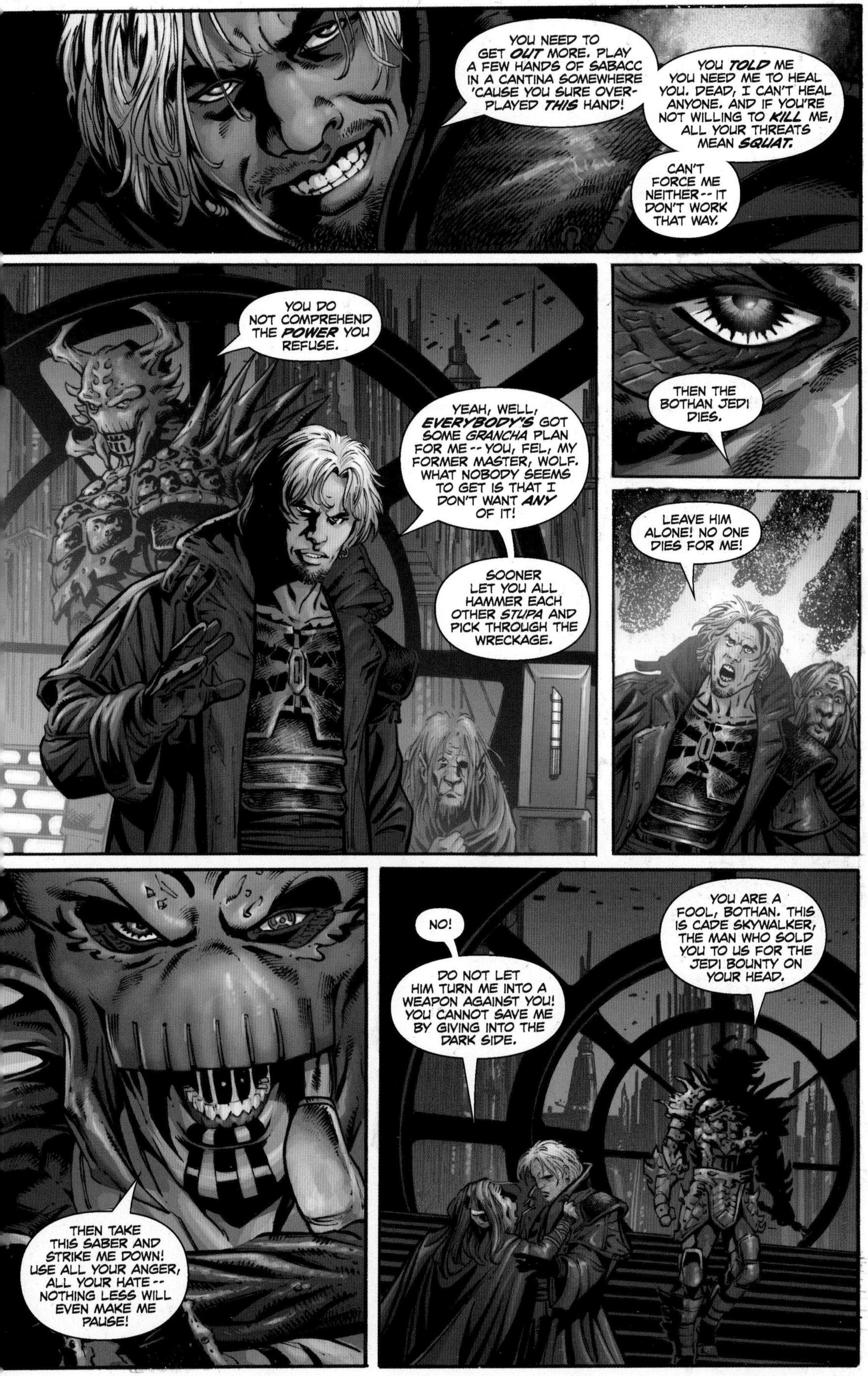
YOU NEED TO GET OUT MORE. PLAY A FEW HANDS OF SABACC IN A CANTINA SOMEWHERE 'CAUSE YOU SURE OVER-PLAYED THIS HAND!
YOU TOLD ME YOU NEED ME TO HEAL YOU. DEAD, I CAN'T HEAL ANYONE. AND IF YOU'RE NOT WILLING TO KILL ME, ALL YOUR THREATS MEAN SQUAT.
CAN'T FORCE ME NEITHER-- IT DON'T WORK THAT WAY.
YOU DO NOT COMPREHEND THE POWER YOU REFUSE.
YEAH, WELL, EVERYBODY'S GOT SOME GRANCHA PLAN FOR ME-- YOU, FEL, MY FORMER MASTER, WOLF. WHAT NOBODY SEEMS TO GET IS THAT I DON'T WANT ANY OF IT!
SOONER LET YOU ALL HAMMER EACH OTHER STUPA AND PICK THROUGH THE WRECKAGE.
THEN THE BOTHAN JEDI DIES.
LEAVE HIM ALONE! NO ONE DIES FOR ME!
THEN TAKE THIS SABER AND STRIKE ME DOWN! USE ALL YOUR ANGER, ALL YOUR HATE-- NOTHING LESS WILL EVEN MAKE ME PAUSE!
NO!
DO NOT LET HIM TURN ME INTO A WEAPON AGAINST YOU! YOU CANNOT SAVE ME BY GIVING INTO THE DARK SIDE.
YOU ARE A FOOL, BOTHAN. THIS IS CADE SKYWALKER, THE MAN WHO SOLD YOU TO US FOR THE JEDI BOUNTY ON YOUR HEAD.

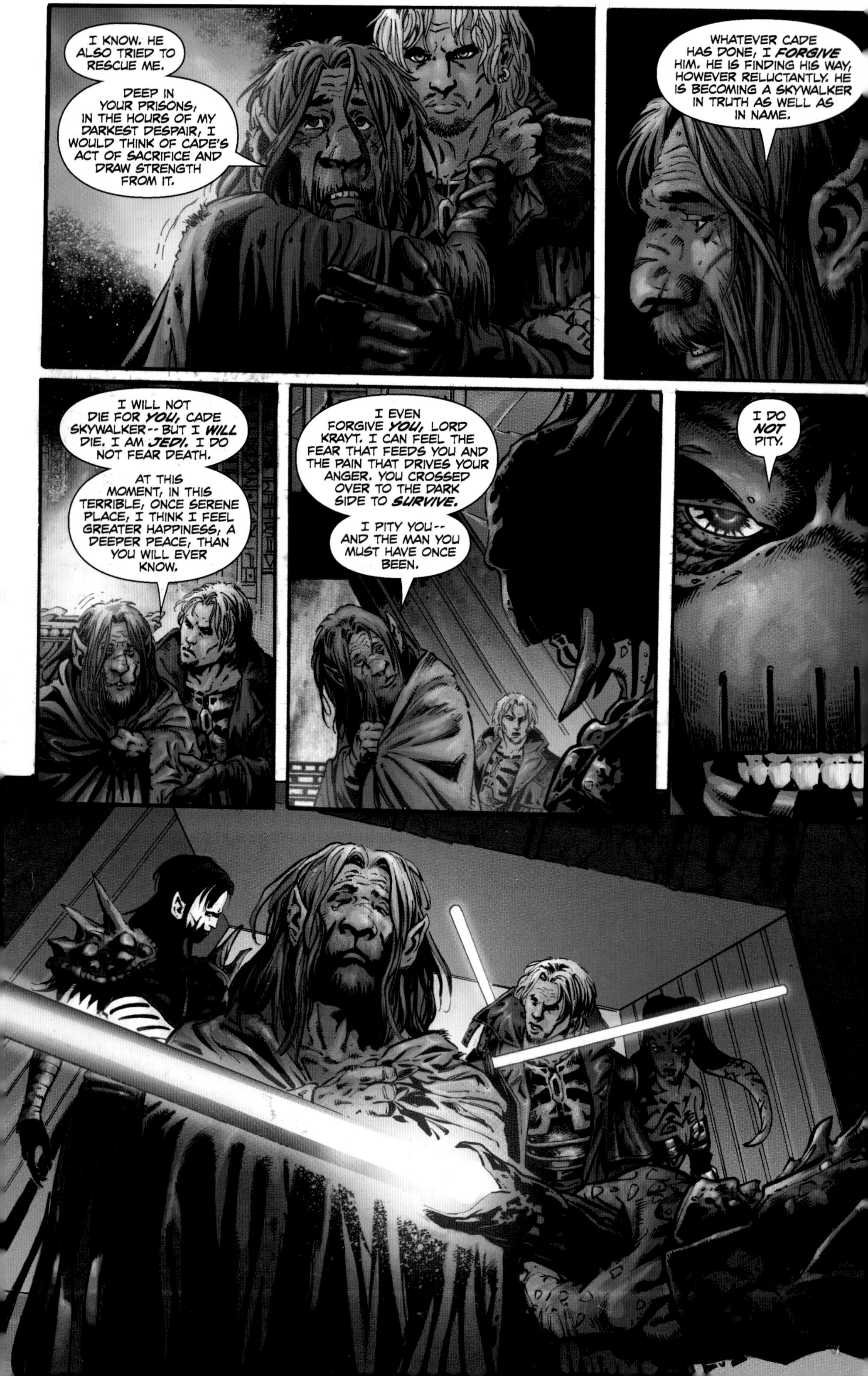
I KNOW. HE ALSO TRIED TO RESCUE ME.
DEEP IN YOUR PRISONS, IN THE HOURS OF MY DARKEST DESPAIR, I WOULD THINK OF CADE'S ACT OF SACRIFICE AND DRAW STRENGTH FROM IT.
WHATEVER CADE HAS DONE, I *FORGIVE* HIM. HE IS FINDING HIS WAY, HOWEVER RELUCTANTLY. HE IS BECOMING A SKYWALKER IN TRUTH AS WELL AS IN NAME.
I WILL NOT DIE FOR *YOU*, CADE SKYWALKER-- BUT I *WILL* DIE. I AM *JEDI*. I DO NOT FEAR DEATH.
AT THIS MOMENT, IN THIS TERRIBLE, ONCE SERENE PLACE, I THINK I FEEL GREATER HAPPINESS, A DEEPER PEACE, THAN YOU WILL EVER KNOW.
I EVEN FORGIVE *YOU*, LORD KRAYT. I CAN FEEL THE FEAR THAT FEEDS YOU AND THE PAIN THAT DRIVES YOUR ANGER. YOU CROSSED OVER TO THE DARK SIDE TO *SURVIVE*.
I PITY YOU-- AND THE MAN YOU MUST HAVE ONCE BEEN.
I DO *NOT* PITY.

HOSK!

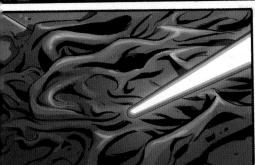

THERE IS NO DEATH. THE FORCE WILL BE WITH YOU, CADE SKYWALKER...

NO!

YOU KARKING SITH MURGLAK!

"NO ONE DIES FOR ME." ISN'T THAT WHAT YOU *SAID*, SKYWALKER? IT'S A *LIE!* YOUR *FATHER* DIED FOR YOU, HOSK TREY'LIS DIED FOR YOU!

KILLED BY THE *SITH!*

I'LL KILL YOU!!!

ANGER! GOOD! TAKE THE SABER! CLAIM YOUR DARK *LEGACY!*

CADE...

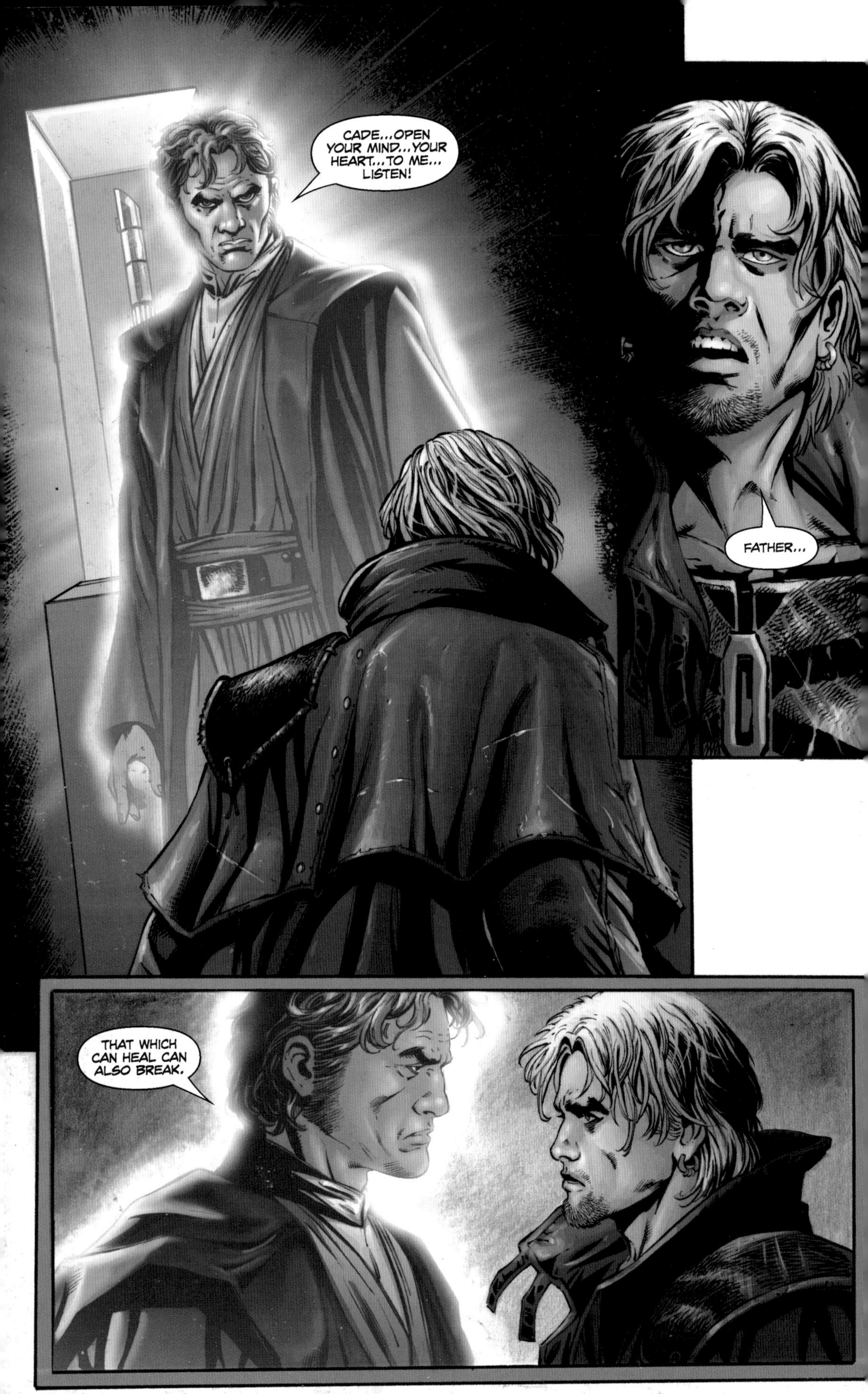
CADE...OPEN YOUR MIND...YOUR HEART...TO ME... LISTEN!
FATHER...
THAT WHICH CAN HEAL CAN ALSO BREAK.

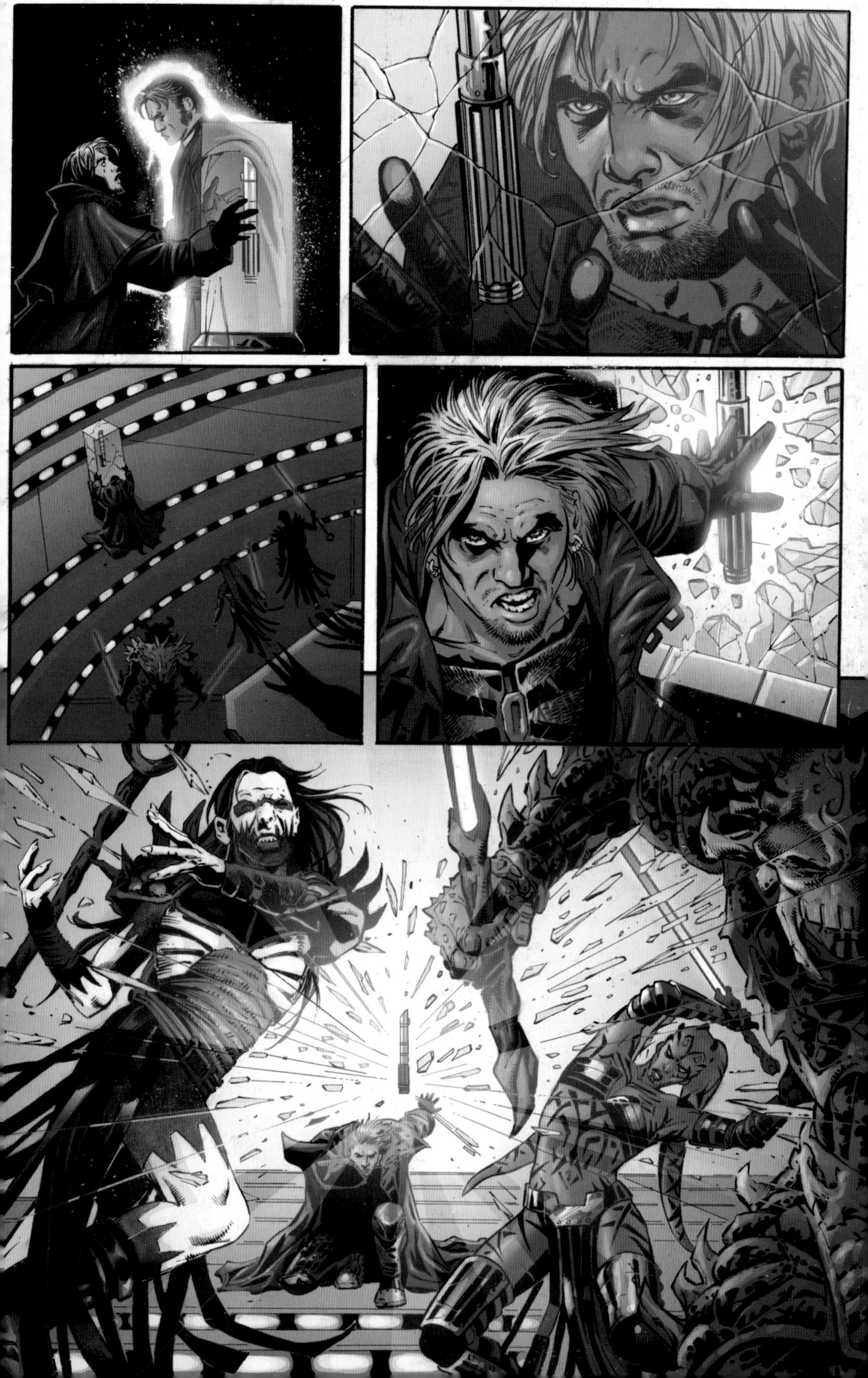

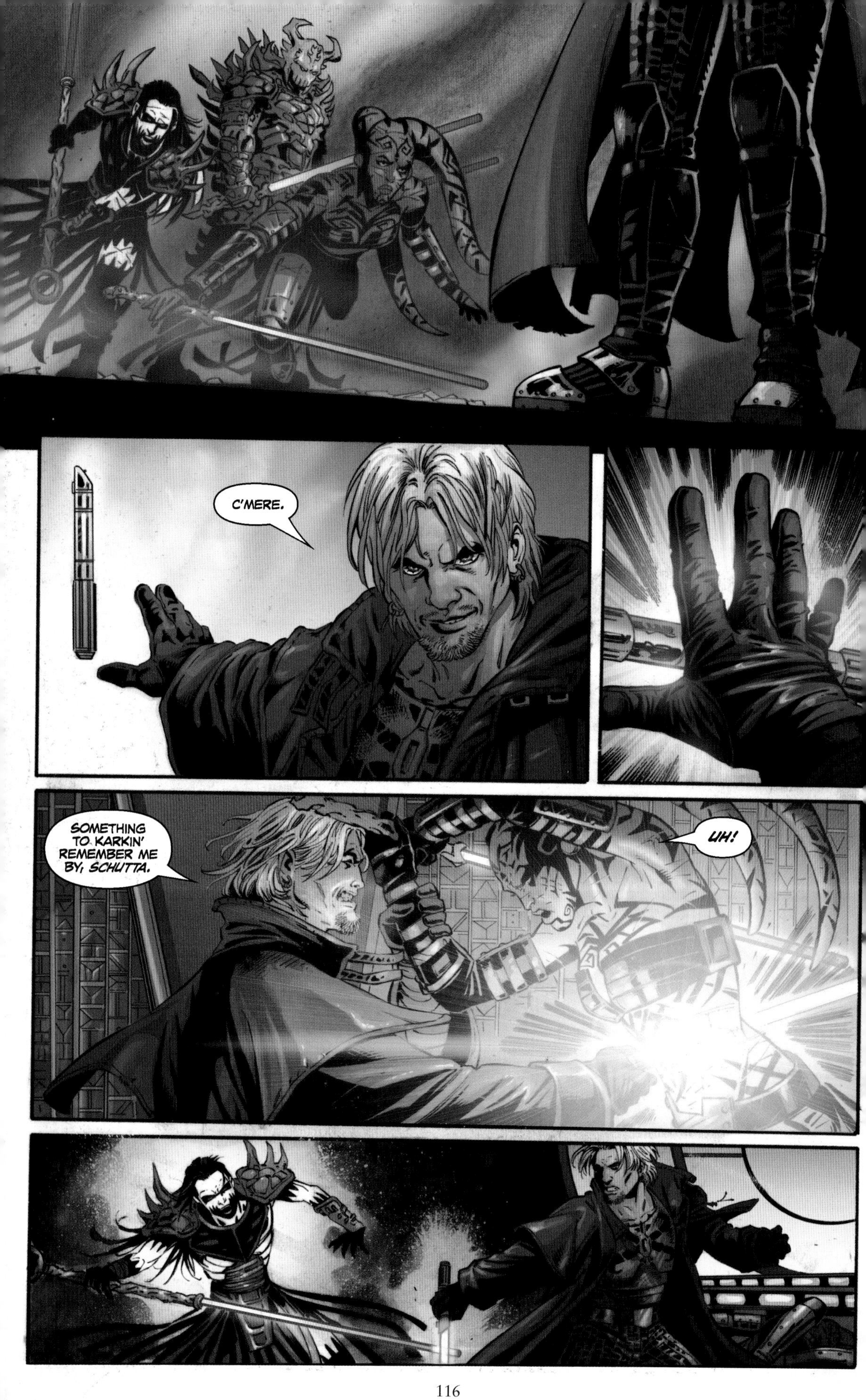
C'MERE.
SOMETHING TO KARKIN' REMEMBER ME BY, SCHUTTA.
UH!

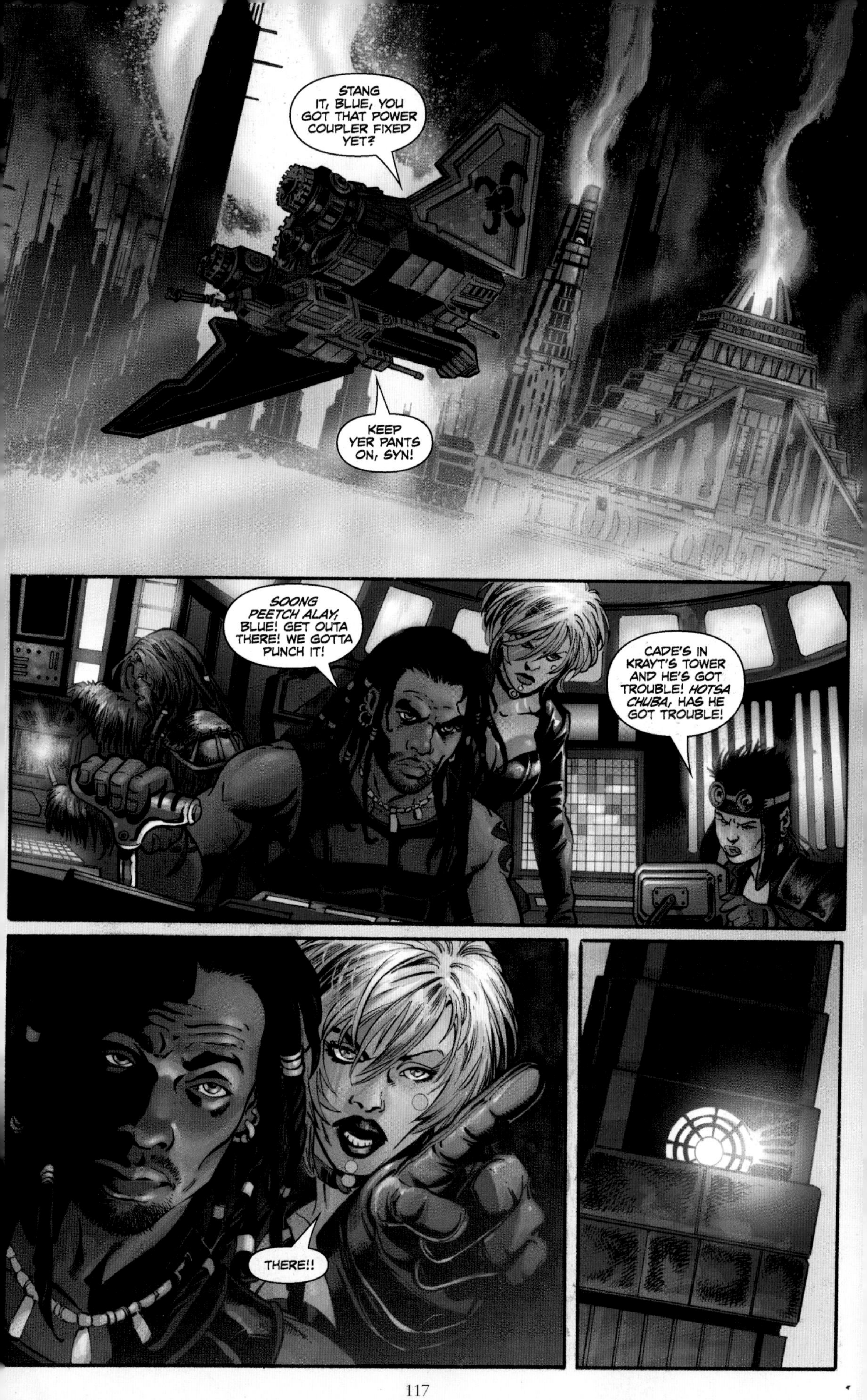
STANG IT, BLUE, YOU GOT THAT POWER COUPLER FIXED YET?
KEEP YER PANTS ON, SYN!
SOONG PEETCH ALAY, BLUE! GET OUTA THERE! WE GOTTA PUNCH IT!
CADE'S IN KRAYT'S TOWER AND HE'S GOT TROUBLE! HOTSA CHUBA, HAS HE GOT TROUBLE!
THERE!!

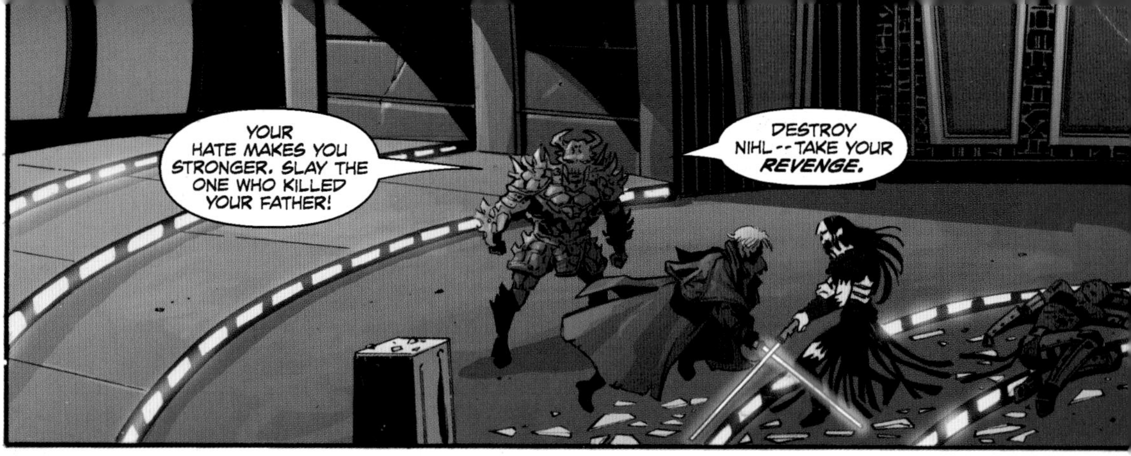
YOUR HATE MAKES YOU STRONGER. SLAY THE ONE WHO KILLED YOUR FATHER!
DESTROY NIHL -- TAKE YOUR REVENGE.
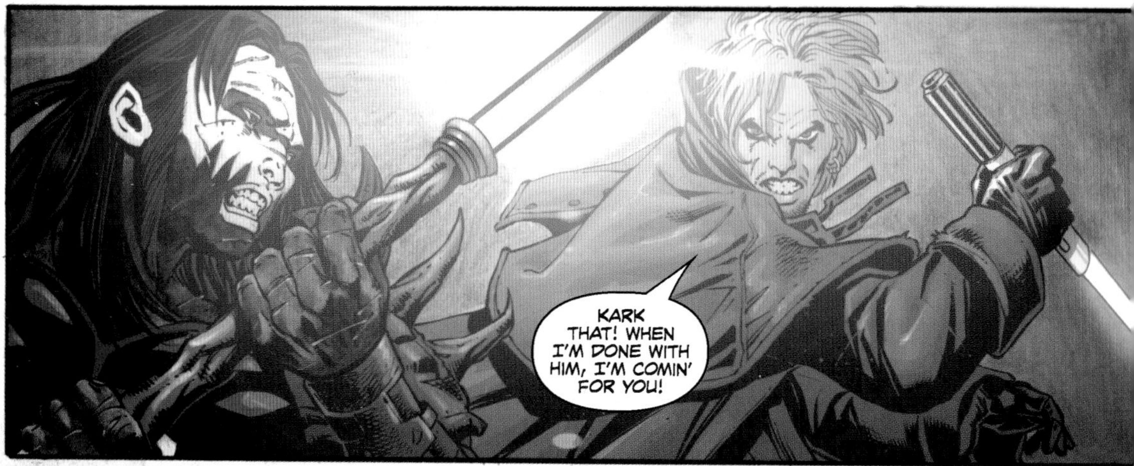
KARK THAT! WHEN I'M DONE WITH HIM, I'M COMIN' FOR YOU!
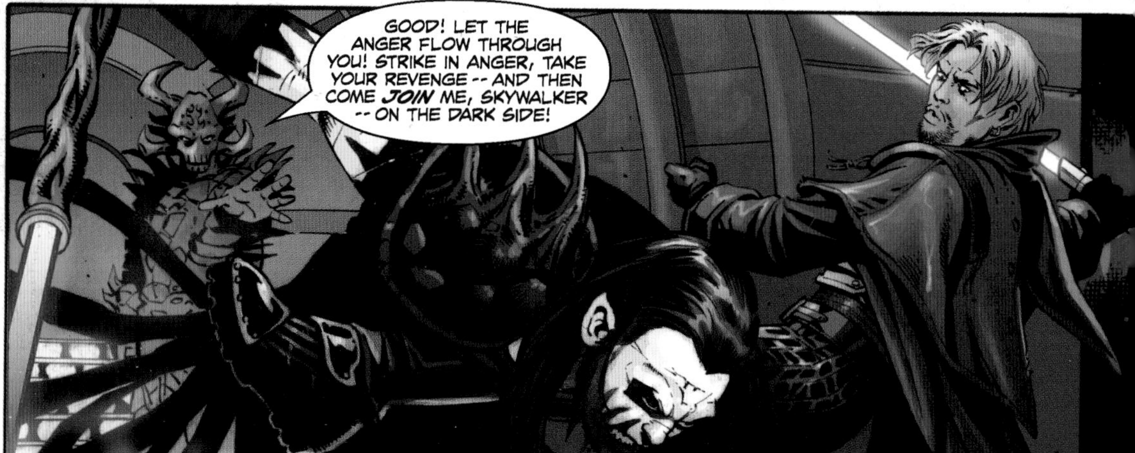
GOOD! LET THE ANGER FLOW THROUGH YOU! STRIKE IN ANGER, TAKE YOUR REVENGE -- AND THEN COME JOIN ME, SKYWALKER -- ON THE DARK SIDE!
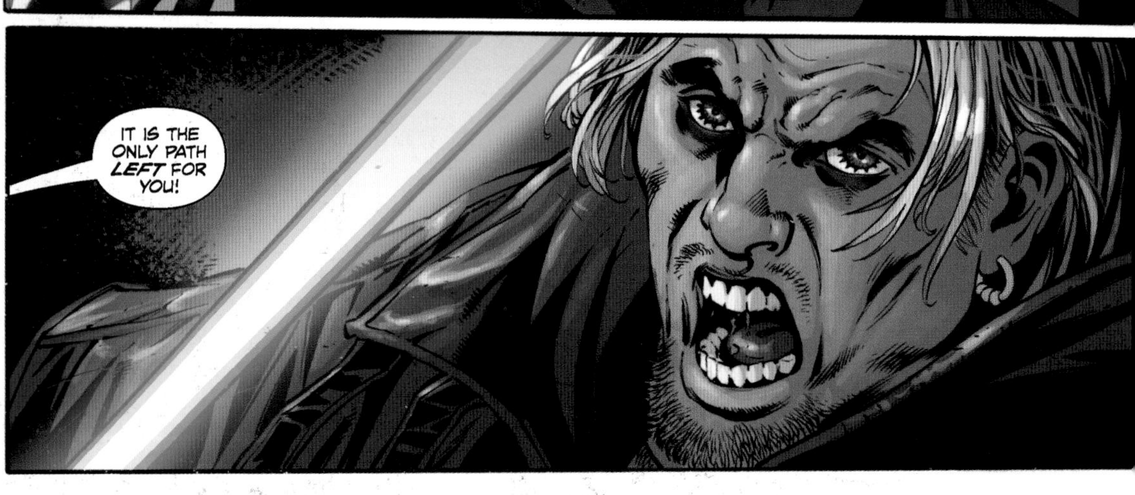
IT IS THE ONLY PATH LEFT FOR YOU!

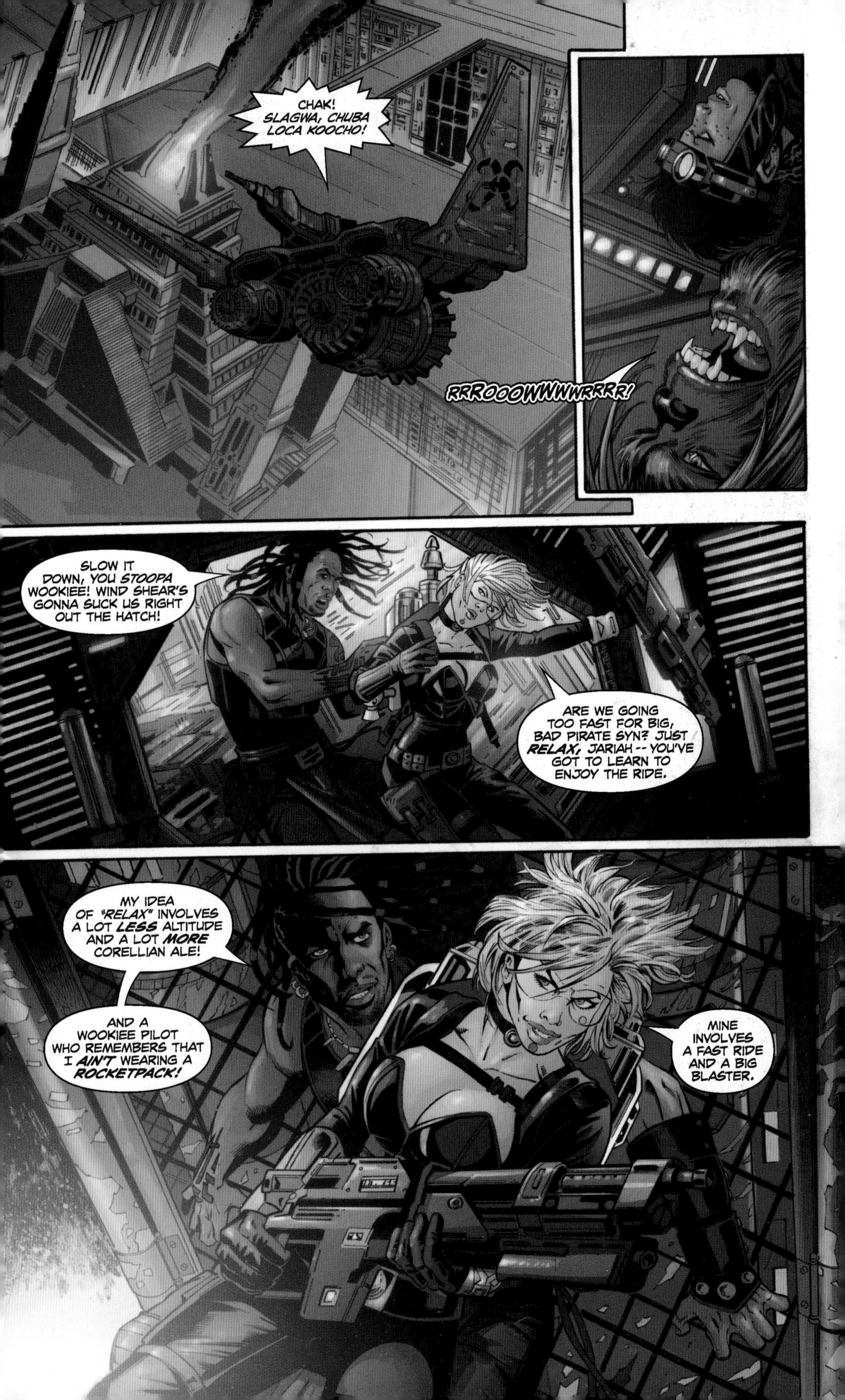
CHAK! SLAGWA, CHUBA LOCA KOOCHO!
RRROOOWWWWRRRR!
SLOW IT DOWN, YOU STOOPA WOOKIEE! WIND SHEAR'S GONNA SUCK US RIGHT OUT THE HATCH!
ARE WE GOING TOO FAST FOR BIG, BAD PIRATE SYN? JUST RELAX, JARIAH -- YOU'VE GOT TO LEARN TO ENJOY THE RIDE.
MY IDEA OF "RELAX" INVOLVES A LOT LESS ALTITUDE AND A LOT MORE CORELLIAN ALE!
AND A WOOKIEE PILOT WHO REMEMBERS THAT I AIN'T WEARING A ROCKETPACK!
MINE INVOLVES A FAST RIDE AND A BIG BLASTER.

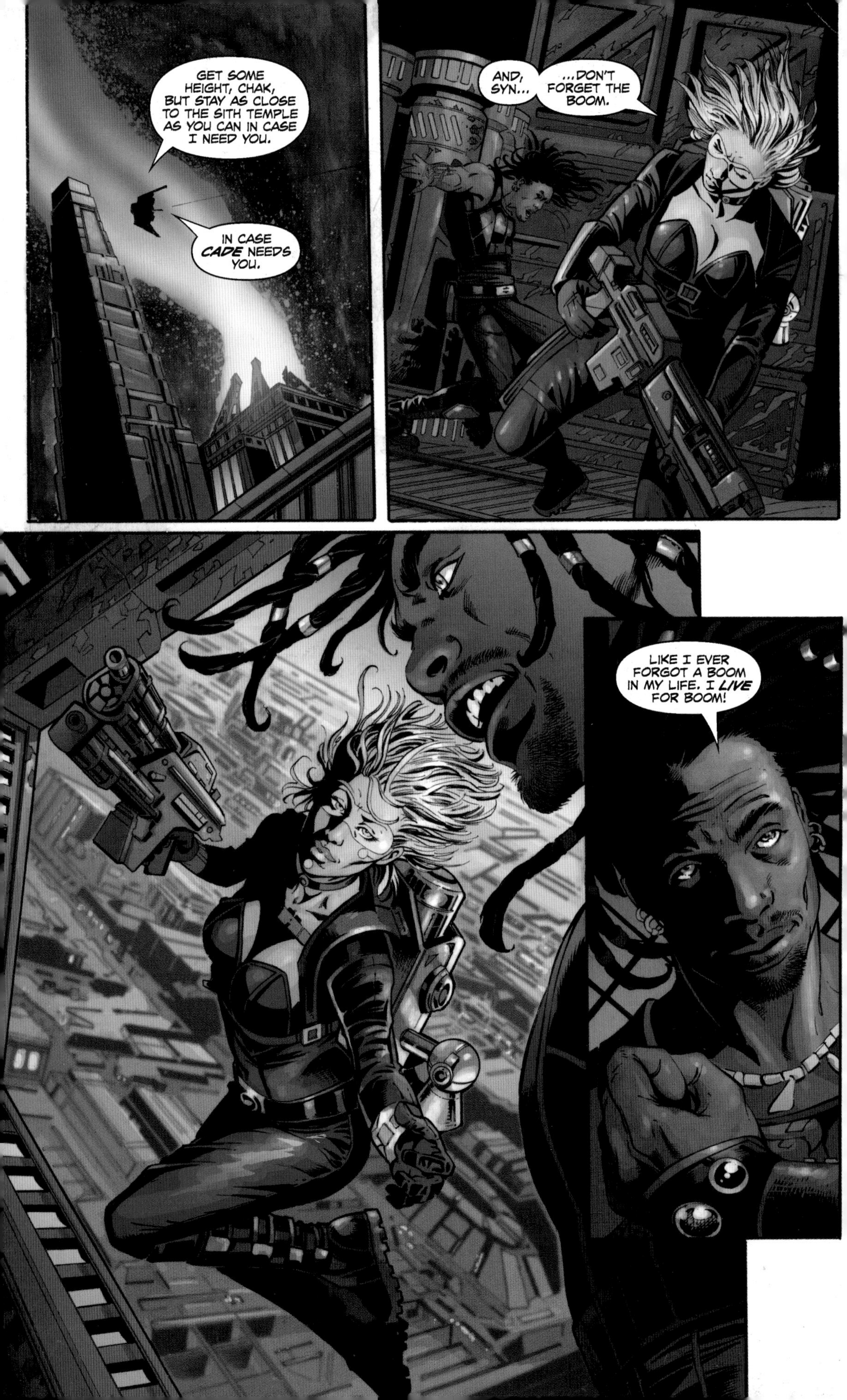
GET SOME HEIGHT, CHAK, BUT STAY AS CLOSE TO THE SITH TEMPLE AS YOU CAN IN CASE I NEED YOU.
IN CASE *CADE* NEEDS YOU.
AND, SYN...
...DON'T FORGET THE BOOM.
LIKE I EVER FORGOT A BOOM IN MY LIFE. I *LIVE* FOR BOOM!

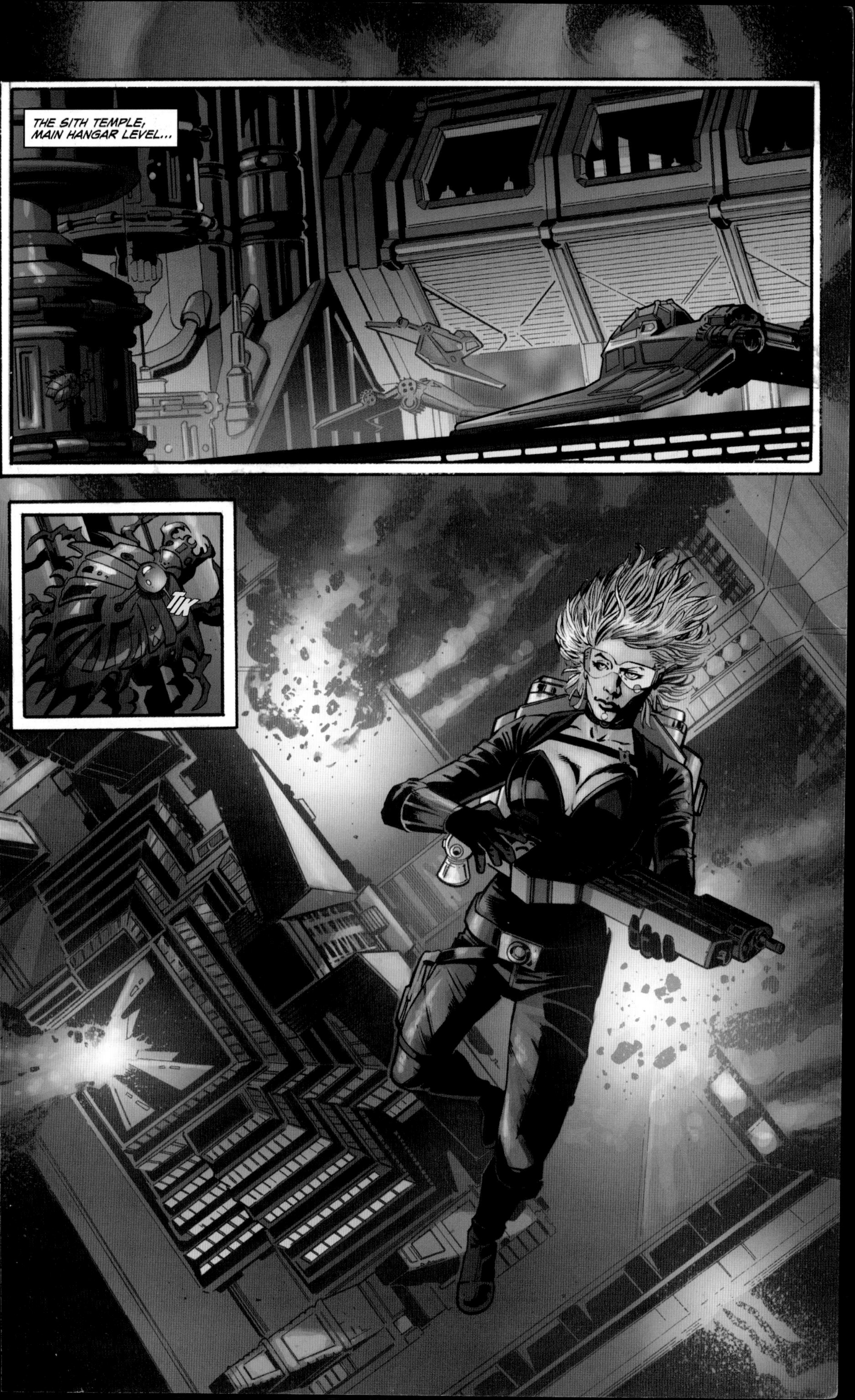
THE SITH TEMPLE,
MAIN HANGAR LEVEL...
TIK

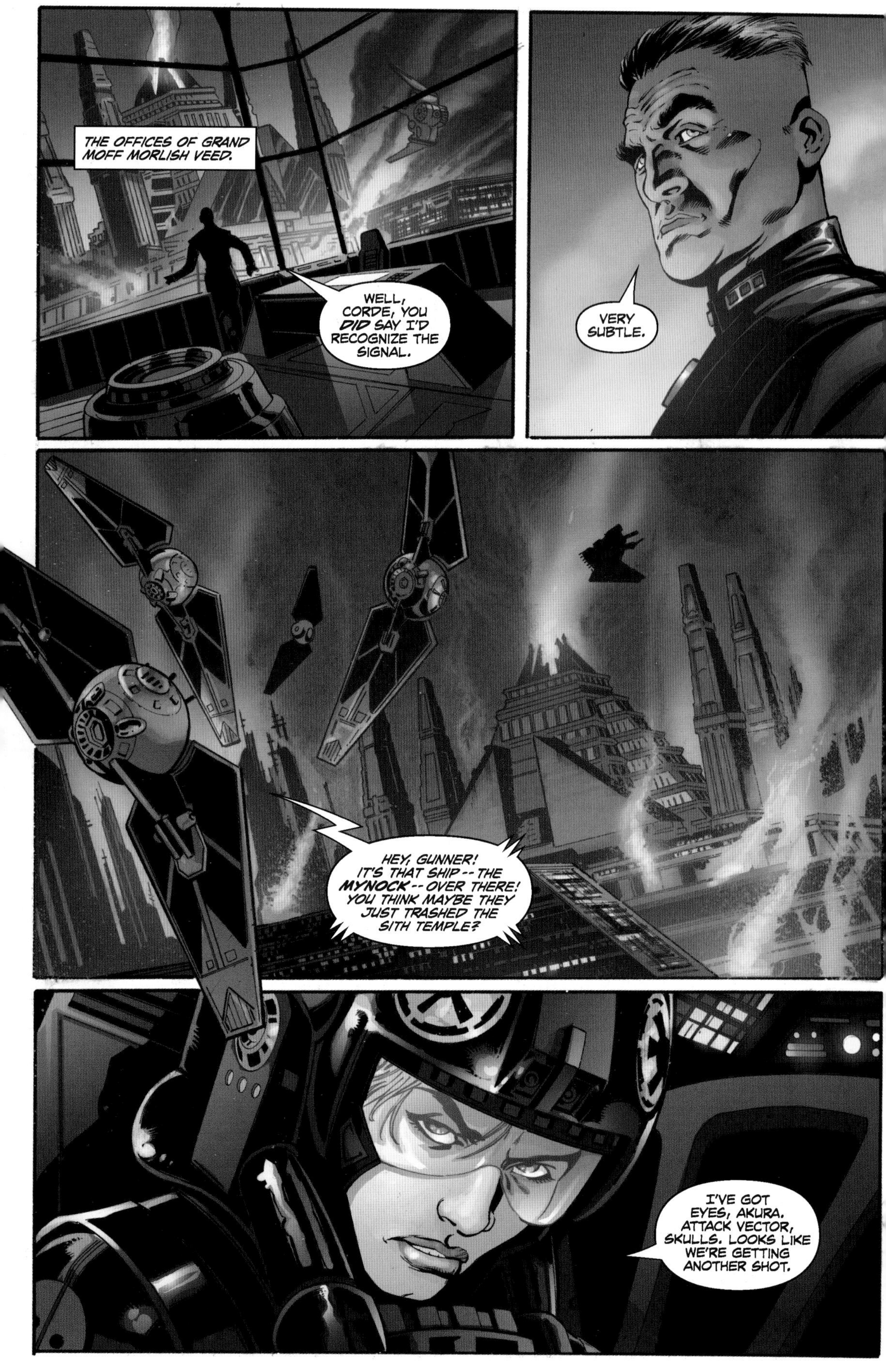

THE OFFICES OF GRAND MOFF MORLISH VEED.
WELL, CORDE, YOU DID SAY I'D RECOGNIZE THE SIGNAL.
VERY SUBTLE.
HEY, GUNNER! IT'S THAT SHIP -- THE MYNOCK -- OVER THERE! YOU THINK MAYBE THEY JUST TRASHED THE SITH TEMPLE?
I'VE GOT EYES, AKURA. ATTACK VECTOR, SKULLS. LOOKS LIKE WE'RE GETTING ANOTHER SHOT.

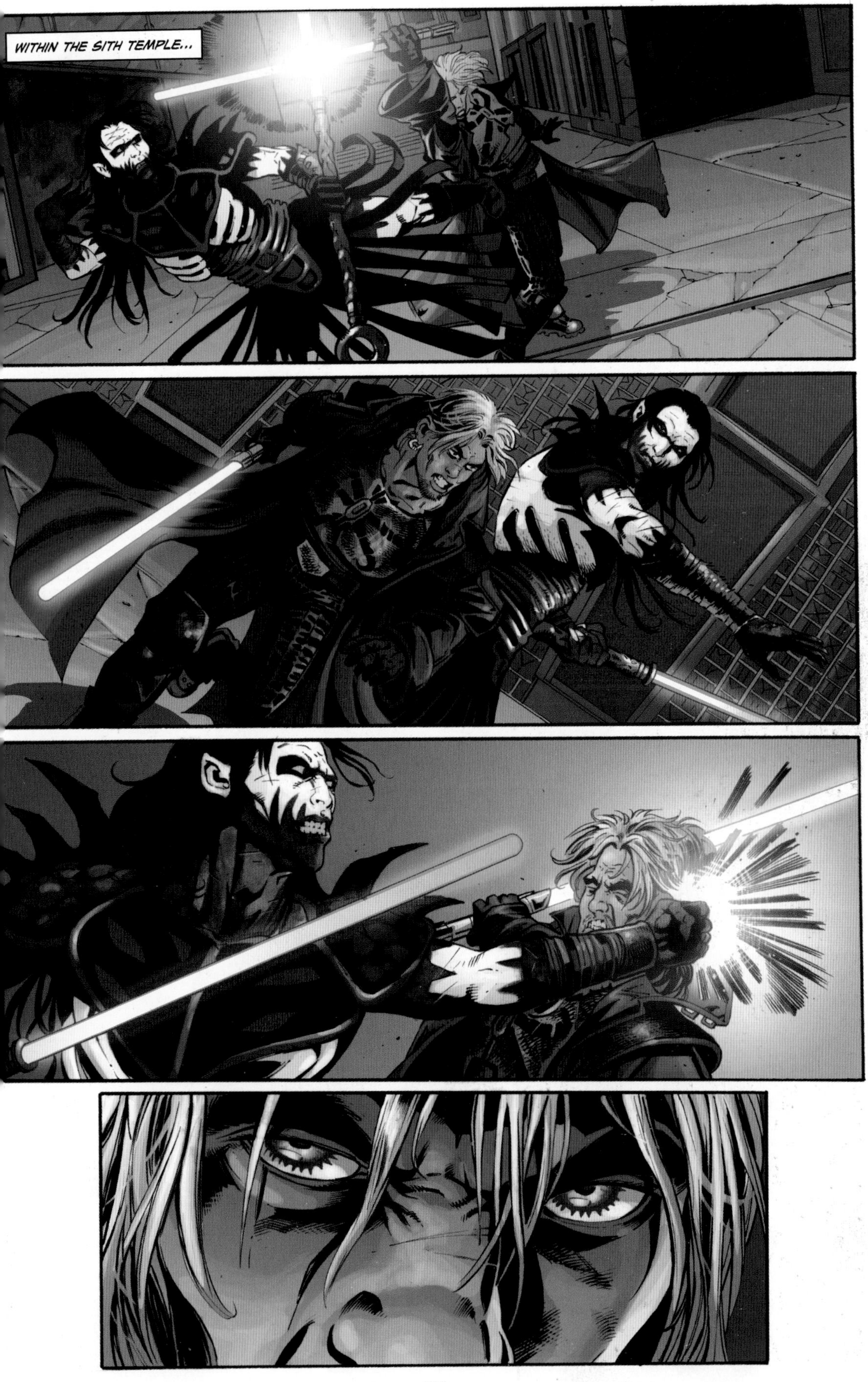
WITHIN THE SITH TEMPLE...

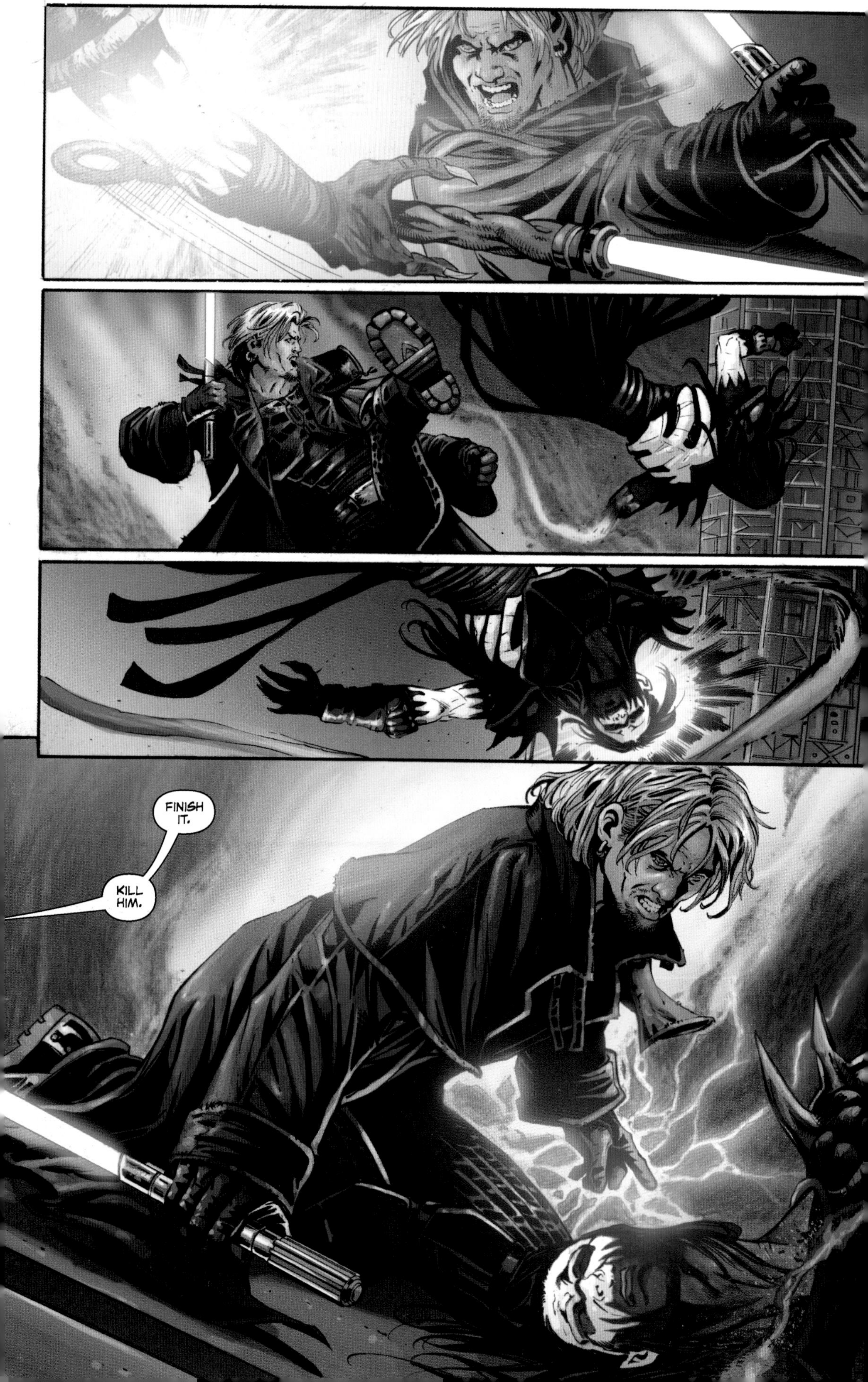
FINISH IT.
KILL HIM.

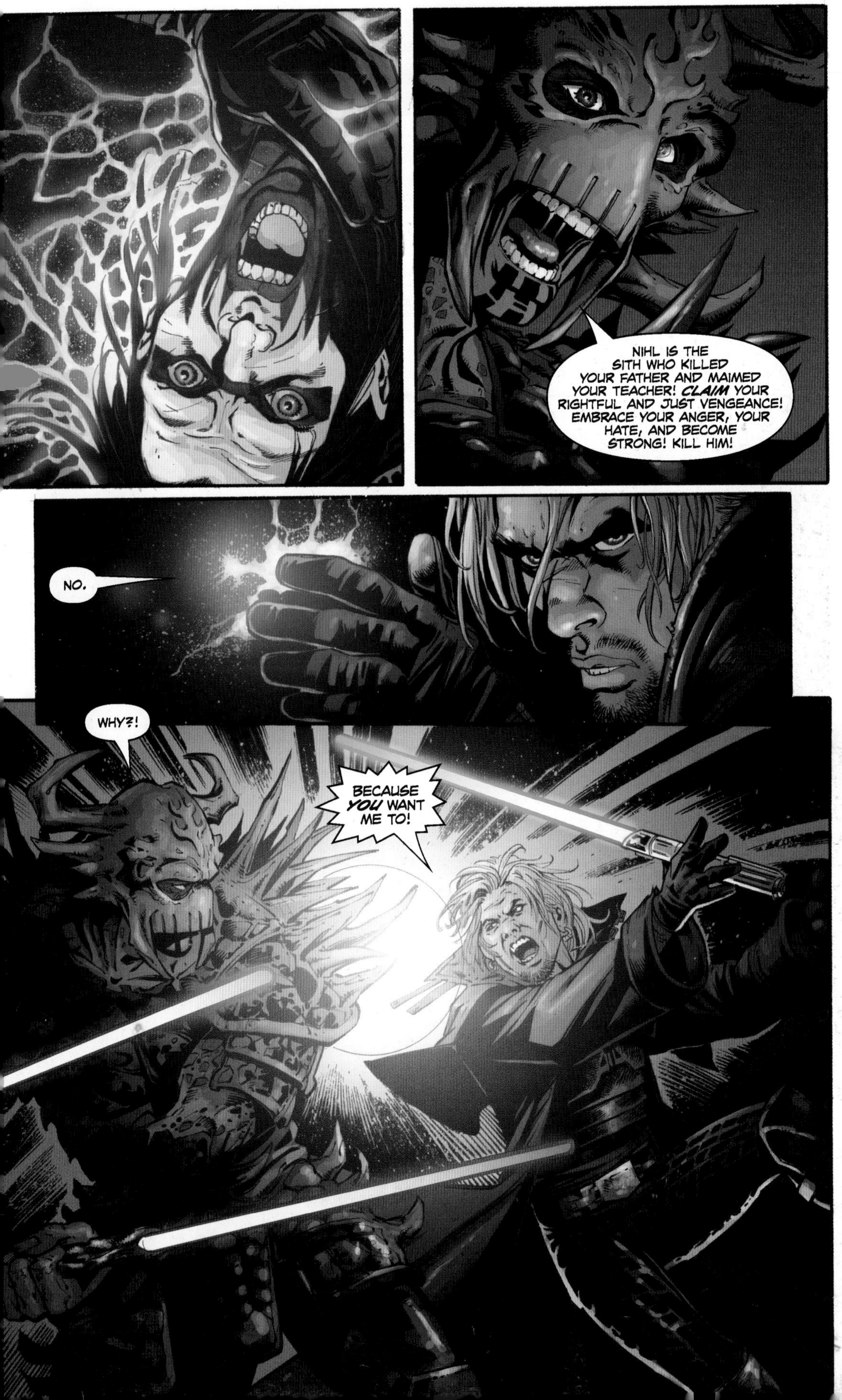
NIHL IS THE SITH WHO KILLED YOUR FATHER AND MAIMED YOUR TEACHER! *CLAIM* YOUR RIGHTFUL AND JUST VENGEANCE! EMBRACE YOUR ANGER, YOUR HATE, AND BECOME STRONG! KILL HIM!
NO.
WHY?!
BECAUSE *YOU* WANT ME TO!

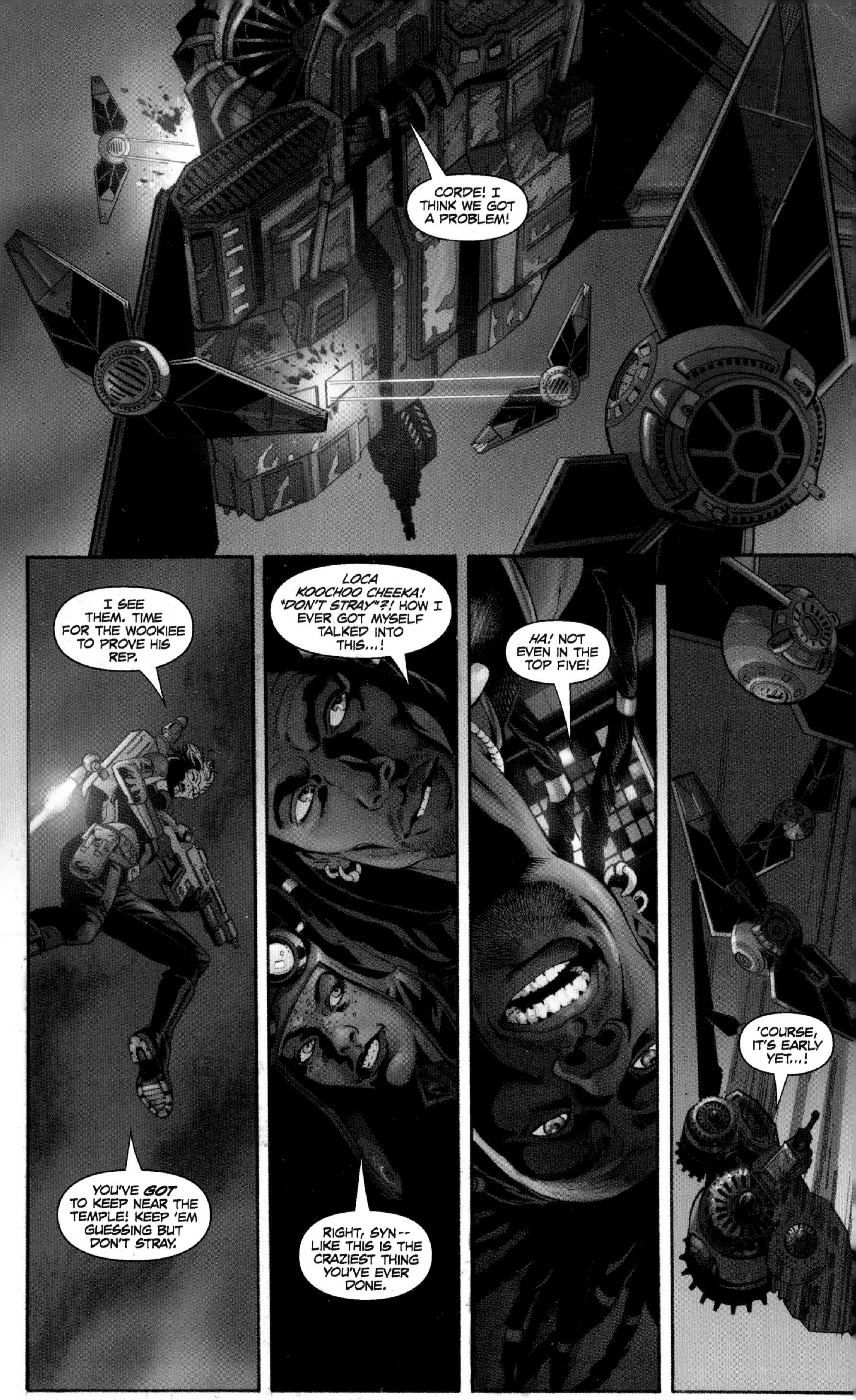
CORDE! I THINK WE GOT A PROBLEM!
I SEE THEM. TIME FOR THE WOOKIEE TO PROVE HIS REP.
YOU'VE GOT TO KEEP NEAR THE TEMPLE! KEEP 'EM GUESSING BUT DON'T STRAY.
LOCA KOOCHOO CHEEKA! "DON'T STRAY"?! HOW I EVER GOT MYSELF TALKED INTO THIS...!
RIGHT, SYN-- LIKE THIS IS THE CRAZIEST THING YOU'VE EVER DONE.
HA! NOT EVEN IN THE TOP FIVE!
'COURSE, IT'S EARLY YET...!

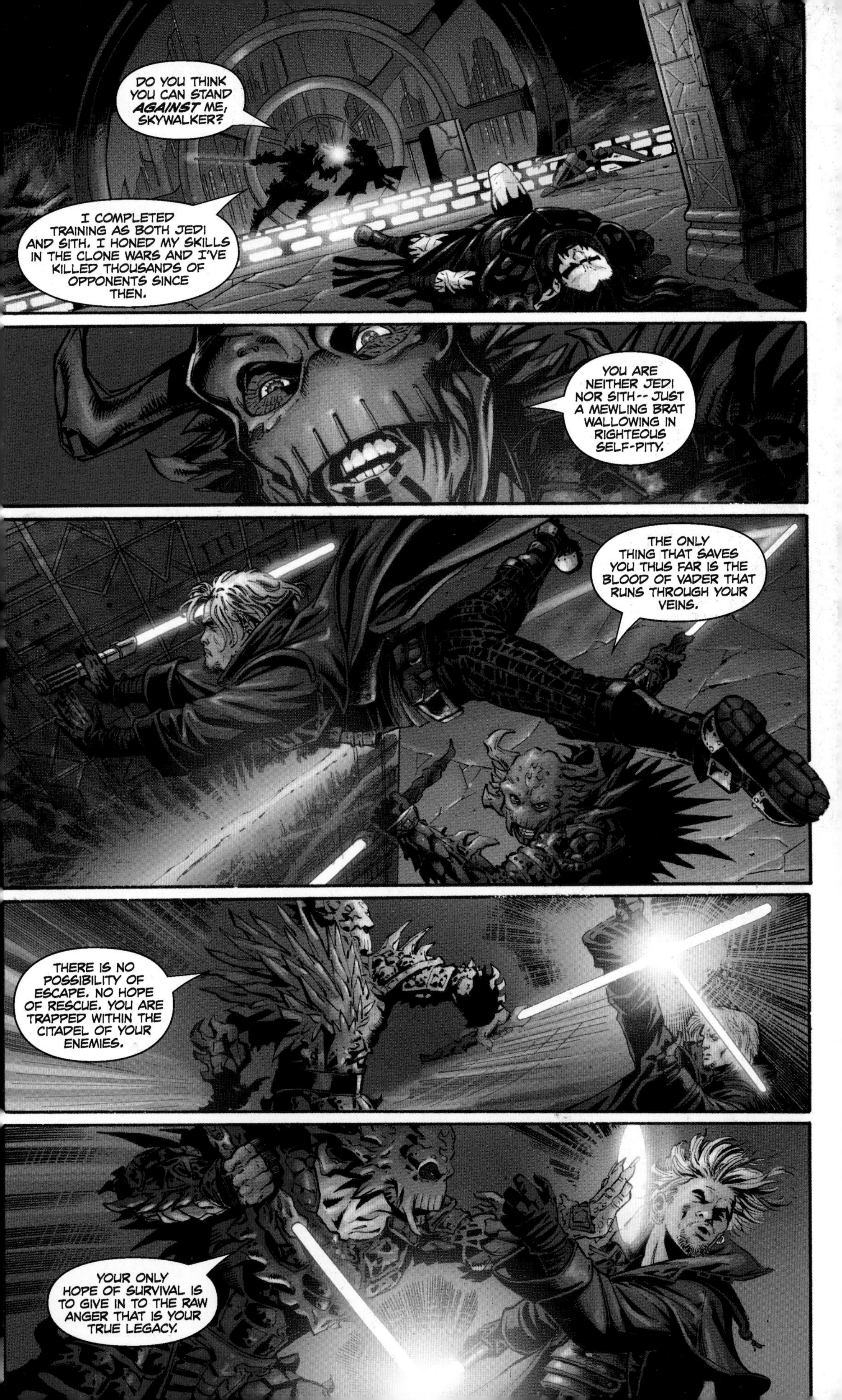

DO YOU THINK YOU CAN STAND AGAINST ME, SKYWALKER?
I COMPLETED TRAINING AS BOTH JEDI AND SITH. I HONED MY SKILLS IN THE CLONE WARS AND I'VE KILLED THOUSANDS OF OPPONENTS SINCE THEN.
YOU ARE NEITHER JEDI NOR SITH-- JUST A MEWLING BRAT WALLOWING IN RIGHTEOUS SELF-PITY.
THE ONLY THING THAT SAVES YOU THUS FAR IS THE BLOOD OF VADER THAT RUNS THROUGH YOUR VEINS.
THERE IS NO POSSIBILITY OF ESCAPE. NO HOPE OF RESCUE. YOU ARE TRAPPED WITHIN THE CITADEL OF YOUR ENEMIES.
YOUR ONLY HOPE OF SURVIVAL IS TO GIVE IN TO THE RAW ANGER THAT IS YOUR TRUE LEGACY.

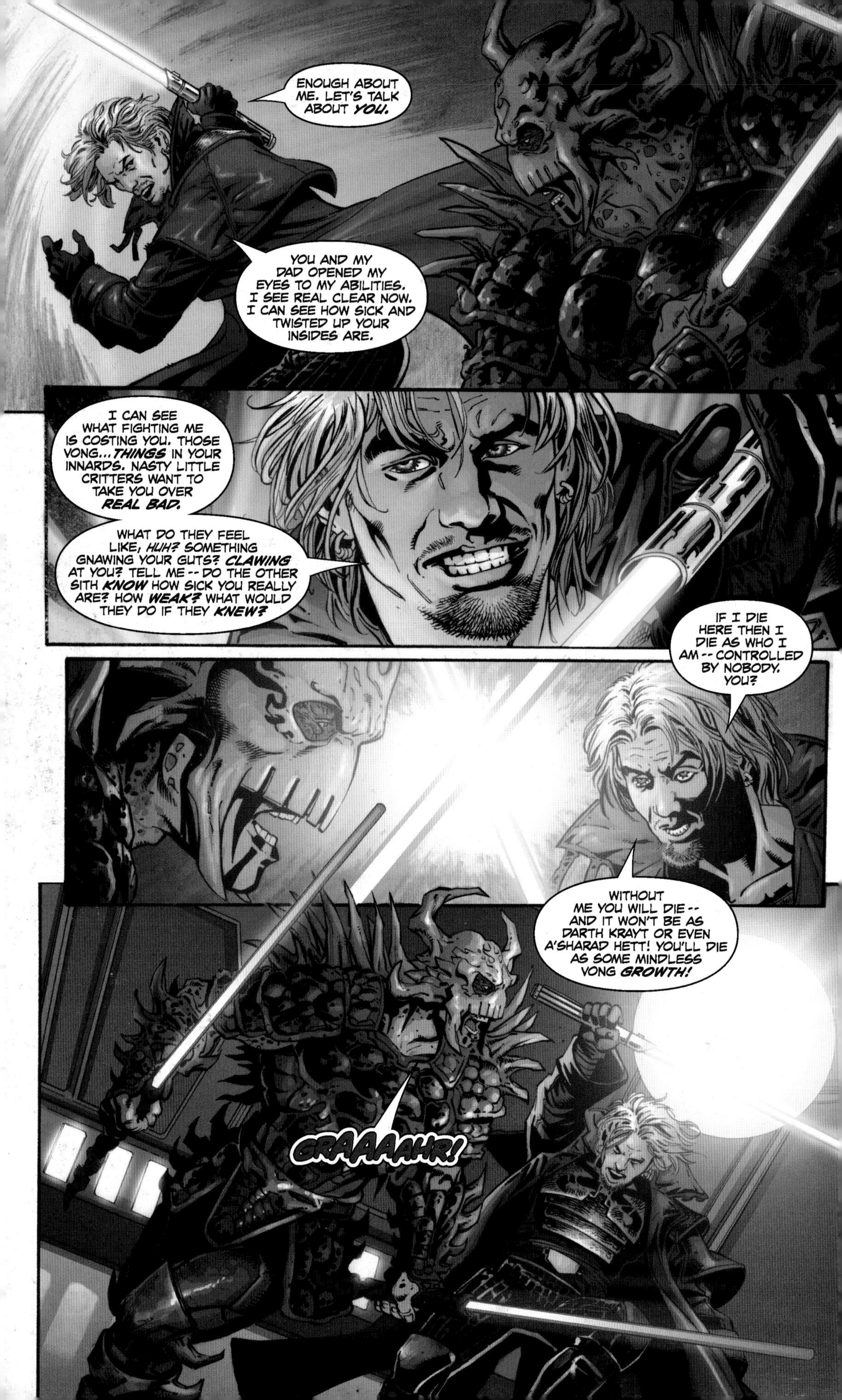

ENOUGH ABOUT ME. LET'S TALK ABOUT YOU.
YOU AND MY DAD OPENED MY EYES TO MY ABILITIES. I SEE REAL CLEAR NOW. I CAN SEE HOW SICK AND TWISTED UP YOUR INSIDES ARE.
I CAN SEE WHAT FIGHTING ME IS COSTING YOU. THOSE VONG...THINGS IN YOUR INNARDS. NASTY LITTLE CRITTERS WANT TO TAKE YOU OVER REAL BAD.
WHAT DO THEY FEEL LIKE, HUH? SOMETHING GNAWING YOUR GUTS? CLAWING AT YOU? TELL ME -- DO THE OTHER SITH KNOW HOW SICK YOU REALLY ARE? HOW WEAK? WHAT WOULD THEY DO IF THEY KNEW?
IF I DIE HERE THEN I DIE AS WHO I AM -- CONTROLLED BY NOBODY. YOU?
WITHOUT ME YOU WILL DIE -- AND IT WON'T BE AS DARTH KRAYT OR EVEN A'SHARAD HETT! YOU'LL DIE AS SOME MINDLESS VONG GROWTH!
GRAAAAHR!

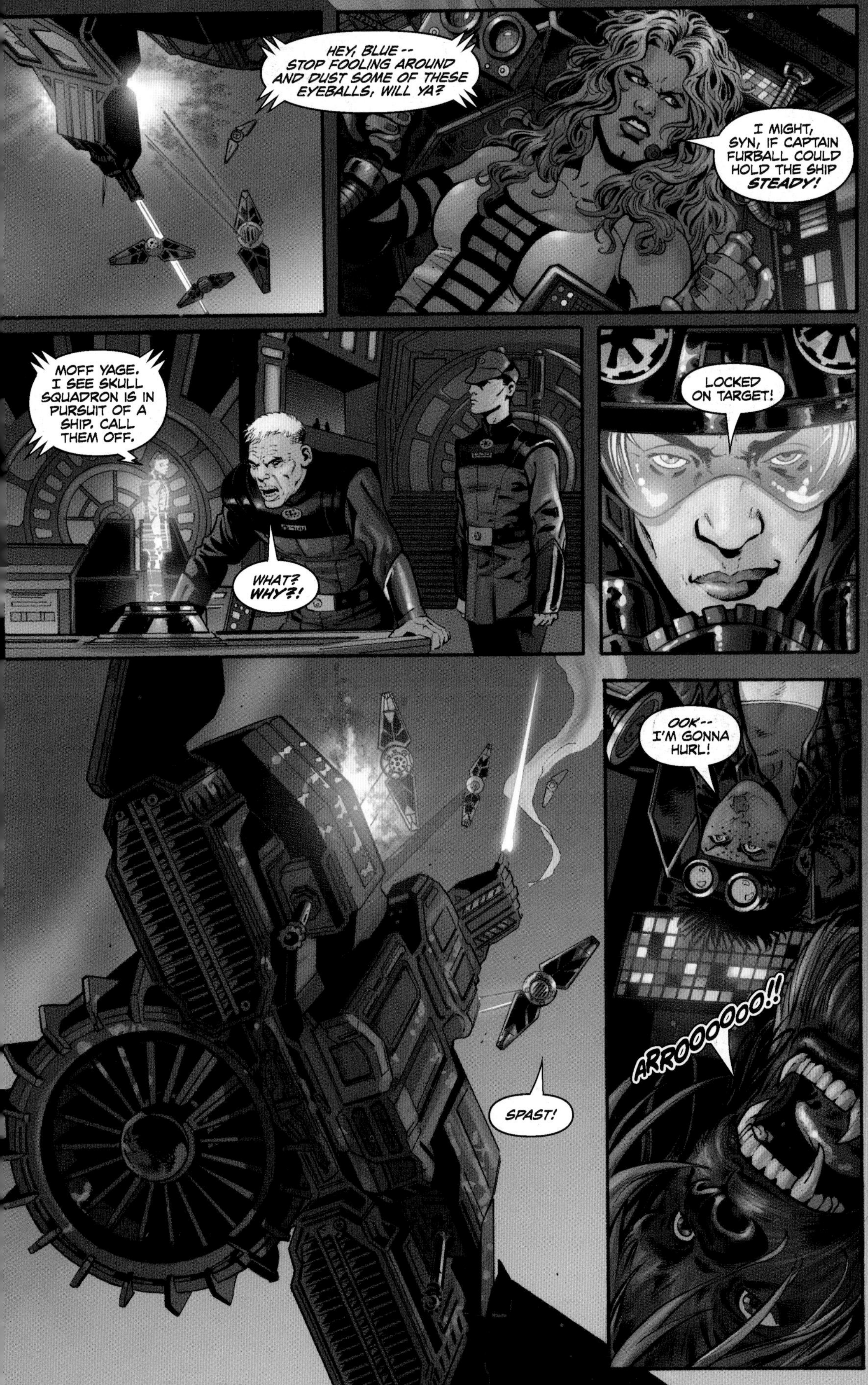
HEY, BLUE -- STOP FOOLING AROUND AND DUST SOME OF THESE EYEBALLS, WILL YA?
I MIGHT, SYN, IF CAPTAIN FURBALL COULD HOLD THE SHIP STEADY!
MOFF YAGE. I SEE SKULL SQUADRON IS IN PURSUIT OF A SHIP. CALL THEM OFF.
WHAT? WHY?!
LOCKED ON TARGET!
OOK-- I'M GONNA HURL!
ARROOOOOOO!!
SPAST!

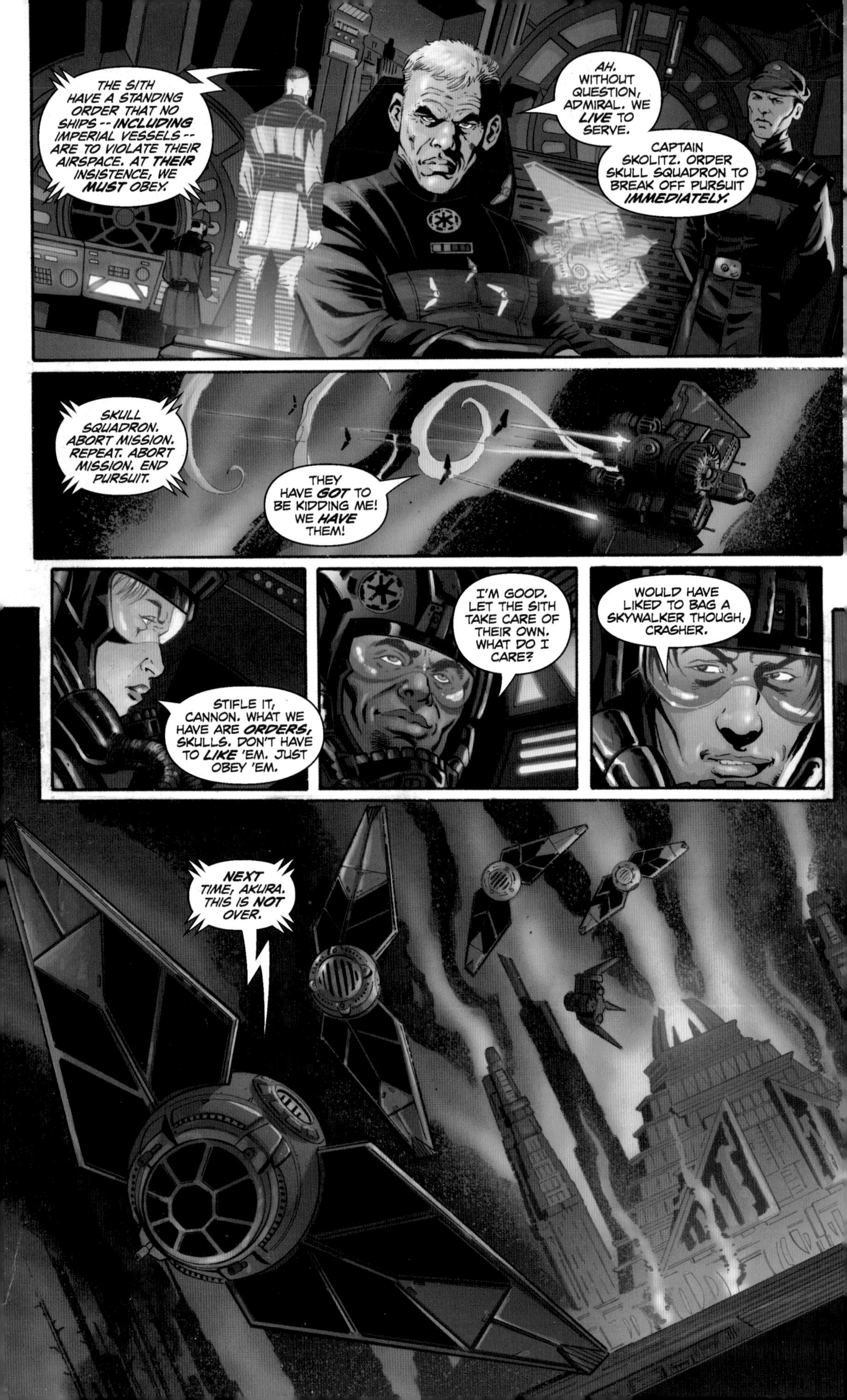

THE SITH HAVE A STANDING ORDER THAT NO SHIPS -- INCLUDING IMPERIAL VESSELS -- ARE TO VIOLATE THEIR AIRSPACE. AT THEIR INSISTENCE, WE MUST OBEY.
AH. WITHOUT QUESTION, ADMIRAL. WE LIVE TO SERVE.
CAPTAIN SKOLITZ. ORDER SKULL SQUADRON TO BREAK OFF PURSUIT IMMEDIATELY.
SKULL SQUADRON. ABORT MISSION. REPEAT. ABORT MISSION. END PURSUIT.
THEY HAVE GOT TO BE KIDDING ME! WE HAVE THEM!
STIFLE IT, CANNON. WHAT WE HAVE ARE ORDERS, SKULLS. DON'T HAVE TO LIKE 'EM. JUST OBEY 'EM.
I'M GOOD. LET THE SITH TAKE CARE OF THEIR OWN. WHAT DO I CARE?
WOULD HAVE LIKED TO BAG A SKYWALKER THOUGH, CRASHER.
NEXT TIME, AKURA. THIS IS NOT OVER.

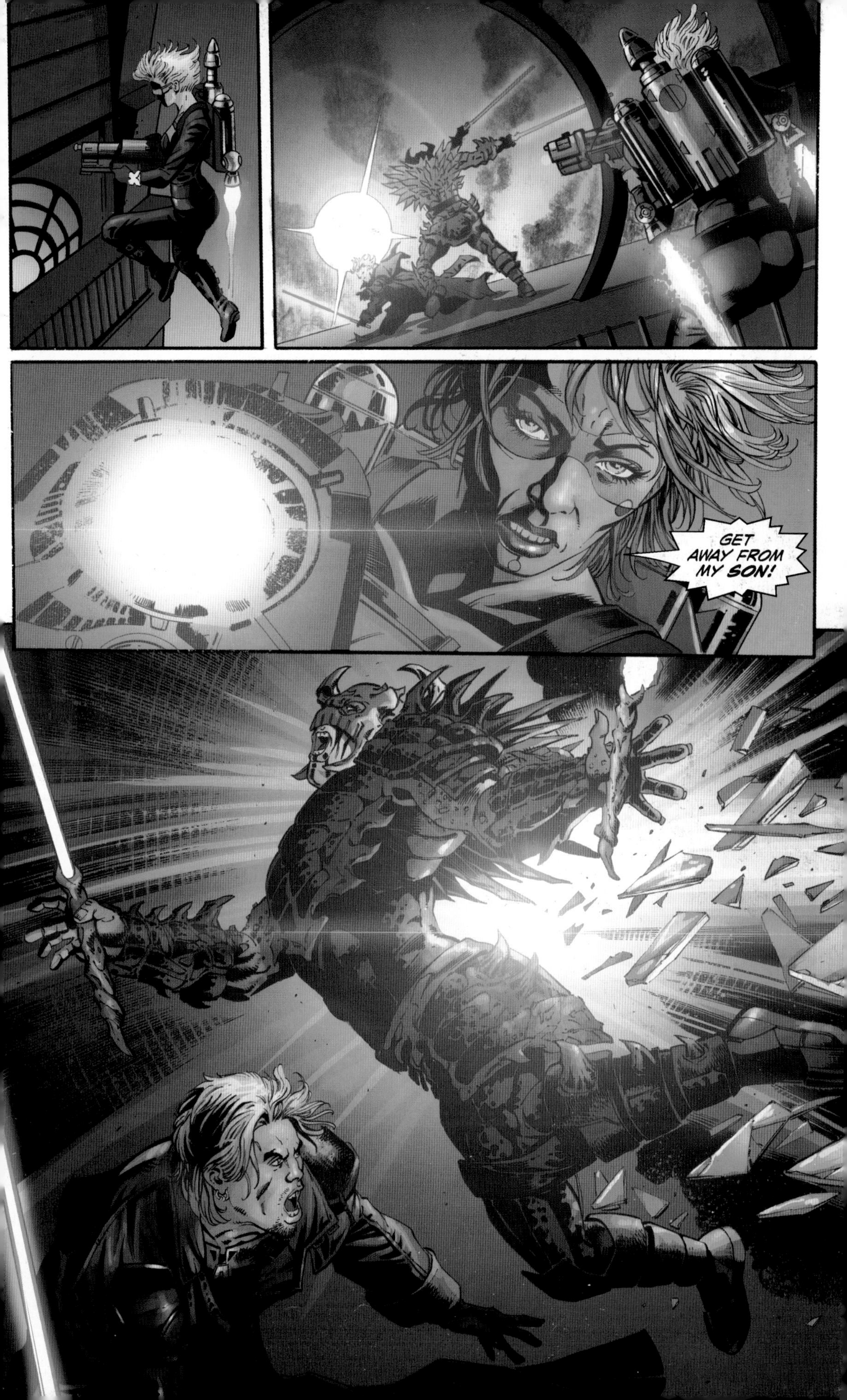
GET AWAY FROM MY SON!

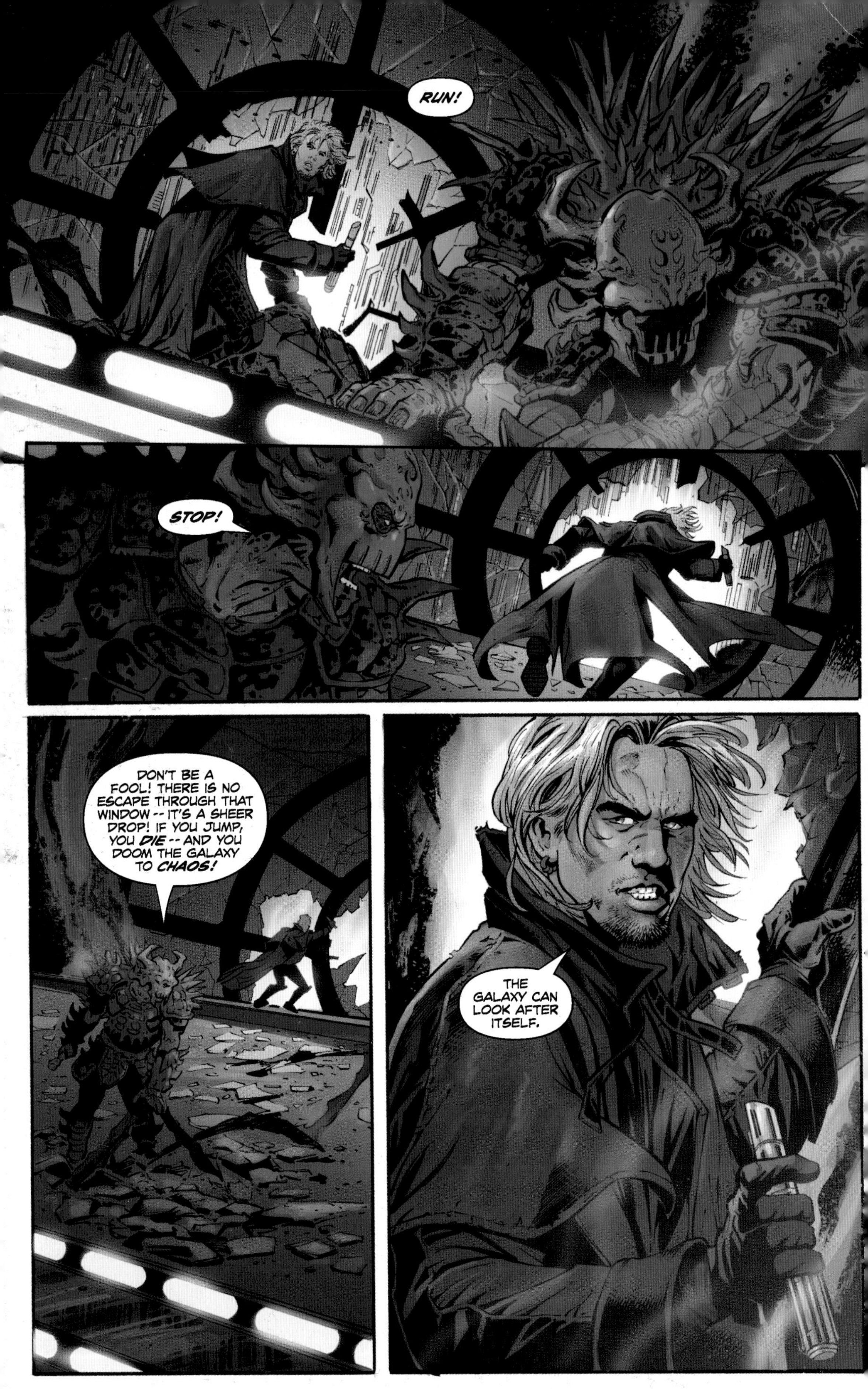
RUN!
STOP!
DON'T BE A FOOL! THERE IS NO ESCAPE THROUGH THAT WINDOW -- IT'S A SHEER DROP! IF YOU JUMP, YOU DIE -- AND YOU DOOM THE GALAXY TO CHAOS!
THE GALAXY CAN LOOK AFTER ITSELF.

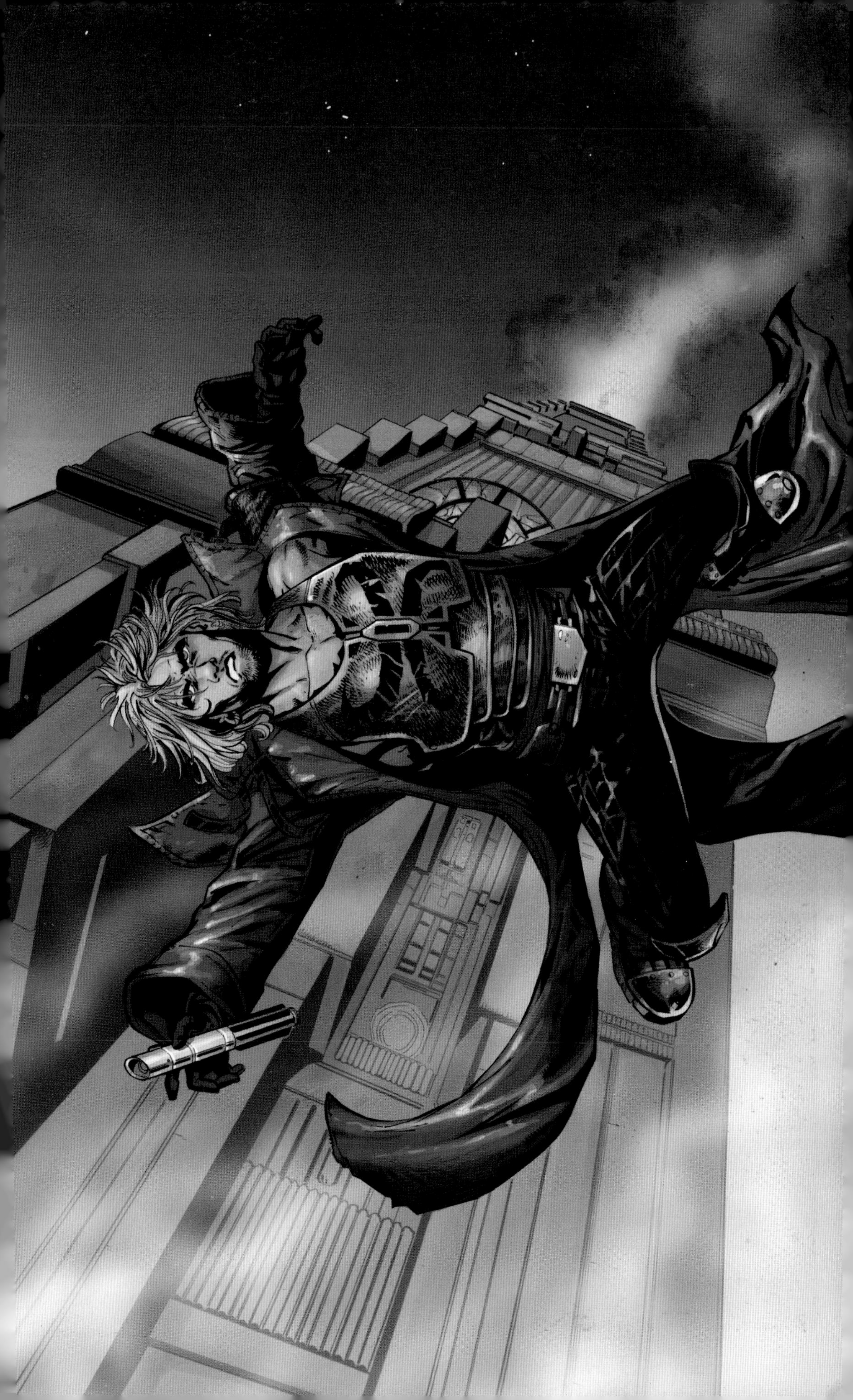

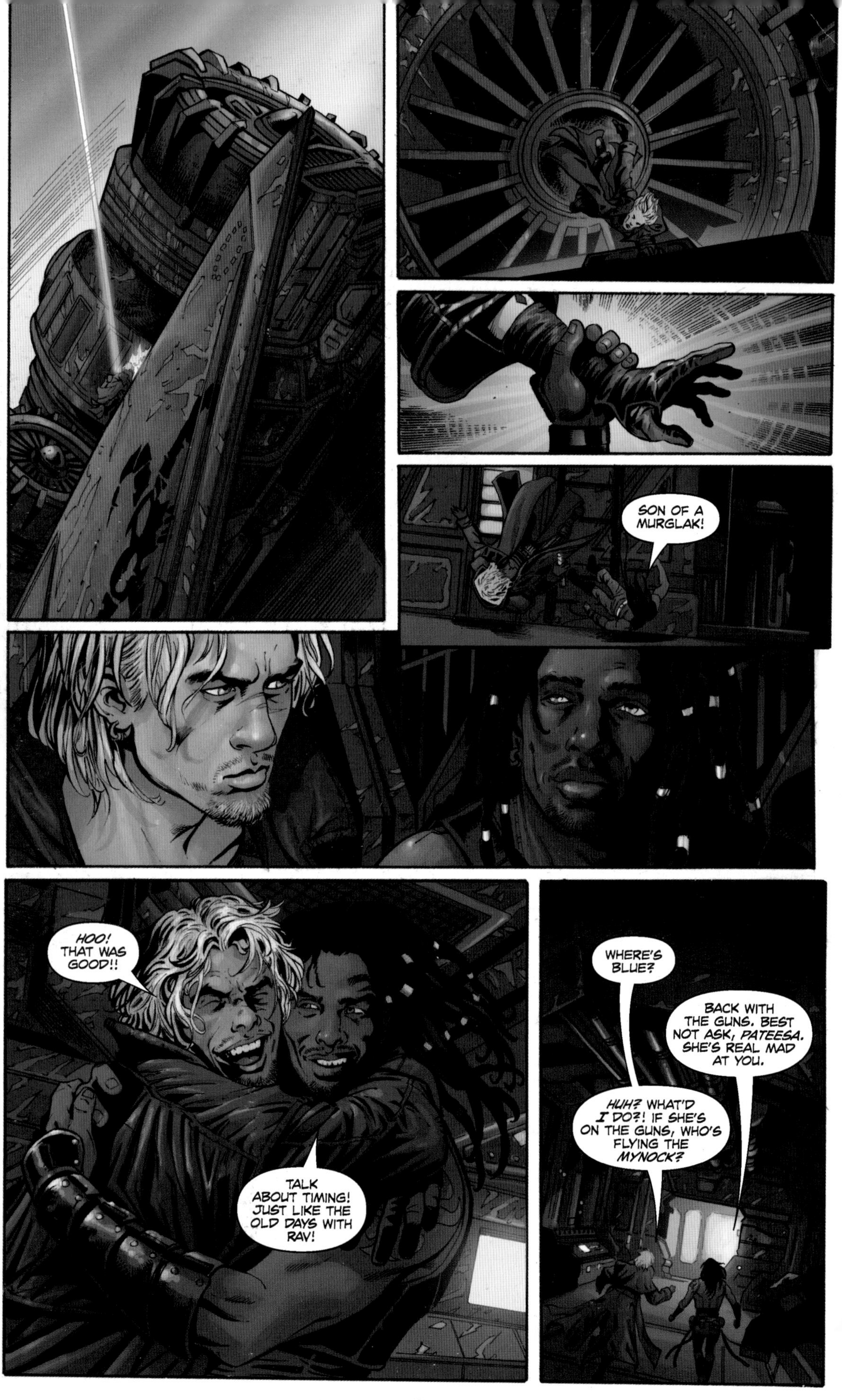
SON OF A MURGLAK!
HOO! THAT WAS GOOD!!
TALK ABOUT TIMING! JUST LIKE THE OLD DAYS WITH RAV!
WHERE'S BLUE?
BACK WITH THE GUNS. BEST NOT ASK, PATEESA. SHE'S REAL MAD AT YOU.
HUH? WHAT'D I DO?! IF SHE'S ON THE GUNS, WHO'S FLYING THE MYNOCK?

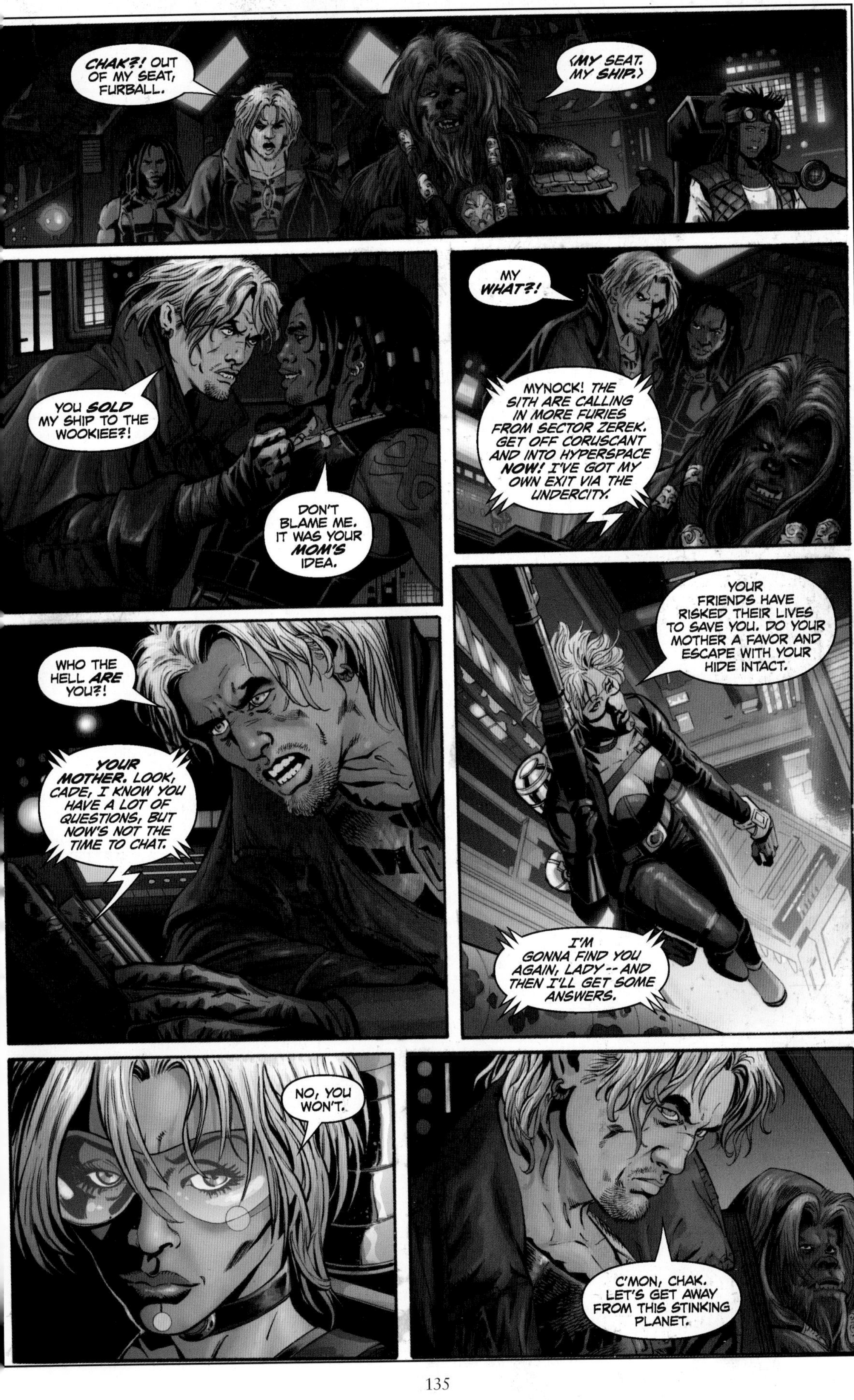
CHAK?! OUT OF MY SEAT, FURBALL.
‹MY SEAT. MY SHIP.›
YOU SOLD MY SHIP TO THE WOOKIEE?!
DON'T BLAME ME. IT WAS YOUR MOM'S IDEA.
MY WHAT?!
MYNOCK! THE SITH ARE CALLING IN MORE FURIES FROM SECTOR ZEREK. GET OFF CORUSCANT AND INTO HYPERSPACE NOW! I'VE GOT MY OWN EXIT VIA THE UNDERCITY.
WHO THE HELL ARE YOU?!
YOUR MOTHER. LOOK, CADE, I KNOW YOU HAVE A LOT OF QUESTIONS, BUT NOW'S NOT THE TIME TO CHAT.
YOUR FRIENDS HAVE RISKED THEIR LIVES TO SAVE YOU. DO YOUR MOTHER A FAVOR AND ESCAPE WITH YOUR HIDE INTACT.
I'M GONNA FIND YOU AGAIN, LADY -- AND THEN I'LL GET SOME ANSWERS.
NO, YOU WON'T.
C'MON, CHAK. LET'S GET AWAY FROM THIS STINKING PLANET.

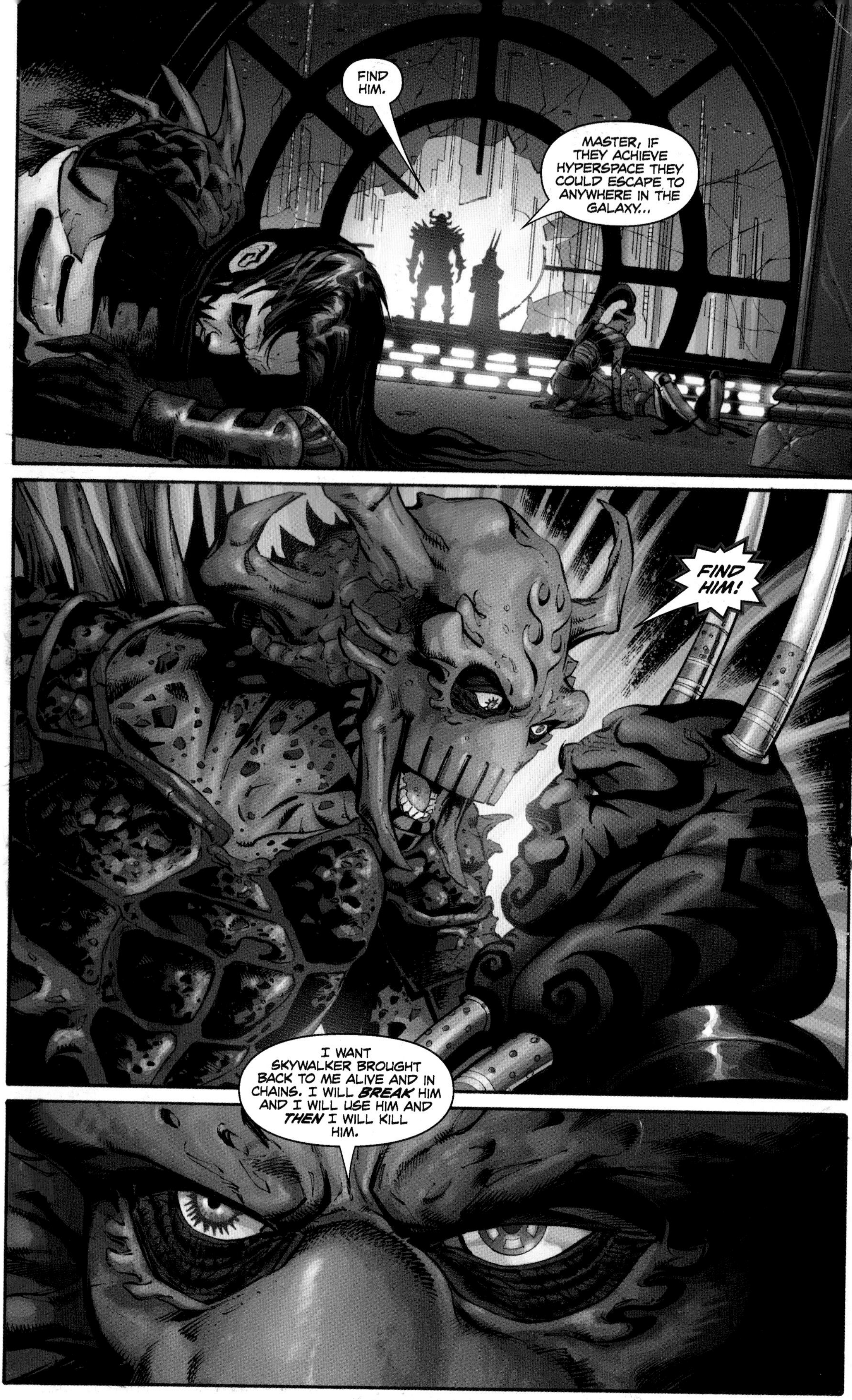
FIND HIM.
MASTER, IF THEY ACHIEVE HYPERSPACE THEY COULD ESCAPE TO ANYWHERE IN THE GALAXY...
FIND HIM!
I WANT SKYWALKER BROUGHT BACK TO ME ALIVE AND IN CHAINS. I WILL **BREAK** HIM AND I WILL USE HIM AND **THEN** I WILL KILL HIM.

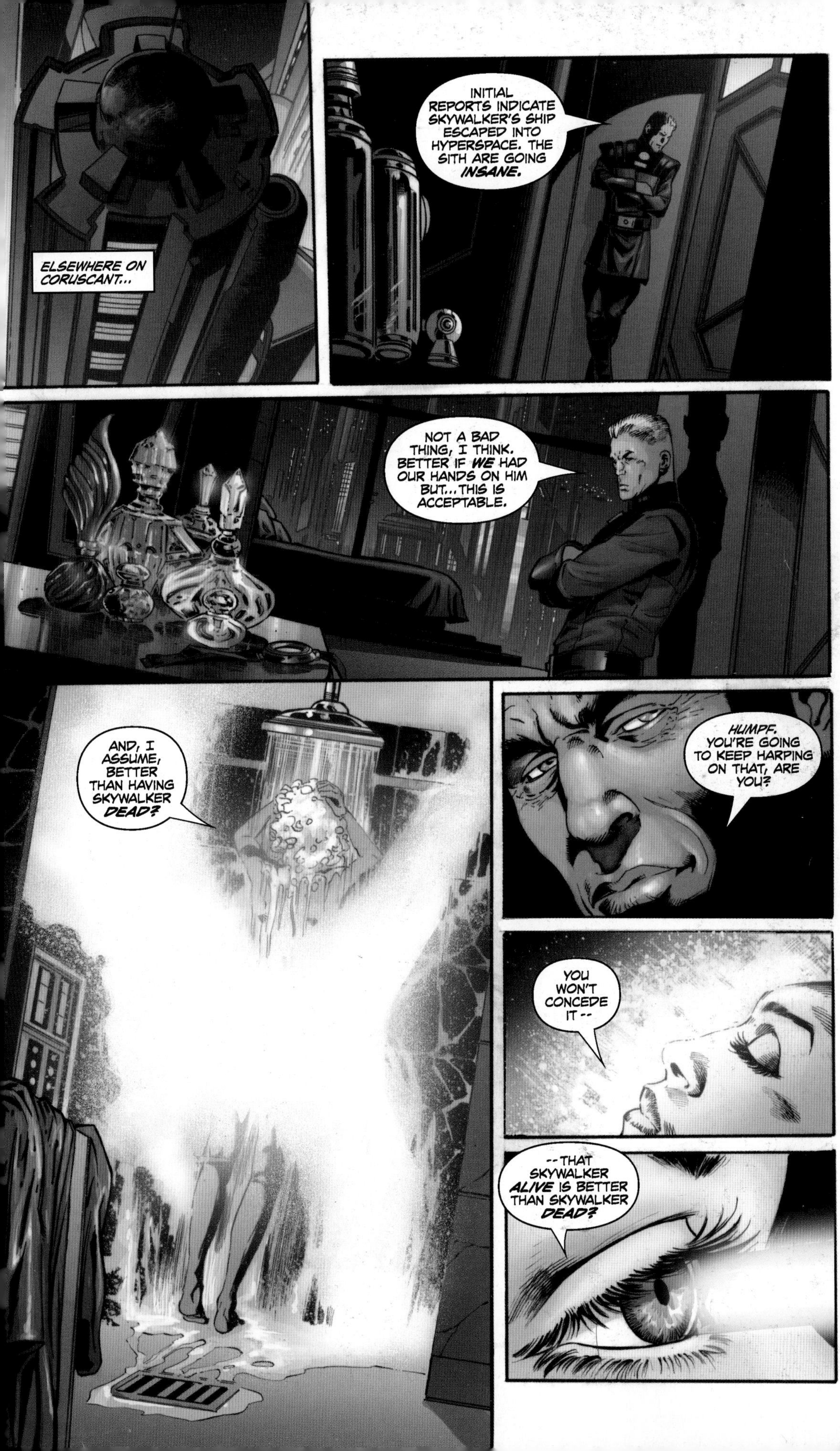
ELSEWHERE ON CORUSCANT...
INITIAL REPORTS INDICATE SKYWALKER'S SHIP ESCAPED INTO HYPERSPACE. THE SITH ARE GOING INSANE.
NOT A BAD THING, I THINK. BETTER IF WE HAD OUR HANDS ON HIM BUT...THIS IS ACCEPTABLE.
AND, I ASSUME, BETTER THAN HAVING SKYWALKER DEAD?
HUMPF. YOU'RE GOING TO KEEP HARPING ON THAT, ARE YOU?
YOU WON'T CONCEDE IT --
-- THAT SKYWALKER ALIVE IS BETTER THAN SKYWALKER DEAD?

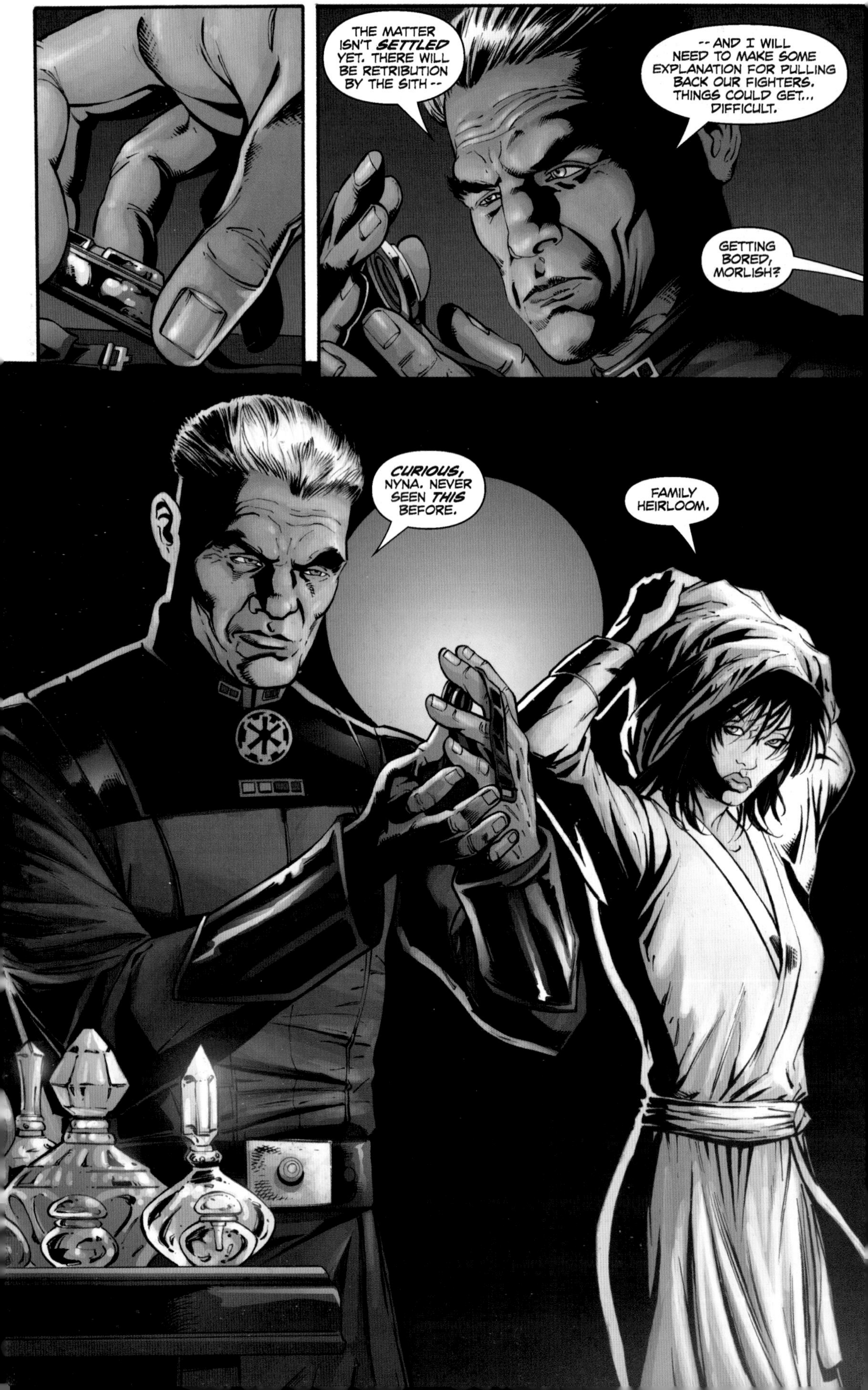

THE MATTER ISN'T *SETTLED* YET. THERE WILL BE RETRIBUTION BY THE SITH --
-- AND I WILL NEED TO MAKE SOME EXPLANATION FOR PULLING BACK OUR FIGHTERS. THINGS COULD GET... DIFFICULT.
GETTING BORED, MORLISH?
CURIOUS, NYNA. NEVER SEEN *THIS* BEFORE.
FAMILY HEIRLOOM.

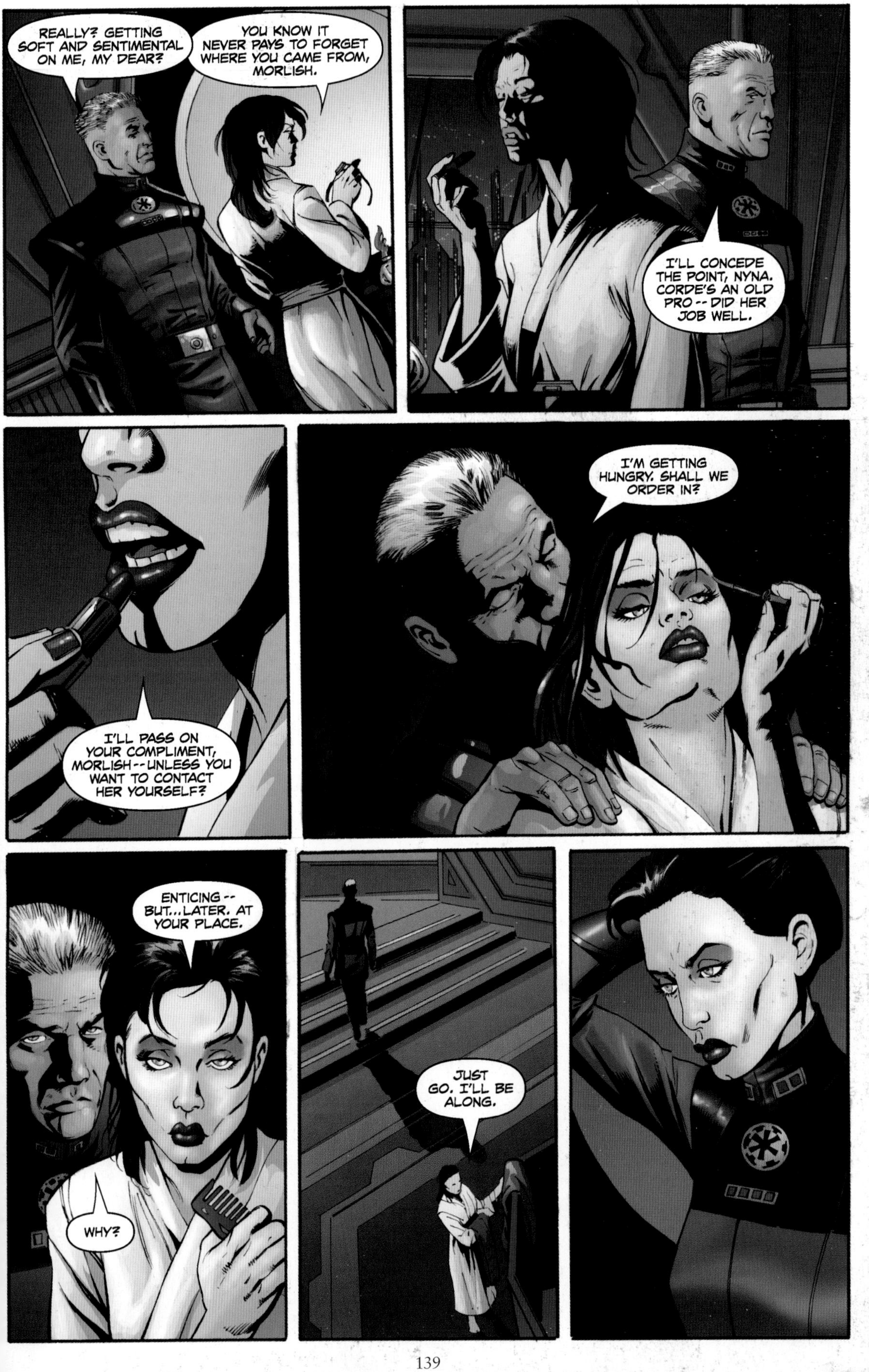
REALLY? GETTING SOFT AND SENTIMENTAL ON ME, MY DEAR?
YOU KNOW IT NEVER PAYS TO FORGET WHERE YOU CAME FROM, MORLISH.
I'LL CONCEDE THE POINT, NYNA. CORDE'S AN OLD PRO--DID HER JOB WELL.
I'LL PASS ON YOUR COMPLIMENT, MORLISH--UNLESS YOU WANT TO CONTACT HER YOURSELF?
I'M GETTING HUNGRY. SHALL WE ORDER IN?
ENTICING--BUT...LATER. AT YOUR PLACE.
WHY?
JUST GO. I'LL BE ALONG.

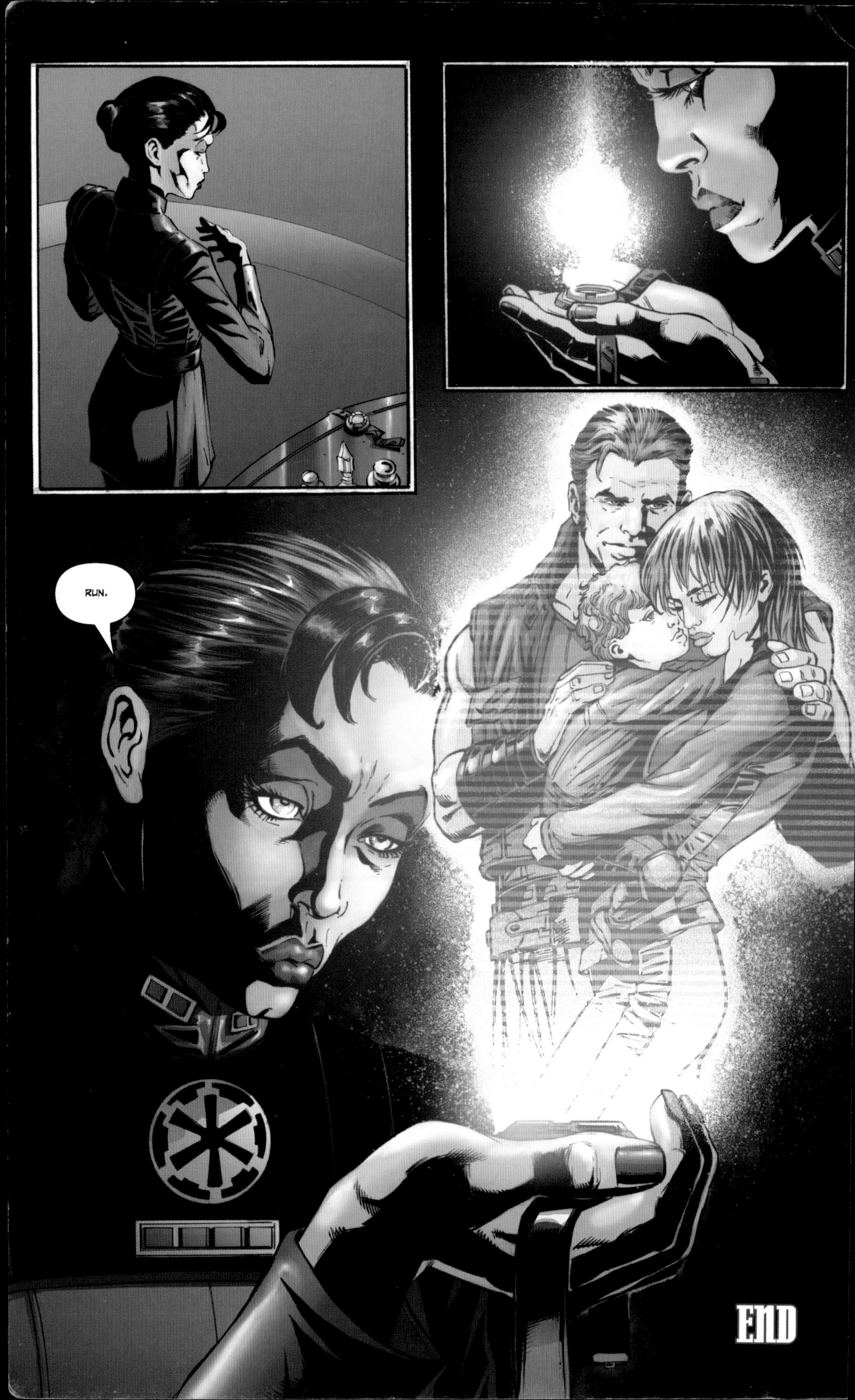
RUN.
END

STAR WARS®

TIMELINE OF GRAPHIC NOVELS FROM DARK HORSE!

OLD REPUBLIC ERA:
25,000—1000 YEARS BEFORE
STAR WARS: A NEW HOPE

Tales of the Jedi—
The Golden Age of the Sith
ISBN: 1-56971-229-8 $16.95

Tales of the Jedi—
The Fall of the Sith Empire
ISBN: 1-56971-320-0 $15.95

Tales of the Jedi—
Knights of the Old Republic
ISBN: 1-56971-020-1 $14.95

Tales of the Jedi—
The Freedon Nadd Uprising
ISBN: 1-56971-307-3 $5.95

Tales of the Jedi—
Dark Lords of the Sith
ISBN: 1-56971-095-3 $17.95

Tales of the Jedi—The Sith War
ISBN: 1-56971-173-9 $17.95

Tales of the Jedi—Redemption
ISBN: 1-56971-535-1 $14.95

Knights of the Old Republic
Volume 1—Commencement
ISBN: 1-59307-640-1 $18.95

Knights of the Old Republic
Volume 2—Flashpoint
ISBN: 1-59307-761-0 $18.95

Jedi vs. Sith
ISBN: 1-56971-649-8 $17.95

RISE OF THE EMPIRE ERA:
1000-0 YEARS BEFORE
STAR WARS: A NEW HOPE

The Stark Hyperspace War
ISBN: 1-56971-985-3 $12.95

Jedi Council—Acts of War
ISBN: 1-56971-539-4 $12.95

Prelude to Rebellion
ISBN: 1-56971-448-7 $14.95

Darth Maul
ISBN: 1-56971-542-4 $12.95

Episode I—The Phantom Menace
ISBN: 1-56971-359-6 $12.95

Episode I—
The Phantom Menace Adventures
ISBN: 1-56971-443-6 $12.95

Jango Fett
ISBN: 1-56971-623-4 $5.95

Zam Wesell
ISBN: 1-56971-624-2 $5.95

Jango Fett—Open Seasons
ISBN: 1-56971-671-4 $12.95

Outlander
ISBN: 1-56971-514-9 $14.95

Emissaries to Malastare
ISBN: 1-56971-545-9 $15.95

The Bounty Hunters
ISBN: 1-56971-467-3 $12.95

Twilight
ISBN: 1-56971-558-0 $12.95

The Hunt for Aurra Sing
ISBN: 1-56971-651-X $12.95

Darkness
ISBN: 1-56971-659-5 $12.95

Rite of Passage
ISBN: 1-59307-042-X $12.95

Honor and Duty
ISBN: 1-59307-546-4 $12.95

Episode II—Attack of the Clones
ISBN: 1-56971-609-9 $17.95

Clone Wars Volume 1—
The Defense of Kamino
ISBN: 1-56971-962-4 $14.95

Clone Wars Volume 2—
Victories and Sacrifices
ISBN: 1-56971-969-1 $14.95

Clone Wars Volume 3—
Last Stand on Jabiim
ISBN: 1-59307-006-3 $14.95

Clone Wars Volume 4—Light and Dark
ISBN: 1-59307-195-7 $16.95

Clone Wars Volume 5—The Best Blades
ISBN: 1-59307-273-2 $17.95

Clone Wars Volume 6—
On the Fields of Battle
ISBN: 1-59307-352-6 $17.95

Clone Wars Volume 7—
When They Were Brothers
ISBN: 1-59307-396-8 $17.95

Clone Wars Volume 8—
The Last Siege, the Final Truth
ISBN: 1-59307-482-4 $17.95

Clone Wars Volume 9—Endgame
ISBN: 1-59307-553-7 $17.95

Clone Wars Adventures Volume 1
ISBN: 1-59307-243-0 $6.95

Clone Wars Adventures Volume 2
ISBN: 1-59307-271-6 $6.95

Clone Wars Adventures Volume 3
ISBN: 1-59307-307-0 $6.95

Clone Wars Adventures Volume 4
ISBN: 1-59307-402-6 $6.95

Clone Wars Adventures Volume 5
ISBN: 1-59307-483-2 $6.95

Clone Wars Adventures Volume 6
ISBN: 1-59307-567-7 $6.95

Clone Wars Adventures Volume 7
ISBN: 1-59307-678-9 $6.95

Episode III—Revenge of the Sith
ISBN: 1-59307-309-7 $12.95

General Grievous
ISBN: 1-59307-442-5 $12.95

Droids—The Kalarba Adventures
ISBN: 1-56971-064-3 $17.95

Droids—Rebellion
ISBN: 1-56971-224-7 $14.95

Classic Star Wars—
Han Solo at Stars' End
ISBN: 1-56971-254-9 $6.95

Boba Fett—Enemy of the Empire
ISBN: 1-56971-407-X $12.95

Underworld—The Yavin Vassilika
ISBN: 1-56971-618-8 $15.95

Dark Forces—Soldier for the Empire
ISBN: 1-56971-348-0 $14.95

Empire Volume 1—Betrayal
ISBN: 1-56971-964-0 $12.95

Empire Volume 2—Darklighter
ISBN: 1-56971-975-6 $17.95

REBELLION ERA:
0-5 YEARS AFTER
STAR WARS: A NEW HOPE

A New Hope—The Special Edition
ISBN: 1-56971-213-1 $9.95

Boba Fett: Man with a Mission
ISBN: 1-59307-707-6 $12.95

Empire Volume 3—
The Imperial Perspective
ISBN: 1-59307-128-0 $17.95

Empire Volume 4—
The Heart of the Rebellion
ISBN: 1-59307-308-9 $17.95

Empire Volume 5—Allies and Adversaries
ISBN: 1-59307-466-2 $14.95

Empire Volume 6—In the Shadows
of Their Fathers
ISBN: 1-59307-627-4 $17.95

Empire Volume 7—The Wrong side of
the War
ISBN: 1-59307-709-2 $17.95

Rebellion Volume 1—My Brother,
My Enemy
ISBN: 1-59307-711-4 $14.95

A Long Time Ago . . . Volume 1—
Doomworld
ISBN: 1-56971-754-0 $29.95

A Long Time Ago . . . Volume 2—
Dark Encounters
ISBN: 1-56971-785-0 $29.95

Classic Star Wars—
The Early Adventures
ISBN: 1-56971-178-X $19.95

Classic Star Wars Volume 1—
In Deadly Pursuit
ISBN: 1-56971-109-7 $16.95

Classic Star Wars Volume 2—
The Rebel Storm
ISBN: 1-56971-106-2 $16.95

Classic Star Wars Volume 3—
Escape to Hoth
ISBN: 1-56971-093-7 $16.95

Jabba the Hutt—The Art of the Deal
ISBN: 1-56971-310-3 $9.95

Vader's Quest
ISBN: 1-56971-415-0 $11.95

Splinter of the Mind's Eye
ISBN: 1-56971-223-9 $14.95

The Empire Strikes Back—
The Special Edition
ISBN: 1-56971-234-4 $9.95

A Long Time Ago . . . Volume 3—
Resurrection of Evil
ISBN: 1-56971-786-9 $29.95

A Long Time Ago . . . Volume 4—
Screams in the Void
ISBN: 1-56971-787-7 $29.95

A Long Time Ago . . . Volume 5—
Fool's Bounty
ISBN: 1-56971-906-3 $29.95

Battle of the Bounty Hunters
Pop-Up Book
ISBN: 1-56971-129-1 $17.95

Shadows of the Empire
ISBN: 1-56971-183-6 $17.95

Return of the Jedi—The Special Edition
ISBN: 1-56971-235-2 $9.95

A Long Time Ago . . . Volume 6—
Wookiee World
ISBN: 1-56971-907-1 $29.95

A Long Time Ago . . . Volume 7—
Far, Far Away
ISBN: 1-56971-908-X $29.95

Mara Jade—By the Emperor's Hand
ISBN: 1-56971-401-0 $15.95

Shadows of the Empire: Evolution
ISBN: 1-56971-441-X $14.95

NEW REPUBLIC ERA:
5-25 YEARS AFTER
STAR WARS: A NEW HOPE

Omnibus—X-Wing Rogue Squadron
Volume 1
ISBN: 1-59307-572-3 $24.95

Omnibus—X-Wing Rogue Squadron
Volume 2
ISBN: 1-59307-619-3 $24.95

Omnibus—X-Wing Rogue Squadron
Volume 3
ISBN: 1-59307-776-9 $24.95

Dark Forces—Rebel Agent
ISBN: 1-56971-400-2 $14.95

Dark Forces—Jedi Knight
ISBN: 1-56971-433-9 $14.95

Heir to the Empire
ISBN: 1-56971-202-6 $19.95

Dark Force Rising
ISBN: 1-56971-269-7 $17.95

The Last Command
ISBN: 1-56971-378-2 $17.95

Boba Fett—
Death, Lies, and Treachery
ISBN: 1-56971-311-1 $12.95

Dark Empire
ISBN: 1-59307-039-X $16.95

Dark Empire II 2nd ed.
(includes Empire's End)
ISBN: 1-59307-526-X $19.95

Crimson Empire
ISBN: 1-56971-355-3 $17.95

Crimson Empire II: Council of Blood
ISBN: 1-56971-410-X $17.95

Jedi Academy: Leviathan
ISBN: 1-56971-456-8 $11.95

Union
ISBN: 1-56971-464-9 $12.95

NEW JEDI ORDER ERA:
25+ YEARS AFTER
STAR WARS: A NEW HOPE

Chewbacca
ISBN: 1-56971-515-7 $12.95

LEGACY ERA:
40+ YEARS AFTER
STAR WARS: A NEW HOPE

Legacy Volume 1—Broken
ISBN: 1-59307-716-5 $17.95

INFINITIES:
DOES NOT APPLY TO TIMELINE

Infinites: A New Hope
ISBN: 1-56971-648-X $12.95

Infinities: The Empire Strikes Back
ISBN: 1-56971-904-7 $12.95

Infinities: Return of the Jedi
ISBN: 1-59307-206-6 $12.95

Star Wars Tales Volume 1
ISBN: 1-56971-619-6 $19.95

Star Wars Tales Volume 2
ISBN: 1-56971-757-5 $19.95

Star Wars Tales Volume 3
ISBN: 1-56971-836-9 $19.95

Star Wars Tales Volume 4
ISBN: 1-56971-989-6 $19.95

Star Wars Tales Volume 5
ISBN: 1-59307-286-4 $19.95

Star Wars Tales Volume 6
ISBN: 1-59307-447-6 $19.95

Tag & Bink Were Here
ISBN: 1-59307-641-X $14.95

FOR MORE INFORMATION ABOUT THESE BOOKS VISIT DARKHORSE.COM!

AVAILABLE AT YOUR LOCAL COMICS SHOP OR BOOKSTORE
To find a comics shop in your area, call 1-888-266-4226. For more information or to order direct, visit darkhorse.com or call 1-800-862-0052 Mon.–Fri. 9 A.M. to 5 P.M. Pacific Time. *Prices and availability subject to change without notice.

STAR WARS ©2007 Lucasfilm Ltd. & ™. (BL8009)